Changing Minds

Changing Minds
Computers, Learning, and Literacy

Andrea A. diSessa

A Bradford Book
The MIT Press
Cambridge, Massachusetts
London, England

First MIT Press paperback edition, 2001
© 2000 Massachusetts Institute of Technology

This book was set in Sabon by Achorn Graphic Services, Inc. and was printed and bound in the United States of America.

Library of Congress Cataloging-in-Publication Data

diSessa, Andrea A.
  Changing minds: computers, learning, and literacy / Andrea A. diSessa.
    p.   cm.
  Includes bibliographical references and index.
  ISBN 0-262-04180-4 (hc: alk. paper), 0-262-54132-7 (pb)
  1. Education—Data processing. 2. Learning, Psychology of. 3. Literacy. I. Title.
  LB1028.43.D57 2000
  370′.285 21—dc21

                                                      99-040215

To Melinda

Contents

Preface   ix

Acknowledgments   xvii

1 Computational Media and New Literacies—The Very Idea   1

2 How It Might Be   29

3 Snapshots: A Day in the Life   45

4 Foundations of Knowledge and Learning   65

5 Intuition and Activity Elaborated   89

6 Explaining Things, Explainable Things   109

7 Designing Computer Systems for People   131

8 More Snapshots: Kids Are Smart   165

9 Stepping Back, Looking Forward   209

Notes and Resources   249

Index   267

Preface

Can computers convey to humans a new increment of intellectual power that rivals what conventional literacy has given us? Can education—science education in particular—be transformed by the computer's presence so that children learn much more, learn it earlier and more easily, and, fundamentally, learn it with a pleasure and commitment that only a privileged few now feel toward school learning? For me, these questions enfold a scope and depth that is frightening and wonderful. The questions are frightening because, in order to answer them with confidence, we need to understand much more than we do today about learning, about how materials (such as text and computers) can make us smarter and help us learn, and about how cultures appropriate a competence base such as a literacy. The questions are wonderful for almost the same reason: trying to answer them brings us to profound and almost timeless questions about people and how they may think and act. The questions are wonderful also because, to my best estimation, both should be answered in the affirmative. Computers *can* make us smarter, if not wiser, and *can* revolutionize education. If this proves correct, civilization has some truly excellent days ahead of it—provided we recognize the possibilities and act in accordance with them.

I can't answer these questions definitively, but I can show why I believe the best data and theory available suggest immense promise for computers and human potential. Twenty-five years of work have only increased my commitment to the view that computers can be the basis of a new literacy and that great improvements in science education can follow. Part of my commitment comes from practical and theoretical successes at understanding the issues and possibilities; part of it comes from a better understanding of critics' reasoning, including why it is they think the way they do! Given the promise, I believe that it is irresponsible not to pursue computational literacies, even if we are still uncertain of the outcome, and I would be personally irresponsible if I did not trouble to put the case forward.

This book is not likely to be an easy read, despite the fact that I worked hard to make it accessible to anyone with a good high school science background or, at minimum, to people who know enough to enter responsibly into discussions of science education. Part of the difficulty is the depth of the issues we must face. There are no easy answers to questions such as "How might people think?"

Another part of the difficulty is breadth. Understanding a literacy involves understanding thinking, understanding how material resources can help us think better, and understanding what it means socially for a culture to become literate. I expect almost all readers will be differentially interested in and prepared to engage this breadth, so I have been careful to provide clues and guideposts for readers to pick and choose what suits them. Despite the challenge of breadth, one of the most exciting things about writing this book has been the chance to put together in one place the many aspects of my own work that bear on these issues. I would be disappointed if no one read it all.

Finally, this book will be difficult because many of the ideas cut against the grain of contemporary thought about learning, about education, and about what good computer software looks like. Coming to understand the depth and influence of this misalignment has been exciting and enlightening, if not always encouraging.

Allow me to forestall a few misunderstandings about the intent of this book. No matter what I do or say, many readers will interpret this book as being about a particular piece of software—Boxer, the system my research group and I are using to experiment with computational literacies. I have been as careful as I can manage to frame the issues at the appropriate level of generality. The prime foci of this book are computational media and new literacies, not Boxer per se. On the other hand, concreteness demands I explain how we worked with students and what they did. Furthermore, Boxer is almost certainly the best-developed exemplar of software intended to support a literacy model of the use of computers in education. Despite the fact that I would love to escape the crush of responsibility for developing and implementing a complex software system, we have had no reasonable alternative in order to undertake the experiments that we felt were needed. In addition, it would be foolish not to show some of the cleverness, I hope, we've installed in Boxer to others who might choose to pursue similar work.

Critics complain that I am unrelentingly positive in my portrayals of students' work. They want me also to explain failures and disappointments, claiming only that will convey a sense of honesty and impartiality. There are practical, scientific, and "political" reasons why I don't include many examples of students' or teachers' or our own failures. The practical reasons are simplest. I have underscored the complexity of the arguments in this book, even as things stand. If I were to qualify every statement and explain the basis and limits of every judgment, the book would lose any semblance of accessibility.

Scientifically, I have tried hard to maintain a sense of balance. My disclaimers of uncertainty already (appropriately) put this book far outside the regime of unqualified confidence that pervades general public discussion of computers and education. If I want to express my convictions and make any contribution at all to public discussion, I cannot lock these ideas in the intricate chambers of pure scientific discourse. In addition, many of our project's failures and difficulties are boring. We could not afford sufficiently fast machines and the programming necessary for a truly smooth and professional interface in our early experiments. How illuminating is it to know this caused difficulty? Many others have demonstrated beyond question that teachers need time and support to teach in new ways. Our specific difficulties in this regard are, for the most part, completely unremarkable. Finally, I have reserved my most somber and uncertain tones for those subjects that I feel most deserve them—social and cultural change, not the potential of students and teachers.

Educational research entails positioning oneself with respect to contemporary landmark points of view. One of the fault lines in current research is how we view teachers and students. On one side, teachers need strict accountabilities, and students won't ever learn unless we discipline their unruly thought patterns and unacademic interests. I have chosen to remind people, as often as necessary, that many if not most of the faults attributed to teachers and students lie in the inability or unwillingness of scientists or citizens who decide public priorities to support them sufficiently. I want to show not that children "naturally" learn anything put in front of them or that all teachers are brilliant, but that there are solid scientific and empirical reasons to believe that much more can be achieved in learning than most expect. Against the sea of demonstrated failure, a few successes deserve special attention for what they show about the directions to pursue for improvement.

Guide to the Book

Chapter 1 begins by introducing the core claim of the book: computers can be the basis for an empowering new literacy (or family of literacies); hence, they can change the way people think and learn. I also introduce three fundamental views on literacy that organize discussion in the remainder of the book. The cognitive view asks the question, "How can we see the advantages that competence with an external representational system—such as text, algebra, graphing, or computer-implemented systems—conveys to individuals?" The material view of literacy puts the emphasis on the external forms of literacy, what particular characteristics they have, and how they combine with our thoughts and actions to create particular new capabilities. The social view of literacy inquires how literate communities surpass the accomplishment allotted to individuals, no matter how brilliant. In addition, the social view holds the key to understanding whether, when, and how computational literacy might actually take hold. The subtle concept of *social niches* is introduced to explore and explain the viability of some (but not other) forms of literacy and to support an appropriately anarchic view of what good literacy does for people. I use examples from everyday life and from the history of science and education to illustrate these ideas.

Chapter 2 introduces a concrete and realistic image of how new computational representations can change the landscape of learning important scientific ideas. I argue that programming is incredibly apt for "speaking" about the mathematics and physics of motion. In addition, programming can make learning about motion far more motivating than any other available means. The chapter ends by speculating on the properties and plausibility of changing schools into tool-rich communities, where teachers do far more than consume what others feel is best for them to use in the way of educational software.

Chapter 3 is a set of accounts of children and teachers who have experimented with us concerning learning with computational media. The intent is to enliven the abstractions of previous chapters with real-world happenings that illustrate important ideas. I hope to give readers a feeling for the data that convinces me that radical improvements in learning are possible.

Chapters 4 and 5 are the cognitive and philosophical core of the book. They introduce the learning theory that explains why computers can be such powerful catalysts of change in education. I explain how intuitive knowledge—a much ignored and maligned component of human competence—is actually the platform on which students build scientific understanding. Computer-based representations support and cultivate this important kind of knowledge especially well.

In addition, chapters 4 and 5 discuss how critical it is to view human beings as engaged actors in the world and not simply repositories of instrumental knowledge. People choose to do some things and not others. They have a sense of self that entails ownership over some activities, but alienation and disconnection from others. I introduce a sketch of a future theory of activities that can help us understand and design more human trajectories of competence. I introduce the goal of *committed learning,* where individuals feel a personal connection to the form of extended action in which they participate.

Chapters 6 and 7 are the most technical in the book. They deal with the material forms for possible new literacies. Most particularly, I undertake to explain how to design computer systems that are both comprehensible and powerful. To this end, I introduce two views of computer systems. The *structural view* explains the logic of the system in its own terms. Structurally simple and powerful systems afford long trajectories of learning and use. On the other hand, a *functional view* of systems explains how they can feel familiar and support fluent everyday activity. The functional view connects computer systems most directly to what people care about. I use imaginary designers of incomprehensible bicycles and the foibles of real calculators to explore the intricate interweaving of function and structure that is the hallmark of the best design.

Chapters 6 and 7 contain two somewhat hidden elements. First, I argue for—and try to show how it is possible to create—two-way literacies, where everyone is a creator as well as a consumer of new material forms. Reading without writing would be an absurdly limited form of literacy in modern society, but far too many people ignore the equivalent of writing for computers. In addition, chapter 7 contains the only technical description of the Boxer software in the book ("A Structure for Cyberspace"). Even readers not interested in principles of design, which Boxer is used to illustrate, will benefit from an up close look at a computational medium. Understanding Boxer will help in understanding the examples given elsewhere in the book, and in understanding their general implications. The description of Boxer also explains how the process of developing learning materials may change with the advent of two-way computational media. In contrast to the dominant paradigm of top-down development by experts, the image of more organic, extended, and open forms of educational materials development, including teachers and students, is a distinctive emblem of what we have been trying to achieve with Boxer.

Chapter 8 returns to accounts of real children and teachers in action. This time, however, we have the benefit of a lot of theoretical preparation for seeing the meaning of new and different things that are made possible by computational media. In particular, I introduce the exotic but wonderful idea that computers can support not just a new fixed form (such as text) for new intelligence, but constant innovation in representational forms, even by teachers and students. If I hadn't seen it with my own eyes, I wouldn't believe it myself! The chapter again highlights the role of the computer in engaging intuitive knowledge and how students can reach surprising levels of accomplishment in programming because of the characteristics of computational media.

Chapter 9 complements the focus on cognitive issues in chapters 4 and 5, and the focus on issues of material form in chapters 6 and 7. We return to social and cultural issues to examine in some detail the resonance or antiresonance of computational literacies with current common sense about computer systems and how people learn. As part of this study, I look at the World Wide Web with respect to how it builds toward the hopes for improved learning presented in this book. Then, I look at the intuitions and implicit assumptions about computers and learning of several important communities, including educators, technologists, and research funders. This study leads to a renewed appreciation for the scale and difficulty of change in the direction of the most optimistic hopes expressed in this book. If the possible rewards of new literacies are opulent, the challenges are commensurate.

Highlights for Different Audiences

A Minimal Read
For those who want a sense of this book's ideas with minimal effort, I suggest the following sections.

Chapter 1: Introduction; A Cognitive View of Material Intelligence (optional)
Chapter 2: Beyond Algebra
Chapter 3: Fish and Water; Ownership by Individuals and Communities; Materials That Live and Grow (optional)

General Audience
The general audience interested in education will need the outline of the book's project in chapter 1, although the theoretical ideas concerning literacy may be less important. The examples of student and teacher work in chapter 3 and, to a lesser extent, the more exotic examples in chapter 8 should be important to this audience. The discussion of learning in chapters 4 and 5 should be accessible to the more dedicated reader; probably the most important new ideas are introduced in "The Structure of Activities and 'Committed Learning'" in chapter 4 and elaborated in the second half of chapter 5. Although chapters 6 and 7 introduce some technical issues, the discussion of Boxer in chapter 7 ("A Structure for Cyberspace") should be accessible and helpful to all.

Technology Designers
The "materials" chapters will be of most interest. Ideas concerning structural and functional understanding of systems (chapters 6 and 7) and concerning alternative social patterns of materials development (the end

of chapter 2 and last third of chapter 7) should be relevant. The discussions of children's and teachers' programming in the chapters describing student and teacher work (chapters 3 and 8) may be of interest.

Theorists of Literacy

The discussion of literacy in chapter 1 should be relevant. In particular, putting social viability in a central position with respect to defining literacy may be a surprising move. The idea of social niches inevitably leads to an expectation of diversity and multifaceted influence for literacy, which is quite different from most general accounts. Discussions of technical and scientific subliteracies, such as algebra and programming, might be of interest to contrast with more conventionally narrow definitions of literacy having to do exclusively with written language. The discussion of meta-representational competence and how computational literacies may fundamentally alter which people create new representational forms should resonate with some accounts of the power of literacy and contrast with others.

Socioculturally Oriented Readers

This group will find chapters 1 and 9 most relevant. "Activity theorists" may be interested to consider the approach taken to understanding activities in chapters 5 and 6. My general approach to understanding the power and influence of artifacts (scattered throughout the book) may be of interest.

Students of Learning and Conceptual Change

Chapters 4 and 5 are most relevant. The discussion of intuitive knowledge may be old hat, but the move toward enfolding activity into epistemology should be provocative.

Acknowledgments

Proper acknowledgments for the work reported in this book—which included a huge software project and the difficult pragmatics of doing truly unusual things in schools—probably deserves another book. At the risk of slighting many contributions, I'll attempt a miniature version. My grateful thanks in no way implies funders' or individuals' endorsement of the ideas in this book.

The most important proximal cause of this book was a year as a Fellow at the Center for Advanced Study in the Behavioral Sciences, supported by a fellowship from the Spencer Foundation (grant no. 19940032). The Spencer Foundation seems to have provided support for my work at precisely the most critical times. In particular, it also supported my work on intuitive knowledge (grant no. B1393) reported in chapters 4 and 5.

The development of Unix Boxer and most of the learning experiments reported here were supported by a pair of grants from the National Science Foundation (NSF), from a program directed by Dr. Andrew Molnar (grant nos. MDR 86-42177 and MDR 88-50363). A more recent grant allowed us to investigate students' metarepresentational competence (grant no. RED 95-53902), reported in chapter 8.

Some additional support for the development of Boxer came in the way of generous equipment donations from Sun Microsystems and a grant from Apple Computer that allowed us to hire a computer science student. The Graduate School of Education of the University of California, Berkeley, provided some direct support for my project and also indirect support in the way of computational infrastructure.

Seymour Papert got me started in computers and education, and inspired many of the early ideas that eventually led to this book. Alan Kay's work helped motivate the move to a serious consideration of a literacy perspective.

Ed Lay has been the chief designer and implementor of Boxer for nearly fifteen years. Boxer was conceptualized under the auspices of the MIT Laboratory for Computer Science under a grant from the Defense Advanced Research Projects Agency (DARPA), Michael Dertouzos, principal investigator. Hal Abelson codirected that work and, critically, sketched the single most difficult algorithm, which made Boxer efficient enough to be practical. Several talented programmers made contributions: Gregor Kiczalis wrote the first version of the editor; Leigh Klotz wrote the core of the Boxer interpreter; Jeremy Roschelle wrote the first real Boxer graphics system; and Michael Travers, introduced to us by Alan Kay, did the initial port of Boxer to the Macintosh platform.

The two teachers who have contributed most to the project are Henri Picciotto and Tina Kolpokowski. Henri has defined "teacher-leader" for me in terms of innovation with computational media. His constant feedback has made Boxer much better. Tina guided our first Boxer course, and her courage and brilliant teaching have continued to inspire.

Several people were instrumental in our school trials. Don Ploger provided many kinds of help and innovation during our two initial NSF grants, and he is still showing how to bring computational media into the real world. Many graduate students made important intellectual and practical contributions. Those whose influence has shown most in this book are Bruce Sherin and David Hammer. I can't omit all the young students whom we tried to help learn and who, in return, taught us so much.

The most helpful feedback on the text of this book was provided by Michael Eisenberg, Richard Noss, and Melinda diSessa. Graduate student members of my research group (including Rafael Granados, Rodrigo Madanes, and Andy Elby) influenced content and style. Two anonymous reviewers of the manuscript also had a significant influence. Kathleen Much of the Center for Advanced Study in the Behavioral Sciences helped improve the writing of many of the chapters. Maurice Anker developed the software extension that created the high-resolution Boxer figures used in this book.

Critics of the ideas presented in this book made important contributions, not all of which were intended. You know who you are.

Although I list them last, my family is first in my heart. Melinda provided advice, help, support, and encouragement, without which this book would have been impossible. My sons, Kurt and Nicholas, are two of those "smart kids" from whom I have learned so much about thought, action, and human potential. I love them, too.

Changing Minds

1
Computational Media and New Literacies—The Very Idea

Literacy in the conventional sense of being able to read and write is both highly valued and commonplace in contemporary society. Although almost everything else—especially values—seems to be in dispute, no one questions the importance of reading and writing as foundational skills. Of course, there is plenty of disagreement about exactly what constitutes literacy and how we should go about bringing up children to become literate. Still, not even the most extremist politicians can expect to win converts by cheering the latest study that shows college students can neither string two sentences together coherently nor read a map.

Because the social value of literacy is so important to this book, it is worth taking a few moments to evoke a more lively sense of the multiple roles literacy plays in our lives. Everyday life is a good place to start. When I get up in the morning, I usually find time to look at the newspaper. I glance through international events, partly just to keep up, partly because I have a few special interests stemming from overseas friends and personal associations from travel. I am not very fond of national politics, but it is interesting to see who is trying to do away with the U.S. Department of Education this year and whether National Science Foundation funding for social sciences will really go away.

I usually look in the business section mainly because that is the most likely place to find technology news, but also because I hope to find useful information that will help me save for retirement and pay for my sons' college education. Sometimes I'll find a good recipe and other times a piece of medical or health information of use to my family.

My interests in newspaper news are partly personal, organized by my own orientations and multiple group memberships, and partly professional. I keep up with some aspects of my work that don't get covered in professional journals (such as what features one gets in an inexpensive home computer these days), and I "accidentally" become a better-informed citizen and voter. For all of this, I lead a bit richer, probably slightly better, and more meaningful life. Many people buy newspapers, and I'm sure they have similar experiences.

Mail time is another bit of everyday life that reminds us how deeply literacy pervades our lives, frequently without our notice: letters from offspring or parents (we'd better write back), magazines, solicitations that every once in a while get noticed and acted on, forms to fill out (taxes!), sometimes with daunting written instructions (taxes!) . . .

Work gives us another perspective on literacy. As an academic, I have a special relation to literacy. It would not be a bad approximation to say my professional life *is* reading and writing. This book, for example, may be the single best representation of at least fifteen years' work on computational media, and it is likely to be only a small percentage of my career writing output. I'm writing now at home in front of a wall of books eight feet high and twenty feet wide; perhaps half of them are professional books. My professional dependence on literacy may be easy to dismiss as atypical in society—and surely it is atypical—but I am not too modest to claim that academia makes significant contributions, particularly in educating the young and in pursuing new knowledge outside of narrow special interests that measure new accomplishments only by dollars or by political or social power. There are many other "niche players" in society for whom literacy is nearly as important as in the lives of academics. Science and high technology are critically literate pursuits. I am certainly glad my personal doctor reads and that some doctors can write well enough to convey new ideas and practices effectively. In a wider scope, business and bureaucracies run on information, reports, memos, spreadsheets, concept papers, and so on.

A third perspective on literacy may be the most obvious and most important. Literacy is infrastructural and absolutely essential to education, to creating people who are knowledgeable and competent. *Infrastructural* means that literacy is not just a result of the educational process, but a driving force within it. Every class has textbooks, not only English class or other overtly literacy-oriented classes. If you can't read well enough or don't have basic mathematical literacy, you can't profit from history, science, or mathematics textbooks. Education has producers as well as consumers. Teachers, too, read to learn more and improve their practice. Someone has to write textbooks. Most teachers, especially the best, also write to help students—notes, handouts, evaluations—even if they are not writing to and for fellow teachers.

Enter the computer, a "once in several centuries" innovation, as Herbert Simon put it. Computers are incontestably transforming our civilization. Comparisons of our current information revolution to the Industrial Revolution are commonplace and apt. Almost no corner of society is untouched by computers. Most dramatically, science and business are not remotely the same practices they were twenty years ago because of the widespread influence of computers.

Education and schooling are, as yet, an ambiguous case. Few can or should claim that computers have influenced the cultural practices of school the way they have other aspects of society, such as science and business. Just look at texts, tests, and assignments from core subjects. They have changed little so far. Numbers tell a more optimistic but still muted story of penetration. In 1995, K–12 schools in the United States had about three computers per "average" thirty-student classroom. A decent informal benchmark I use is one computer per three students before core practices can be radically changed. This is the ratio at which students can be working full-time, three to a machine, a number that I know from personal experience can work very well, or each student can work alone one-third of the time, well above the threshold for infrastructural influence. One computer per ten students seems some distance from one per three, but consider that schools have been adding regularly to their stock of computers by about one-half computer per classroom per year. At that rate, average schools can easily meet my benchmark in a decade and a half. More than 10 percent of the high schools in the country are *already* above the threshold benchmark.

I fully expect the rate of computer acquisition to accelerate. That one-half computer per classroom is a fraction of what school districts spend per pupil, let alone per classroom, each year. Add the facts that in, say, ten years, computers will be easily ten times more powerful (thirty is a more responsible scientific estimate), that they will cost less, and that there will be vastly more good learning materials available, and I see inevitability. Despite amazing entrenchment, general conservatism, small budgets, and low status, schools will soon enough be computer-rich communities, unless our society is suicidally reluctant to share the future with its young.

Assuring ourselves that schools will have enough computers to do something interesting is a long way from assuring ourselves that something good—much less the very best we can manage—will happen. That is precisely what this book is about. What is the very best thing that can happen with computer use in education? What might learning actually be like then? How can you assure yourself that any vision is plausible and attainable? What sort of software must be created, and what are the signposts to guide us on the way to realizing "the best"?

I've already set the standard and implicitly suggested the key:

Computers can be the technical foundation of a new and dramatically enhanced literacy, which will act in many ways like current literacy and which will have penetration and depth of influence comparable to what we have already experienced in coming to achieve a mass, text-based literacy.

Clearly, I have a lot of explaining to do. This is not a very popular image of what may happen with computers in education. For that matter, it is not a very unpopular image either in the sense of having substantial opposition with objections that are deeply felt or well thought out. Instead, I find that most people have difficulty imagining what a *computational literacy,* as I propose to call it, may mean, or they dismiss it as easy and perhaps as already attained, or they find it immediately implausible, almost a contradiction in terms, so that it warrants little thought.

I need to identify and reject an unfortunate cultural artifact that can easily get in the way of thinking seriously about relevant issues. *Computer literacy* is a term that has been around since the early days of computers. It means something like being able to turn a computer on, insert a CD, and have enough keyboarding and mouse skills to make a few interesting things happen in a few standard applications. Computational literacy is different. In the first instance, the scale of achievement involved in computer literacy is microscopic compared to what I am talking about. It is as if being able to decode, haltingly, a few "typical" words could count as textual literacy.

If a true computational literacy comes to exist, it will be infrastructural in the same way current literacy is in current schools. Students will be learning and using it constantly through their schooling careers and beyond in diverse scientific, humanistic, and expressive pursuits. Outside of schools, a computational literacy will allow civilization to think and do things that will be new to us in the same way that the modern literate society would be almost incomprehensible to preliterate cultures. Clearly, by computational literacy I do not mean a casual familiarity with a machine that computes. In retrospect, I find it remarkable that society has allowed such a shameful debasing of the term *literacy* in its conventional use in connection with computers; perhaps like fish in the ocean, we just don't see our huge and pervasive dependence on it.

I find that substituting the phrase *material intelligence* for *literacy* is a helpful ploy. People instinctively understand intelligence as essential to our human nature and capacity to achieve. Material intelligence, then, is an addition to "purely mental" intelligence. We can achieve it in the presence of appropriate materials, such as pen and paper, print, or computers. This image is natural if we think of the mind as a remarkable and complex machine, but one that can be enhanced by allowing appropriate external extensions to the mechanism, extensions that wind up improving our abilities to represent the world, to remember and reason about it. The material intelligence—literacy—I am referring to is not artificial intelligence in the sense of placing our own intelligence or knowledge, or some enhanced version of it, into a machine. Instead, it is an intelligence achieved cooperatively with external materials.

In the remainder of this introductory chapter, I have one overarching goal. I want to examine traditional literacy in some detail, including both micro- and macrocomponents. The microfocus shows a little about how traditional literacy actually works in episodes of thinking with a materially enhanced intelligence. The macrofocus introduces some large-scale and irreducibly social considerations that determine whether a new literacy is achievable and how. Much of the rest of the book builds on these views of conventional literacy, extrapolating them to consider what exactly a computational literacy might mean, what it might accomplish for us, whether it is plausible, and how we can act to bring it about.

Three Pillars of Literacy

Before getting down to details, we might find it useful to set a rough framework for thinking about the many features and aspects of literacy. I think of literacy as built on three foundational pillars. First, there is the material pillar. That is, literacy involves external, materially based signs, symbols, depictions, or representations. This last set of terms, as well as others, holds an essential magic of literacy: we can install some aspects of our thinking in stable, reproducible, manipulable, and transportable physical form. These external forms become in a very real sense part of our thinking, remembering, and communicating. In concert with our minds, they let us act as if we could bring little surrogates of distant, awkwardly scaled (too big or too small), or difficult to "touch" aspects of the real world to our desktop and manipulate them at will. We can read a map, check our finances, write our itinerary, and plan an automobile trip across the United States. Even more, we can create and explore possible worlds of fantasy or reality (as in a scientific exploration) with a richness, complexity, care, and detail far transcending what we may do with the unaided mind.

The material bases for literacy are far from arbitrary, but are organized into intricately structured subsystems with particular rules of operation, basic symbol sets, patterns of combination, conventions, and means of interpretation. These subsystems all have a particular character, power, and reach, and they also have limits in what they allow us to think about. Associated with them are particular modes of mediated thought and connections to other subsystems. Written language, the prototype of literacy, has an alphabet, a lexicon, a grammar, and a syntax, and above these technical levels are conventions of written discourse, genres, and styles, and so on. Written language is expansive in what may be thought through it, it is variable in its level of precision—we can use it carefully or casually, from a jotted note to a formal proof—and it is generally a wonderful complement to other subsystems, for example, as annotation over the graphical-geometric component of maps.

Other subsystems have a different character. Arithmetic, for example, is much narrower in what you may write about with it. You can't write much good poetry or philosophy in numbers. But what it does allow us to think about, it does with great precision. We can draw inferences (calculate) using arithmetic either perfectly or with as much precision as we care to spend time to achieve. The power of arithmetic is tightly connected with other components of human intellect. For example, scientific understanding frequently is what liberates arithmetic as a useful tool; an engineer can calculate how big a beam is needed in a building because we understand scientifically how size, shape, and material relate to strength. Other important mathematical subsystems—algebra, calculus, graph drawing and interpreting, and so on—also have their own character. Each has its own structure, expressive range, associated modes of thought, and "intellectual allies."

The material pillar of literacy has two immensely important features: the material subsystems of literacy are technologically dependent, and they are designed. It is not at all incidental to contemporary literacy that paper and pencils are cheap, relatively easy to use, and portable. Think back to quills and parchment, or even to cuneiform impressions or rock painting or carving, and consider what you have done today with letters that would have been impossibly awkward without modern, cheap, portable implements. Think what difference the printing press made in creating a widespread, popular, and useful literacy.

Coming directly to the heart of this book, computer technology offers a dazzling range of inscription forms (spreadsheets, electronically processed images and pictures, hypertext, etc.), of reactive and interactive patterns (think of game interfaces—from text typed in and new text returned in reaction, to intense, real-time reflex interaction, to contemplative browsing of a visually based interactive mystery story), of storage and transmission modes (CDs to worldwide networking), and of autonomous actions (simulations, calculation). With all these new forms and more to come, it seems inconceivable our current material literacy basis could remain unaffected.

I noted also that all these inscription forms, both the historical ones and those in current and future development, have been designed—either in acts of inspiration (e.g., the invention of zero or the pulldown menu) or slowly over generations by an accumulation of little ideas and societal trial and error. We have much to gain by thinking carefully about what the whole game of literacy is and about what we can do with computers that can either hasten or undermine new possibilities.

The second pillar of literacy is mental or cognitive. Clearly the material basis of literacy stands only in conjunction with what we think and do with our minds in the presence of inscriptions. A book is only a poor stepping stool to a nonreader. Material intelligence does not reside in either the mind or the materials alone. Indeed, the coupling of external and internal activity is intricate and critical.

This mutual dependence has both constraining and liberating aspects. Our minds have some characteristics that are fixed by our evolutionary state. Nobody can see and remember a thousand items presented in a flash or draw certain kinds of inferences as quickly and precisely as a computer. On the positive side, our ability to talk and comprehend oral language is at least partly physiologically specific, and without this physical equipment, written literacy would also probably be impossible. Similarly, I believe that new computer literacies will build on and extend humans' impressive spatial and dynamic interactive capabilities far more than conventional literacy does. I have much more to say about these issues later, mainly in chapters 4, 5, and 8.

New computational inscription systems should therefore build on strengths in human mental capacities, and they must also recognize our limitations. Intelligence is a complex and textured thing. We know little enough about it in detail, and we will certainly be surprised by its nature when it is materially enhanced in quite unfamiliar ways. The simultaneous tracking of our understanding of intelligence and knowledge along with materially enhanced versions of them is, for me, among the most scientifically interesting issues of our times. It may be among the most practically relevant issues for the survival and prospering of our civilization.

The third pillar of literacy is social, the basis in community for enhanced literacies. Although one may imagine that an individual could benefit in private from a new or different material intelligence, literacy in the sense investigated in this book is unambiguously and deeply social. Let's take a look at the boundary between the social and the individual to get a feeling for the issues.

Sir Isaac Newton (1642–1727) is generally credited with inventing the calculus as part of building the intellectual infrastructure for his own accomplishments in understanding mechanics, the science of force and motion. His feat was one of those rare but especially impressive events in the history of science when a new material intelligence emerged out of the specific needs of an investigation; that new intelligence clearly contributed to Newton's ability to state and validate his new scientific accomplishments.

Fundamentally, the calculus is a way of writing down and drawing inferences about (i.e., calculating) various aspects of changing quantities. Newton wanted to reason about instantaneous properties of motion that were difficult to capture using prior conceptions and representations. A planet traveling around the sun is constantly changing its speed. Averages and constant speed situations, which were handled adequately by prior techniques, simply weren't up to dealing with facts about instants in a constantly and nonuniformly changing situation. The calculus allowed Newton to capture relations in those instants. Thinking about laws of nature that work in instants and at points in space has turned out to be one of the most fundamental and enduring moves of all time in physics. Nature's causality is local: there is no such thing as "action at a distance" (or "at a later time") in modern physics.

Newton's calculus sounds like a case of a new material intelligence emerging in the hands of an individual, which enabled and in part constituted a fundamental advance for all of science, but the details of the story betray important social components. In the first instance, Newton's accomplishment was clearly not developed on a blank slate. He borrowed and extended techniques, even graphical techniques, that had been around certainly since Galileo (1564–1642), fifty years earlier. (Galileo, in turn, cribbed many of these from his predecessors.) Newton himself said, "If I have seen farther than most, it is because I stood on the shoulders of giants," and this was as true for the calculus as for his laws of physics.

Neither was the development of calculus finished in Newton's work. G. W. Leibniz (1646–1716), most believe, independently developed the calculus at about the same time. Indeed, the notational form mainly in use today is Leibniz's, not Newton's. Although I can't prove it, I believe the reasons for this fact are in important measure pedagogic. Leibniz's notation is easier to learn; it is powerfully heuristic in suggesting useful techniques and ways of thinking about change; and it even makes obvious certain important theorems. For example, in Leibniz's notation the rate of change of a quantity, x, given a small change in another, t, looks like just what it is, a ratio, dx/dt. (The d in dx and dt stands for a change, or "delta," in the quantity.) Newton's notation is opaque, $\dot{x}$. In Leibniz's notation, the "change of variable theorem,"

$$\frac{dz}{dy} \bigg/ \frac{dx}{dy} = \frac{dz}{dx}$$

looks obvious, even if it is not. "Cancel the dys" appears to prove the theorem. Newton is not so helpful. His notation dealt easily only with changes in time, which he called "fluxions," so he pretty much had to state this theorem for the case that y is time, and he had to do it in words that hide the real generality of the theorem. Newton's statement of the theorem used the term *velocity* to describe dz/dy and dx/dy, whereas Leibniz's notation makes change over time only a special case: "The moments [spatial rate of change] of flowing quantities are as [the ratio of] the velocities [time rate of change] of their flowing or increasing."

The morals of Leibniz's contributions are both obvious and subtle. Obviously, once again, science is a strongly cumulative social enterprise. To reach their full potential, contributions must be both shared and extended by others. I would extend this precept beyond the bounds of professional science: incremental material intelligence in the hands of a genius, or even in the hands of a scientific or technological elite, is small in comparison to the huge possibilities of popular new literacies.

The second moral from Leibniz is more subtle, but it explains why I spend two chapters on the material basis of computational media. The inscripted form of thought is critically important. I've suggested that Leibniz has helped generations of scientists and mathematicians in training, even if his purely conceptual accomplishment was entirely redundant with Newton's. I can highlight this claim with a somewhat speculative thought experiment. The fact is that calculus has become absolutely infrastructural in the educational process of scientists, engineers, and a broad range of other technical professions. All learners in these categories are funneled through freshman calculus, if they did not already study calculus in high school. Further learning is dependent on this prerequisite. Upper division textbooks, for example, assume it in their exposition.

This move to infrastructural status for calculus was not easy. It took more than two centuries! In the twentieth century, a few bold universities decided it was possible and useful to teach calculus in the early and universal (that is, for all technical students) infrastructural mode. It succeeded, more or less, and gradually more schools jumped on the bandwagon. They had the advantage of knowing that teaching calculus this way was possible, and they could capitalize on the know-how of the early innovators. In the meantime, other professors and textbook writers for other classes began to take the teaching of calculus for granted. They became dependent on it. Calculus came to be infrastructural.

Focus on two critical phases. First, suppose calculus was just 10 percent more difficult to learn. Would those early innovators have had the courage to guess it might succeed? Similarly, at the second phase, if 10 percent fewer students "got it," would these innovators have declared success, and would others have followed and had enough success for the whole project to succeed? Finally, might Leibniz's notation have made that small difference by which the snowball of calculus got over the crest to start the eventual avalanche of infrastructural adoption?

I am not interested in verifying any particular account of these events. The general principles are clear. The emergence of a material intelligence as a literacy, as infrastructural, depends on complex social forces of innovation, adoption, and interdependence, even if (as I have argued is generally false) it originated with an individual or a small group. Furthermore, under some circumstances at least, small differences in learnability can make huge differences in eventual impact.

Here are the implications of this history of calculus with respect to the broader aims of this book. We may now have sufficiently learnable and powerful computational inscription systems to have dramatic literacy implications. For example, learning some important parts of mathematics and science may be transformed from a pleasurable success for a few but a painful failure for most to an infrastructural assumption for our whole society, and this transformation depends in an essential way on details of material form and on social forces, which it behooves us to understand.

A Cognitive View of Material Intelligence

My goal for this section is to illustrate and explicate some of the details of how material intelligence works to enhance the power of individual human beings. I have chosen to look at a small part of the works of Galileo for several reasons. The first is a version of the invisibility of water to fish. I want to take us a little away from our familiar everyday world of literacy so that some things we otherwise take for granted may stand out.

The second reason to consider Galileo is that doing so illustrates a somewhat technical and scientific component of literacy. Making mathematics and science easier and more interesting to learn was my first motivation for thinking about computers, and it is still my primary concern. I firmly believe computers will also have revolutionary literacy effects in art and the humanities generally, but this book is rich and complex enough dealing with mathematics and science. As a bonus, this little story leads directly into my own experiences in using computers to teach children about motion.

The last reason to look at Galileo and to return to the early part of the seventeenth century is to remind us, by contrast with what exists today, that literacy is created. What we had is not what we have, and without the slightest doubt it is not what we will have. The process of literacy creation happens on the scale of decades, if not centuries, even for some relatively small components of literacy. If we want to think about new literacies—and I think we must, given their importance—we must also free ourselves to think about the coming decades, not just next year.

Let me start this little parable of Galileo and literacy as it first appeared to me—as a puzzle. Just at the beginning of his treatment of motion in *Dialogues Concerning Two New Sciences,* at the outset of what is generally regarded as his greatest accomplishment, Galileo defines uniform motion, motion with a constant speed. The section that follows this definition consists of six theorems about uniform motion and their proofs. Below, I reproduce those theorems. Despite the unfamiliarity of the language, I urge you to try to follow along and think what, in essence, Galileo is getting at in these theorems and how we would express it in modern terms.

THEOREM 1   If a moving particle, carried uniformly at constant speed, traverses two distances, then the time intervals required are to each other in the ratio of these distances.

THEOREM 2   If a moving particle traverses two distances in equal intervals of time, these distances will bear to each other the same ratio as their speeds. And conversely, if the distances are as the speeds, then the times are equal.

THEOREM 3   In the case of unequal speeds, the time intervals required to traverse a given space are to each other inversely as the speeds.

THEOREM 4   If two particles are carried with uniform motion, but each with a different speed, then the distances covered by them during unequal intervals of time bear to each other the compound ratio of the speeds and time intervals.

THEOREM 5   If two particles are moved at a uniform rate, but with unequal speeds, through unequal distances, then the ratio of the time intervals occupied will be the products of the distances by the inverse ratio of the speeds.

THEOREM 6   If two particles are carried at a uniform rate, the ratio of their speeds will be the product of the ratio of the distances traversed by the inverse ratio of the time intervals occupied.

A modern reader (after struggling past the language of ratios and inverse ratios) must surely get the impression that here there is much ado about very little. It seems like a pretentious and grandly overdone set of variations on the theme of "distance equals rate times time." To make matters worse, the proofs of these theorems given by Galileo are hardly trivial, averaging almost a page of text. The first proof, indeed, is difficult enough that it took me about a half-dozen readings before I understood how it worked. (See the boxed text.)

In fact this *is* a set of variations on distance equals rate times time. Allow me to make this abundantly clear. Each of these theorems is about two motions, so we can write "distance equals rate times time" for each. Subscripts specify which motion the distance (d), rate (r), and time interval (t) belong to.

$$d_1 = r_1 t_1$$
$$d_2 = r_2 t_2$$

In these terms, we can state and prove each of Galileo's theorems. Because Galileo uses ratios, first we divide equals by equals (the left and right sides of the equations above, respectively) and achieve:

$$\frac{d_1}{d_2} = \frac{r_1}{r_2}\frac{t_1}{t_2}$$

THEOREM 1   In the case $r_1 = r_2$, the r terms cancel, leaving $d_1/d_2 = t_1/t_2$.

THEOREM 2   In the case $t_1 = t_2$, the t terms cancel, leaving $d_1/d_2 = r_1/r_2$. Conversely, if $d_1/d_2 = r_1/r_2$ then $t_1/t_2 = 1$ or $t_1 = t_2$.

THEOREM 3   In the case of $d_1 = d_2$, the d terms cancel, leaving $(r_1/r_2)(t_1/t_2) = 1$, or $t_1/t_2 = r_2/r_1$.

THEOREM 4   This is precisely our little ratio lemma, $d_1/d_2 = (r_1/r_2)(t_1/t_2)$.

THEOREM 5   Solve the equation above for t_1/t_2; $t_1/t_2 = (d_1/d_2)(r_2/r_1)$.

THEOREM 6   Solve for r_1/r_2; $r_1/r_2 = (d_1/d_2)(t_2/t_1)$.

For direct contrast, I reproduce Galileo's proof of theorem 1, which is *one-sixth* of the job we did with algebra, in box 1.

So now we've redone a significant piece of work by one of the great geniuses of Western science, with amazing ease. Solving problems is always easier after the first time around, but the difference here is almost mindboggling. What we did would constitute only an exercise for a ninth-grade mathematics student.

That, in fact, is the key. Galileo never had ninth-grade mathematics; he didn't know algebra! There is not a single "=" in all of Galileo's writing.

The fault is not with Galileo or with the education provided by his parents or with the schooling of the times. Algebra simply did not exist at that time. To be more precise, although solving for unknowns that participated in given relations with other numbers had been practiced for at least half a millennium, the modern notational system that allows writing equations as we know them—and also the easy manipulations to solve them—did not exist. Fifty years after Galileo's main work, René Descartes (1596–1650) would have a really good start on modern algebra. Later, by the end of the seventeenth century, algebra had stabilized to roughly the modern notation and manipulative practices, although it would be the twentieth century before algebra became a part of widespread technical literacy.

Box 1

If a moving particle, carried uniformly at a constant speed, traverses two distances the time-intervals required are to each other in the ratio of these distances.

Let a particle move uniformly with constant speed through two distances AB, BC, and let the time required to traverse AB be represented by DE; the time required to traverse BC, by EF; then I say that the distance AB is to the distance BC as the time DE is to the time EF.

Let the distances and times be extended on both sides towards G, H and I, K; let AG be divided into any number whatever of spaces each equal to AB, and in like manner lay off in DI exactly the same number of time-intervals each equal to DE. Again lay off in CH any number whatever of distances each equal to BC; and in FK exactly the same number of time-intervals each equal to EF; then will the distance BG and the time EI be equal and arbitrary multiples of the distance BA and the time ED; and like-wise the distance HB and the time KE are equal and arbitrary multiples of the distance CB and the time FE.

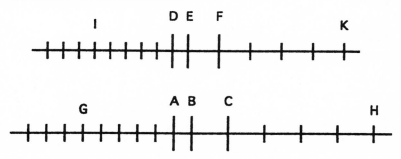

And since DE is the time required to traverse AB, the whole time EI will be required for the whole distance BG, and when the motion is uniform there will be in EI as many time-intervals each equal to DE as there are distances in BG each equal to BA; and likewise it follows that KE represents the time required to traverse HB.

Since, however, the motion is uniform, it follows that if the distance GB is equal to the distance BH, then must also the time IE be equal to the time EK; and if GB is greater than BH, then also IE will be greater than EK; and if less, less. There are then four quantities, the first AB, the second BC, the third DE, and the fourth EF; the time IE and the distance GB are arbitrary multiples of the first and the third, namely of the distance AB and the time DE.

But it has been proved that *both* of these latter quantities are either equal to, greater than, or less than the time EK and the space BH, which are arbitrary multiples of the second and the fourth. Therefore, the first is to the second, namely the distance AB is to the distance BC, as the third is to the fourth, namely the time DE is to the time EF.
Q.E.D.

(From Galileo, *Dialogues Concerning Two New Sciences*. Translated by H. Crew and A. de Salvio [Northwestern University, 1939], pp. 155–156.)

In net, an average ninth-grade mathematics student plus a particular inscription system yields a material intelligence that surpasses Galileo's intelligence, at least in this domain of writing and "reasoning about" simple quantitative relationships.

We can learn more about the power that material intelligence conveys to individuals by thinking more about this example. Notice first that the equations are shorter, more concise than Galileo's natural language. Compactness has many advantages, besides saving paper. It usually results in statements that are easier to remember. Every mathematically literate person remembers, probably literally and iconically, $d = rt$, and possibly $E = mc^2$. Some even remember the solution to the quadratic equation,

$$x = \frac{-b \pm \sqrt{b^2 - 4ac}}{2a}$$

(I didn't have to look it up!). Galileo's sentences, as well written as they are, are less compact and less memorable. Our memories are better with good external inscriptions, even if we do not use the material form as memory by rereading what we wrote a while ago. Literacies leave traces of themselves in autonomous thinking, making us smarter even when we're not in the presence of the material form.

Inscription systems and associated subliteracies are a little like miniature languages in that they select a certain kind of thing to talk about and certain things to say about them. They have a certain vocabulary, one might say. Thus, each system is apt for some things and less apt for others. Every good new system enlarges the set of ways we can think about the world. If we happen to have in hand a system that is apt for learning or inquiring into a new area, we make progress quickly. If it turns out that a fairly easy inscription system enlightens a new area, then we can teach the inscription system first, and students will learn the area much more easily than those who had to work without or had to invent the system. This is a general version of where we came in: any high school student who knows algebra and Descartes's analytic geometry can learn all of Galileo's accomplishments concerning motion in very short order.

Part of expressing the right things is picking the right level of abstraction. For example, Galileo sometimes talks about two motions of one particle and sometimes about two distinct particles. These details are irrelevant, however; the algebraically expressed relations apply to any pair of motions. An even higher level of abstraction than that of equations turns out to be worse than one that is too detailed. To say that distance, rate, and time "are related" misses important, relevant details.

Algebra has been so spectacularly successful at picking a good level of abstraction and displaying the right kind of relations that in some parts of science, one may understandably, but incorrectly, view progress as a march from one equation to the next, from Newton ($F = ma$) to Maxwell

$$(\nabla \times E = -\frac{1}{c}\frac{\partial B}{\partial t}, \text{etc.})$$

to relativity (Einstein's $E = mc^2$) to quantum mechanics (Schroedinger's equation,

$$i\hbar\frac{\partial}{\partial t}\Psi = -\frac{\hbar^2}{2m}\nabla^2\Psi).$$

Yet we must not forget: (1) Algebra did not always exist; it was invented, just as other systems have been and will be developed, especially with the advent of computers. (2) Algebra is not apt for all areas of science; it has not been nearly as important in biology as in physics, and I am quite sure it will never be so central in cognitive science.

Coming to see or hypothesize patterns—discovery—is an important mental act that can be aided by literacies, especially those based on simple, systematic representational systems. Systematic representational systems aid discovery because they convert abstract "intellectual" patterns into spatial, visible ones. James Maxwell discovered an important electromagnetic phenomenon essentially because a missing term broke a nice pattern in a set of equations. There's a miniature example here in Galileo's six theorems. Why are there six? Might there be more, or perhaps fewer would do? Probably only the most diligent and perceptive reader noticed the pattern in Galileo's discourse, but, at least in retrospect, the algebraic form makes it evident: Start with the ratio form of $d = rt$. The first three relationships eliminate in succession each of the three basic quantities—rate, distance, and time—by declaring a ratio equal to one; the second three express the full relationship, solving one at a time for distance, rate, and time ratios. We note also, therefore, that the first three relations are special cases of the last three.

Casting a wider net, graphs are another obvious case where a written literacy makes pattern detection easier. A graph that swoops up shows us instantly that a quantity is increasing faster and faster.

I have been listing ways in which written inscription systems can make us smarter, illustrating some details of material intelligence using algebra as an example. Inscription systems and associated subliteracies can effectively improve our memories, even without our rereading what we wrote. They may be well adapted to saying clearly, precisely, and compactly the particular things that need to be said in a particular field of study. They may also extend our abilities to detect patterns and make discoveries. The last example I want to deal with here is at the heart of intelligence: reasoning—the ability to draw inferences.

Look again at what I did with Galileo's six theorems and think how those results would appear in the minds of modern, algebra-literate knowers. I do not think an investigation is necessary. We know that $d = rt$ is a part of our current mathematical and scientific cultures, but Galileo's "six laws of uniform motion" are not. We can certainly tell what they are about, but they are not cornerstone pieces of our basic understanding. The reason is fairly obvious. The modern algebraic form is simply much better adapted to exactly what needs to be said. It produces a compact, precise, memorable statement at exactly the right level of abstraction. But what about Galileo's theorems? Have we lost them? Hardly. These theorems are so easy to derive algebraically that a student could easily manage the task, and a scientist would do it so effortlessly that no one would think to consider it a new result.

Think about it this way. Theorems are necessarily true given the axioms and definitions out of which they flow, so why do we bother writing the theorems at all? We do so simply because reasoning is sometimes expensive, and we just can't afford to reason from basic principles each time. We struggle to derive a result once, then essentially memorize it so that we have it quickly available whenever we need it. If reasoning suddenly becomes inexpensive, we can keep just the definitions and axioms in our own minds and derive particular theorems at need. In this case, reasoning became inexpensive because of a new modicum of material intelligence. We can quickly and easily see many implications of an algebraic expression by pushing symbols around. Galileo's intellectual terrain had six small hills. The algebraically enhanced version is one tall, powerful mountain of a result that covers the whole area of those six hills and more besides, using the glue of algebraic reasoning to hold it all together.

I find this a provocative image. Not only can new inscription systems and literacies ease learning, as algebra simplified the proofs of Galileo's theorems, but they may also rearrange the entire intellectual terrain. New principles become fundamental and old ones become obvious. Entirely new terrain becomes accessible, and some old terrain becomes boring.

A Social View of Material Intelligence

When I first introduced social components of literacies, I made two basic points. First, as with any of the major intellectual accomplishments of society, there is always a gradual, cumulative development that involves many people. The second point is about the conversion of a material intelligence in a technical sense (which Newton and Leibniz had) into a true widespread literacy. The simplest version of the latter story is that a community decides a material intelligence is powerful and valuable enough that it is worth the considerable effort of teaching it to all new-comers. The community then puts in place an infrastructure for teaching it—freshman calculus or ninth-grade algebra, for example.

In this section, I want to expand these points, particularly the second, into a more faithfully complex view of the social processes surrounding literacy. We need, most of all, to begin to address the following central questions:

1. What determines whether a literacy can exist? and
2. What determines its nature?

In this way, we may be able to make a more intelligent assessment of whether computational literacies can come to exist, what they may be like, and, as important, how we may design and foster them.

Let me begin with a modest first try at a definition of literacy:

Literacy is a socially widespread patterned deployment of skills and capabilities in a context of material support (that is, an exercise of material intelligence) to achieve valued intellectual ends.

The "intellectual" part is merely to emphasize that we're not talking about skillfully operating a piece of heavy equipment to dig a hole. The "patterned deployment" part is to avoid lumping all versions of wide-spread material intelligence under one umbrella. Unless we distinguish, for example, patterns in using algebra from patterns in using ordinary text, we can't be specific enough to rule in or rule out particular future literacies. Essentially different patterns in the deployment of literacy skills need to be understood separately, possibly on different principles. Algebra doesn't work cognitively or socially like reading and writing natural language. Computational literacy will exhibit still other patterns.

This initial definition turns out to have a great deal of ambiguity in it. Keep in mind that the important thing we want to do is think about possible future literacies, rather than present ones where we have a better sense of what is included in a literacy and what is not. Ambiguity makes it difficult to decide what literacies are sensible and possible. Looking for ambiguities, start in the middle, with "material support." What materials? What support? With conventional literacy, presumably we mean text, but do we mean text in newspapers, in books, on notepads, on computer screens, on blackboards, or indiscriminately all of these at once? And what kind of support? In the previous section, I listed a fairly big collection of ways algebra supports intellectual accomplishments, yet that list is scarcely complete. Indeed, I do not believe that it can in principle be complete, for new physical inscription systems bring about new possibilities.

Scanning across the definition we also meet "skills and capabilities." Which ones? No respectable account of all the skills and capabilities that humans possess has been produced, and just as with "support," we cannot expect any closed list to suffice. Innovation in the material means of possible literacies may make any list of essential skills obsolete. The invention of graphing made curve recognition skills relevant to intellectual pursuits in a whole new way, and in fact it redefined those skills with a new vocabulary. Trivially, but not inconsequentially, a certain kind of manual dexterity and hand-eye coordination became relevant with the invention and adoption of the computer mouse. More profoundly, any given skills may change their effect on and relevance to valued accomplishments with the development of other skills. For example, arithmetic may be a valued skill, but it changes its entire context—its community association, if not its essential meaning—when quantitative sciences give arithmetical computation new reach. Not just accountants but also engineers and scientists use arithmetic, and for each, it is relevant in a different way. For accountants, arithmetic may be "keeping track"; for engineers, it may be "deciding on an element of design"; and for scientists, it may be "tracing implications of a theory."

Finally, values, as in "valued intellectual ends," add another dimension of ambiguity in the proposed definition of literacy. Whose values, and of what sort? Scientists' parsimony, citizens' political empowerment, artists' aesthetics, a child's joyfulness in play?

Although I wring just a bit more specificity out of our preliminary definition in a moment, there is a fundamental lesson here. We must recognize an inescapable diversity in the phenomenon of literacy. There is no essential, common basis of literacy along any of the dimensions listed or along any other similar ones. There are no fixed basic human skills on which it builds. If oral language is a central competency, it is one among an open set of competencies we have or can build. Even oral language itself is open to innovation; we talk in different ways about different things depending on many other components of our material (and immaterial) intelligence. For example, we anticipate and build on non-speech intelligences in our talk—say, reciting $F = ma$ or announcing preliminary guesses of successor equations whose ultimate value will be tested substantially in different, more material modes. This is not to say that intrinsic human intelligence is infinitely malleable, but that existing and future intelligences draw on and engage it in such complex and intricate ways that guessing essential commonalties is not much more than an entertaining parlor game.

Similarly, saying what we get out of literacies is at best a tentative and culturally relative pursuit. We might identify intellectual powers (e.g., improved memory, more "logical" reasoning capability, precision in expression, metadiscursive competencies such as better understanding or manipulation of context dependencies in expression, etc.) or instrumental capabilities (say, "mastering nature"). However, these outcomes certainly vary across different material forms and practices; they are value related and hence depend on culture.

Construed scientifically, this claim of fundamental diversity is contentious and probably unpopular. In a different context, it would deserve a lot of exposition in defense. In this context, however, I believe the claim is properly conservative and at least heuristically correct. Whether or not the claim proves ultimately true, we simply cannot afford to limit our explorations of possible future literacies to extrapolations of what we think we understand about literacy now. Every claim for the essence of literacy can suggest how we may do better with computers, but computer-supported literacies may also work in completely different ways. At this stage, we need generative ideas as much as we need restrictive ones.

Still, can't we do better than "anything goes"? Yes, we can. What do the following have in common: newspapers, magazines (from *People* to *Soldier of Fortune* to *National Geographic*), scientific papers, pulp fiction, poetry, advertisements, tax forms, instruction manuals, and financial prospectuses? The seemingly innocuous but essential observation is that, although they use mostly the same basic material form, they each serve different groups of people in different ways. Variations in form and patterns of use from one to another are comprehensible as adaptations to serve particular purposes in particular contexts.

Let me introduce some terminology. I call each of the specialized forms in which we find literacy exercised in production and consumption a *genre*. This use of the term is a little different from the conventional use in literary criticism, especially when we extend *genre* to cover patterns in the production and consumption of algebra or of new computational inscription forms. However, the basic idea of a recognizably distinct use of a common material substrate is preserved as long as we also emphasize that genres serve particular groups of people in particular ways.

This latter idea—that any genre fits the needs and circumstances of a community—I describe with the phrase *the genre fits a social niche*.

Consider the following example, which I call the subway romance novel–reading niche. A few years ago when I rode the subway regularly in Boston, I undertook an informal study. I noted each day how many people were in my car, how many were reading, and what they read. I noticed that a large percentage of people read (a surprisingly small proportion of these read newspapers), and a reasonable proportion of these riders read romance novels. Think about all of the factors that go into the creation and perpetuation of this genre in its niche.

1. It goes without saying that the romance novel niche rests on the well-established universal literacy basis developed in public education. I doubt this niche could self-generate without that prerequisite; the effort to learn to read is too great for the incremental value of being able to read a romance novel.

2. Almost all subway romance novel readers are women. This says a lot about the position of women in our society.

3. The Western concept of romantic love is an essential constituent. Whatever currents created and sustained the idea, romance is at the heart of romance novel reading. Other cultures would not recognize the sense or value of this genre.

4. Similarly, whatever personal value is perceived in the genre, it is important that there is no public social sanction against reading such novels. There's a delicate balance here. How many fewer public readers of *Playboy* are there because of the very modest and sporadic disapproval it brings? Religious fundamentalist cultures disdain and suppress both romance novels and pornographic magazines.

5. The price of production and cost of paper are relevant. A fifty-dollar romance novel wouldn't sell. Similarly, it is important that writers of these novels can make a living writing or else that it is possible to write while moonlighting. How important is the ubiquitous corner drugstore or newsstand to distribution?

6. The invention of the printing press and paper are relevant technical accomplishments. Cuneiform tablets just wouldn't work.

7. The requisite unoccupied commuting time relies on the existence of mass transit and whatever public values and political processes were necessary to create it. I haven't any idea what proportion of romance novel consumption comes from subway reading, but I'll bet it is significant enough that the demise of subways would be a blow, maybe even a fatal one, to publishers. It is also important that the trains are not outrageously crowded or noisy and that the readers' investment in and nature of their jobs doesn't force out pleasure reading.

These observations are almost the opposite of any claim that there is an essence to the operation and power of literacy. The conditions for creating and sustaining a genre in its social niche reach deeply into and depend delicately on all sorts of physical, social, cultural, institutional, and historical conditions.

We can consolidate this view of literacy in a central hypothesis.

A literacy is the convergence of a large number of genres and social niches on a common, underlying representational form.

Genres are the variously refined and specialized styles of the underlying form, as a romance novel is a specialized sort of text. The social niche defines the complex web of motivating, enabling, and constraining factors that, first and foremost, allow a stability in the form of the genre and in its characteristic pattern of production and consumption. The social niche not only establishes the conditions for existence, but should also explain the defining characteristics of a genre. Existence and nature were the two basic questions that started this inquiry into the social basis of literacies.

The term *niche* is borrowed from ecology, where species—their characteristics and their survival—are studied according to the niche they occupy in the complex web of dependencies in which they participate. Does a particular species have enough land to forage; is it physically adapted to eat available food; are conditions right for the production of that food; are natural predators limited in some way? Genre is to social niche as species is to ecological niche. The challenging game in both inquiries is to discover and identify the necessary and possible types of interdependency. More than any other aspect of this metaphor, I believe that the complexity and range of types of interdependency for social niches of current and future literacies will match or exceed the complexity and range we are still discovering in ecology.

One aspect of a social niches inquiry is manifestly even more complex than for ecological niches. At least for biological niches, the basic chemistry of life is stable. We are all carbon-based life forms that use DNA to pass information from generation to generation. In contrast, our interest in genres and social niches is predicated on a substantial change of the basic material substrate—from static and mainly linear forms to essentially dynamic, multiply connected, and interactive computational media. This change is the main reason for the inquiry, but it also makes the inquiry more difficult and less definitive.

What we know and what we don't know is put in high relief by the concept of social niches. Multiple genres and niches explicitly represent inescapable diversity that strongly motivates broad exploration into new niches now that the "chemical basis of life" in this new "ecology" is moving to electronic forms. On the other hand, social niches also emphasize limits and our scientific accountability, stemming from the basic requirement to assess and explain viability of new social niches. We can't make just any new literacy, no matter how good it might be for us. Social viability is a harsh master. The "skills basis" and "support for intellectual ends" of our first proposed definition of literacy are put in a larger context, including dimensions such as economics and cultural history. Everything we know about each of these dimensions is relevant in principle.

To summarize, a social niches view of literacy comprehends the variability we know from conventional literacy as inescapable. We need to make room for both pulp novels and scientific papers. Each genre fits a different context in a different way. Recognizing that diversity, we are prepared for a future that could be very different. At the same time, we know that not everything can work. In understanding what works and what might work, we need to examine many perspectives on the viability of a niche and the fit of a genre to it.

I wish to cover three other general issues about literacy, genres, and social niches here. The first emphasizes the uncertainty of the central hypothesis concerning social niches and literacy. The question is whether a large number of genres and niches must be involved in a literacy, or would a few—or even one very important one—do? It seems clear that the current widespread textual literacy works because of the existence of a large number of niches that use basically one common representational form. What about all possible future literacies? My bet is that the most important literacies will always work in this way, and the work described in this book assumes that. This issue marks an important choice point determining the kind of software systems we design. Do we design a large number of pieces and kinds of software to fit into a diversity of niches? Or do we follow the pattern from the case of written text and try to create a rich medium capable of supporting a protean array of niches? The work described in this book follows the latter course—aiming to change minds with a single, if extremely versatile, material form. The issue of forms and niches is further explored, for example, under the banner of multifunctionality in chapters 6 and 7, and then also in chapter 9.

Second, I want to make explicit yet another layer of complexity in the analysis of social niches. Start with an image. Think of a grand canyon of textual literacy carved up into quasi-hierarchical subliteracies and sub-subliteracies, which are, metaphorically, branches, gulches, rivulets, and microrivulets built into the texture of the canyon. People read; they read novels (or scientific works); they read pulp fiction (or historical novels); they read pulp romance novels (or science fiction). Down the scientific reading branch, there are subbranches for distinct genres such as treatises, papers, and so on.

The grand canyon view of literacy concentrates on form. But it hides both many uniformities and irregularities. Consider this irregularity: treatises in both philosophy and in mathematics are treatises and not papers or novels, yet they are noticeably different from each other, for understandable reasons: the forms of argument in mathematics and philosophy are different, and this difference propagates into the literary form. Consider also the following (hidden) regularity: you may be tempted to think the influence of the scientific community resides only in "its" genres, but sometimes scientists behave more or less as a bloc with respect to other genres. This might happen because of communitywide characteristics such as economic class, level of education, and so on, so the influence of the scientific community on nonscientific genres is scattered about the grand canyon and not made clear in its structure. We can't see, for example, that the scientific community as a whole is irrelevant to the subway romance novel–reading niche, but that it may be very relevant to science fiction or film. We can't tell that wiping out scientists wouldn't affect romance novels, but that making secretaries' jobs more interesting perhaps would.

I think of this blindness as a problem of perspective. If we choose to think of social niches as geometric forms, then they are forms in a high-dimensional space, not the two or three of the grand canyon. If we choose to look at them from one perspective or another—say, material form, community, or values—we will see the niches grouped in different ways, with different relations among them. Take the grand canyon view (form, subform, etc.), tilt it on its side to get a community view, and you may notice that Jane Austen novels and books such as *Relativistic Quantum Fields* have much more in common than you might have thought.

Finally, let me list a few perspectives on social niches and comment briefly on them mainly because they are relevant to future prospects. We'll come back with more extensive discussion of these perspectives in chapter 9, after we've prepared a better understanding of the possibilities for computational literacies.

1. *Values, interests, motivations.* I know of no really good scientific theory of these, but without question we must take them into account in designing or studying social niches. Of the list of values I mentioned earlier—including scientific, political, artistic, and playful sensibilities—I take two to be most important. Naturally, my personal interests are building on and developing scientific aesthetics—for example, wanting to understand how things work and a great appreciation for the power and parsimony of theories. The other central kind of value may be surprising. It is, at least emblematically, whatever interests can lead a child into extended, self-motivated activity. I think the dawn of computational media is precisely the right time to remake the experience of science and mathematics learning in schools so that interests and values are not ignored. This revision will be a major topic in chapters 4 and 5.

2. *Skills and capabilities.* Textual literacy draws on certain human competencies and not others. For example, the immense competence of humans in dealing with both dynamic and spatial configurations is barely engaged by conventional literacies. We can do better electronically.

3. *Materials.* The material form of future computational literacies is a huge open question, and it may be the place where our directed skills as designers can have most leverage. We can wait for things to happen by accident, or, with due respect for what we do not know, we can move deliberately in the direction of the best we can imagine.

The form of future inscription systems is one thing, but delivery and use are another. With delivery at least, we seem in fine shape technologically for many possible literacies. Unlimited inexpensive or free distribution on CD-ROM (or DVD or other future versions) and via network is already a reality. A really portable personal computer for every teacher and school child could make an immense difference in richness of social niches, I am convinced. We are within a short technological and economical hop of ubiquitous availability. Politically and with respect to a sufficiently clear and convincing public image of what we might achieve, we probably have a longer distance to go.

4. *Community and communal practices.* Current community structures are important, but future possibilities are equally important, if not more so. It is probably too arrogant to think we can design new communities, but as network communications become universal on computers, we may be able to promote productive changes.

5. *Economics.* Hardware is much less the issue than software. It is still difficult to make money with educational software. The research and development of future literacies is an issue of public trust if ever there was one, but the issue doesn't even appear on the agenda of any government agency. If the conclusions of this book are correct—or even a responsible good guess—we are making a terrible mistake by this omission.

6. *History.* Cultural and technical history are powerful currents. The development of a computational basis for new literacies is orthogonal, if not antithetical, to most current trends. I discuss history (and some other of the issues listed above) more in chapter 9. In the best case, blindly following current directions means a delay, possibly a long one. In the worst cases, we'll do things such as standardize suboptimal technology, of which the awkward QWERTY keyboard, which we all are stuck using, is emblematic.

2

How It Might Be

Chapter 1 set the scale of the enterprise—a powerful new material intelligence for human civilization—and opened inquiry into the material, cognitive, and social foundations for new literacies. But what might a computational literacy be like? This chapter presents two concrete images of what the future may hold. One is oriented mainly cognitively and the other mainly socially. Because it is too easy to wax poetic about unimaginable future revolutions, I want to strike a careful balance between present and future. Both of these examples are rooted in experiences we have already had, but I also want to extrapolate toward what I believe to be genuine but profound future possibilities.

Beyond Algebra

Algebra brought certain kinds of reasoning from the province of geniuses such as Galileo into the grasp of average high school students, but suppose there were some new representational form that was (1) easier to learn; (2) learnable at earlier ages; (3) even better adapted to describing important aspects of motion; (4) synthetic—that is, it could produce motion for all to see rather than just analyze or describe it; (5) more useful than algebra for a broader range of subjects; and (6) an incredible lot of fun to play with. Surely such an advance would be adopted immediately by schools.

Let me jump in the deep end with both feet. Suppose that by the end of elementary school, students were literate with computer programming. I am taking computer programming languages to be a material form for

Figure 2.1
The tick model, which defines uniform motion.

a hypothetical new literacy, and I'm assuming that programming is within the grasp of elementary school students. I want to look directly at how such students could approach something like Galileo's six motion theorems and also the next step in his research program—defining and exploring the properties of uniformly accelerating motion. Evidently we're looking at going algebra one better by introducing some basic ideas of motion five grades earlier (than high school physics) on the basis of a new and different literacy. I will use Boxer, the prototype computational medium my colleagues and I have been working on, as the example notational system.

The three elements in figure 2.1 constitute a computer program that represents uniform motion. We call it the *tick model* because, at its core, it shows what happens at each "tick of the clock."

The tick model, like almost any program, has two parts. The *informational* part, or data, is simply a number that represents the speed of the moving object. In Boxer, this corresponds to a data box with an appropriate name, say **s**, for speed. That is the first box in figure 2.1.

The second and third boxes define the *procedural* part of the program, what happens with the data. These are doit (do it) boxes. The second box in figure 2.1 represents the overall "shape" of the process. In this case, it is very simple. In order to **run**, you **loop** (repeat over and over) the simple action, **tick**. **Tick**, in turn, is also very simple. **Tick** does a **move s**, which commands a graphical object to move the short distance specified by the speed, **s**. With every tick of the clock (perhaps **tick** should sound a little click), our object moves a little bit. For simplicity we can make our computer loop through one tick each second.

Each of these parts is independently important. **Run** tells us that exactly the same thing happens over and over; the process is uniform. **Tick**, of course, says what happens over and over, and **s** quantifies the physical

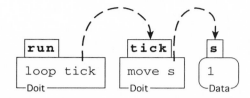

Figure 2.2
Showing the dependencies in the tick model.

process. A bigger **s** means a proportionally greater speed. Figure 2.2 shows the program "from top to bottom" with dotted lines to emphasize dependencies.

What I'd like to do now is consider the properties—the advantages and some disadvantages—of this representational form as an aid to thinking and learning about motion. I use more or less the same set of properties we discussed earlier in considering calculus and more particularly algebra. In fact, I use algebra, along with text and to a minor degree calculus, in making comparisons to programming, which will highlight particular features of each representational scheme.

Let us start with expressiveness. Simply and directly, programming is marvelously adapted to expressing many things about motion. The tick model illustrates the fit between motion and programming well. All the important features of uniform motion appear, and they appear pretty much in independent places. I would call the latter property "information factoring"; you need to look in only one place to see one of the essential features. Look at **run** and you see the uniformity of the process. Look at **tick** and you see the nature of the process at each instant. A simple, numerical parameter is shown by **s** and the use of **s** in tick shows exactly the nature of the parameter's influence.

Compared to text, the tick model shows the characteristic strengths of a technical representational system. It is concise, with all the advantages accrued by compact form—including, usually, memorability. It is also precise. Not only do numbers have a natural fit in the representation, but the process depicted is quite unambiguous, if the reader is familiar with the computational meaning of the program. The latter conceptual clarity is hardly mysterious. Programming languages such as Boxer are precisely languages that express certain kinds of processes without ambiguity. Learning the language means learning how to interpret these inscriptions. Once you have learned that, every instance where the language aptly describes a situation is an instance where you reuse your basic understanding effectively.

Aptness is critical. Every inscription system is apt for some things and less apt for others. Programming, like arithmetic, is evidently not very apt for poetry or for discussing the nature of computational media, but it happens to be quite superb for motion. Being apt for a wide range of things, of course, is pretty much the question of multiple niches for a computational medium. I won't try to discuss the extent and limits of programming's aptness in any detail here.

There is a slightly tricky point about precision and conciseness when we are talking about text and programming as media. Language always affords you the option of developing an intricate technical vocabulary and expressive figures of speech to tune its general capabilities to a particular use. Not only can you invent technical terms, but you can talk about other representational forms. For example, you can speak an equation by saying "distance equals rate times time." There are limits, however, to this enfolding of other inscription systems. In the first place, you have to do the work of building the technical vocabulary or learning the other representational system under discussion, and then you still don't get all of its advantages. I have frequently written little programs in my head at night in bed before falling asleep, but then, unless the program is completely trivial, I realize I'll have to try it in the morning to see whether it correctly does what I wanted.

Programming, like text, happens to be excellent at enfolding more specific representation subsystems and at accepting "tuning" toward specific purposes (as in adding a specialized vocabulary). These capacities turn out to be among its most important strengths (see chapter 7).

Comparing to algebra illuminates other important properties of the tick model. Algebra—for instance, $d = rt$—is arguably a bit more concise and better adapted to a familiar class of word problems: "How long does it take Johnny to . . . ?" But its very high level of abstraction, important to some central aspects of its power, is also a serious problem in other ways. Algebra does not distinguish at all effectively among motion

($d = rt$), converting meters to inches ($i = 39.37 \times m$), defining coordinates of a straight line ($y = mx$) or a host of other conceptually varied situations. Distinguishing these contexts is critical in learning, although it is probably nearly irrelevant in fluid, routine work for experts. The tick model picks apart uniform motion and sets it in a clear, well-developed process framework. Given how poorly adapted both language and algebra are to the central details of physics concepts generally (and given other issues, described below), I am amazed at how well we have managed to teach these things with older media. Even so, it is no surprise that we have had to wait years more than I believe is necessary—until after algebra instruction—before teaching motion concepts. Accepting the wait, students still almost always get stranded at the high level of abstraction of algebra and symbol pushing, at least for a time. "Plug and chug" is the well-known phenomenon of novices' avoiding all conceptual analysis by grabbing a seemingly relevant equation and "grinding" the algebra.

The conceptual aptness of programming for motion has a third and equally important component beyond a process orientation and an appropriate level of abstraction. I mentioned before that one of the most fundamental and enduring moves of all time in physics was the move to understanding nature's laws as local, as unfolding only at instants of time and independently at each point in space. The emblem for that grandly important principle here is the **tick** procedure itself, which represents the heart of motion, what happens at each instant. Programming turns out in general to be really well adapted to local principles. We previously looked at the insufficiency of algebra to describe local principles, which forced Newton to invent calculus. Not only are our hypothetical sixth-grade children getting started learning physics much earlier and in some ways better than they could with algebra, but they are also being introduced to some of the critical postalgebra ideas aptly captured in current instruction only by calculus.

I can at least sharpen focus on the tip of this iceberg with another remark about the tick model. The following observation is allowed by looking at the tick model and understanding what it means as a process describing motion. The total distance traveled by an object is just the sum of all the **s**'s, which are the distances moved each "tick." In the simplest case this is just t times s, where t is the number of ticks. We have just derived the basic relationship that we used to redo Galileo's six theorems; $d = rt$ (in this case $d = st$) is within easy inferential reach of the tick model. Furthermore, we can proceed to a generalization if **s** is changing each instant. Distance traveled is still the sum of all the speeds, **s**. Calculus-literate readers will recognize this as an important special case of the Fundamental Theorem of Calculus. The conventional way of writing this theorem is $d = \int s\, dt$, where $\int$ is Leibniz's sign for the integral operation, corrupted in a wonderfully heuristic fashion from S, for sum.

Going back to Galileo, we shouldn't be surprised that he had difficulty maintaining a focus on the local nature of motion, although some of his best accomplishments came when he managed to do that. An excellent case in point is that he did not derive his versions of $d = rt$ as I did above, by focusing on the instants and small bits of motion that accumulate into a larger motion. Instead, he embedded his motions in still larger motions—going in the opposite direction! (Amazingly, this method works, although, as you are invited to check in the proof quoted in the previous chapter, it involves both complexity and cleverness.)

The tick model is not the same as knowing algebra and $d = rt$, nor is it the same as knowing calculus. In particular, both algebra and calculus allow some inferences that are difficult to express in computer programs. Yet programming prepares the ground to an amazing degree for these later inscriptional accomplishments.

The last feature of representational forms that I want to discuss with respect to the tick model is how particular forms help in detecting patterns and making discoveries. This modest-seeming consideration actually opens up into an advantage of the tick model that may dwarf any of its advantages in power and generality. Programs are not just analytic and a basis for reasoning. They are also synthetic. They can be run.

Running the tick model causes an object to move across the screen at a certain speed. Adjusting **s** adjusts how fast it goes. Replacing **loop** with **repeat t** (where **t** represents equally the amount of time during which the process runs, or the number of repetitions) means we can play with how long an object moves and how far it goes. Programming turns analysis into experience and allows a connection between analytic forms and their experiential implications that algebra and even calculus can't touch.

Figure 2.3
An enhanced tick model, with acceleration.

"Make it experiential" is perhaps the single most powerful educational heuristic that I know. Experts aren't left out either. The synthetic power of computer programs, for example, to simulate weather or global warming transcends all other inscription systems. The capacity to simulate is defining the modern information age for many scientists and engineers. The tick model may be a small step, but it crosses over into that new world.

Allow me two steps of elaboration of the tick model. Figure 2.3 shows the tick model enhanced by a new variable **a**. In an analytic mode, you can see that **a** gets added to **s** at each tick. If you think about it some, you'll be able to understand some properties of **a** and how it affects motion. In fact, **a** is the tick-model version of the concept of acceleration. Beyond analysis, it is easy to imagine children playing with this enhanced tick model to get an excellent intuitive understanding of acceleration, as well as an analytic one. A salient example phenomenon is that **a** exerts "delayed" control on an object: if you set **a** to be a positive number, over time the object speeds up more and more. If you then set **a** to be negative, the object doesn't either stop or change its motion in any abrupt way. A negative **a** just nibbles away at a big **s** until it becomes small.

One more step: figure 2.4 shows a version of the tick model in which numbers have become vectors. A vector is shown in Boxer as an arrow (in a box) that may be adjusted by grabbing and moving the tip. **Move** takes a vector and causes an object to move the length of the arrow in the direction pointed by the arrow. What could be easier? **v** is a "fancy" version of speed, called velocity, that specifies direction as well as amount. You can see that at each instant **v** gets changed to the sum of the old **v** and **a**, just like the numbers in figure 2.3. For those who don't know what it means to add vectors: if you had a computer, you could just click

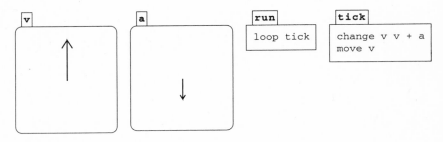

Figure 2.4
A tick model in which numbers have been replaced with vectors. (For simplicity, data and doit type labels are suppressed here and in later figures. Box type is still discernible by the shape of the corners of the box.)

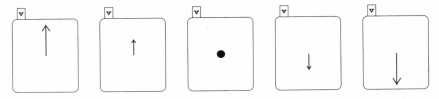

Figure 2.5
A sequence of velocities, each dragged downward from the previous velocity by the acceleration (**a** in figure 2.4).

on the **change v v + a** line a few times to see what happens. You'd see that the tip of **v** moves as specified by **a**, in the direction **a** points and a distance equal to its length, just as **v** moves a graphical object. Figure 2.5 shows snapshots of **v** being dragged downward, through 0 (no velocity, indicated by ●), by **a**.

We have whizzed past a slew of Galileo's accomplishments on the superhighway of a marvelous notation system. (Naturally, it would have been better to stop and look at some sights along the way.) But now that we're here, consider two little examples. If we **run** the figure 2.4 tick model as shown, we'll see an object rise (frame 1 and 2 in figure 2.5 shows moving upward while slowing down) to a peak, seeming to stop for an instant (the middle frame in figure 2.5 shows no velocity) and then fall down. This resembles what happens if we toss a ball. In fact, this is just how Galileo managed to describe a ball toss. Perhaps the most surprising thing about this description of a toss is that the form of the program is pretty much the same as where we started. It is describing a process that is *the same at every instant*, except that **v** is changing. Most people, and almost all students, find this uniformity amazing. Few are prepared to believe going up works in exactly the same way as falling. Even more, essentially everyone believes the peak of the toss is very special, expressed by some sort of balancing (say, balancing of the upward toss force with downward gravity). In contrast, the top of a toss is really an innocuous happenstance, that adding **a** to **v** will drive **v** through its zero-length position.

The tick model does not teach these things automatically and without a teacher, but it is an excellent way to experience, think, and talk through how Galileo's model works. What happens if you pull **v** to the side so that it slants diagonally to the right? The moving object then makes a trajectory like a diagonally tossed ball. But because **a** always moves the tip of **v** directly downward, **v** always slants to the right or, said differently, always has a component of rightward motion. Is this how the world works? It is, in an important idealization, but most find it initially unbelievable. Making unbelievable but accurate descriptions feel plausible is surely something to work through.

Dragging the tip of **a** around while the tick model is running makes for an engaging and sometimes quite challenging game. Getting the object to stop where you want it to, for example, involves setting **a** to bring **v** to its no-length state exactly at the place you choose to stop. No mean feat. This is just the kind of job the pilot of a spaceship has in order to dock with an orbiting satellite or space lab. In fact, according to Newton, **a** exactly represents the effect of direction and magnitude of spaceship thrusters.

We have come through expressive aptness, conceptual precision, and so on to a really new place. From here, it is easy to imagine sixth-grade students getting personally and creatively involved in designing spaceships and all sorts of games. Galileo's and Newton's sometimes forbidding abstractions have been resituated in a fabric of doing—play—that can be owned by children. We can be instrumental and say that mathematics and science can be motivating and engaging in a way that far transcends words, algebra, and calculus. We can talk about "time on task" and notions of learning through rich feedback. Alternatively, we can say merely that we have managed to bring mathematics and science into a child's world in a way that shames "you'll need this for the next course" or "just do the exercises." This last phrasing may be the most important, and I spend a lot of time with it in chapters 4 and 5.

Here is the point of this section in a nutshell. As part of a new literacy, a new representational form, programming, can lead to deeper learning, learning much earlier with fewer unpleasant glitches, and learning in a way that transforms the experience of students substantially from doing what adults say in semicomprehension into a really rich and appropriately kidlike experience, more like what they want to do and can do without adults intruding awkwardly.

The hanging hypothetical component of the story is the key. Can sixth-grade children really become literate in programming well enough, with little enough trouble, that much of learning can be transformed as I suggested above? I have not been scrupulous in hiding for dramatic effect that this whole hypothetical scenario is much less hypothetical than it might seem. We have been through the path traced above with "genuine" sixth-grade children, right down to some boggling surprises for them (e.g., that an upward toss and a downward fall work the same way) and the really pleasant times when students demanded more "work time" to finish their programmed motion games. It is particularly easy for me to imagine sixth-grade students getting personally and creatively involved because I have seen it again and again. Plus, we provided these students the necessary literacy in a few weeks. I'll add relevant detail in chapters 3 and 8.

Tool-rich Cultures

Having lived in three scientific communities—physics, cognitive and education research, and computer science for a time—I have been deeply struck by the relative impoverishment of schools with respect to tool creation and use. Scientific communities, in general, are without question tool-rich cultures. Scientists use telescopes, microscopes, particle accelerators, Bunsen burners, test tubes, analytical balances, vacuum pumps, multimeters, oscilloscopes, stroboscopes, oceangoing submersibles, culture dishes, and video machines for human and material performance analysis. Now, thousands of pieces of software help mathematicians, medical researchers, physicists, psychologists, and so on collect, sort, analyze, and present data. There are even metatools—tools to build tools—for example, in the university science department shop and in programming languages and software toolkits. Collecting and displaying tools of the trade is an excellent way of chronicling the history of the scientific enterprise.

Other important classes of tools are easy to miss. Beyond machines and equipment, it is particularly important in this book to recognize representational tools such as algebra, calculus, tables, and all the rest. Without stretching too far we can include reference books and even libraries. Just slightly more exotic are all the many techniques and skills for operating physical and representational devices (graphing is a tool!). Arguably, especially in view of considerations I take up directly in later chapters, even "purely" intellectual capability—habits of mind tuned to particular services in scientific inquiry—should count as tools.

From our social niches point of view, the position of these devices within the scientific communities and cultures is more important than their nominal classification as tools. First and foremost, tools are instrumental to higher purposes. They are seldom, if ever, ends in themselves. For example, the moment a new, better tool or technique emerges to serve a needed function, the old tool or technique is abandoned. As much as I valued my old, artfully made, and trusted Pickett slide rule (colored yellow, just slightly tinted green, at the peak of human visual acuity), it fell instantly into disuse in some forgotten drawer as soon as cheap scientific calculators became available.

As long as these tools serve their purposes well, however, they carry traces of the fundamental values and goals of the community. They accomplish the jobs that define and justify the very existence of the community. Tools are badges of membership, symbols of commitment and accomplishment, frequently tinged with affects such as pride and sometimes (for beginners) embarrassment.

These tools are in a deep sense owned by their communities. The principles by which the tools work are frequently community property and taught to newcomers. Many are fabricated by and for the community.

Schools are quite another matter. In the category of physical tools, one begins to run out of examples after listing books, black- or whiteboards, pencils, pens, and paper. Yes, a few science classrooms have equipment for laboratory activities, but it is marginal to the main practices of lecture, reading, and paper-and-pencil problem solving. In contrast to computers, devices such as VCRs, overhead projectors, video disk machines, and so on barely show above the noise in widespread educational practice.

Representational tools and techniques at first present a more positive face. Indeed, the expressed purpose of schooling brings a reasonable dose of scientific and mathematical tools to classrooms. Yet even here, a closer look at social positioning reveals problematic differences compared to the scientific community. The gaps are easiest to see from the viewpoint of students. Scientific tools in school are almost always ends in themselves, or they are related vaguely and artificially to "doing well in school" or "preparing for the future." Problems are assigned and understood by everyone as thinly veiled occasions to exercise tool knowledge or skills rather than as reasons for the existence of the tools. Many schools are really designed around incompetence in the sense that any real understanding is a sign to move on to the next topic. Pride in accomplishment is seldom reached.

The net result of these facts is that school—at least the academic component of school—feels artificial to most students. Students enjoy little sense of ownership, personal commitment, or exercise of competence. Because the purposes of the tools they learn are not their purposes, because how they work is seldom a topic for students, important learning mechanisms are undermined. (Knowing how tools work and understanding the jobs they do provide help in bootstrapping adequate skills in using them.) These points are elaborated and extended in chapters 4 through 7.

Teachers may be a little better off because their agendas dominate school activities, but what intellectual and physical tools serve *their* aims and needs? Again, curricular scientific and mathematical tools are mainly targets rather than means to an end, although some few of them may count as instruments in the service of teachers' higher goals. Most teachers make few if any of their own tools and materials, however; textbooks come from outside the community, filtered through political mandates and textbook manufacturers' needs and perceptions of educational goals and means. The larger pattern of disenfranchisement and underprofessionalization of teachers is a widely recognized structural problem in education in the United States.

I believe computational media and associated new literacies may be exactly the infrastructural change that can support converting schools, particularly mathematics and science classes, into vital communities of tool building and sharing. The new genre of software I have in mind is a set of open, reconfigurable, repurposeable tools for student tasks, tasks that are more like design and student research than conventional activities such as exercises and short problem solving. Such a shift in student activity is consistent with much that is recommended in many current educational reform documents. Nevertheless, I believe those reform efforts could be immensely aided with suitable material support, a point that is almost never taken to heart. Reform needs implements, not just implementation plans.

For now, the Boxer vectors that we discussed earlier can serve as an example of such tools. Vectors, in fact, were produced as a simple toolkit by a graduate student member of our research group. The transition that I pointed out—from vectors as an expressive language for laws and properties of motion to vectors as a synthetic resource for students' own, self-motivated projects—is a critical one that needs to be generalized and repeated hundreds of times with different tools. Student programming literacy may be a common basis for these transitions. Starter kits for student design and research, kits built with open programming interfaces, will be a common form of product in this genre. In the next chapter, I discuss a teacher-created set of materials—the infinity box—that served as springing-off point for core student creativity via programming. (Anticipating the discussion directly below, I note that the infinity box and several other productions by its teacher-creator have served other teachers, as well as students, as resources.)

Making educational tools directly serve valued student goals, however, is only a piece of the image. I believe we can revitalize teachers' professional experience by fostering their central participation in the production of such tools as well as their roles as coach and mentor to students. We would be making a fairly radical departure from current assumptions and practice in which teachers are barely trusted to copy worksheets, let alone create (or even modify!) substantial new materials. In what world might this departure really be possible?

In the first instance, my experience with teachers has convinced me that we have thousands of creative, energetic, and competent teachers on whom we can draw. We don't need to imagine that every teacher is exceptional. Five to ten percent of the teaching force as active participants in a culture of creative innovation through tools would be quite sufficient. Although we can always use more innovative teachers, I don't believe their numbers are the most critical barrier. Here is an alternative list of barriers:

1. *Lowering the threshold of technical expertise necessary to produce cogent educational tools.* This, of course, is nearly a defining goal for computational media. I won't say more here than if sixth-grade students can make substantial creative use of a medium, I believe teachers will be able to do so as well.

2. *Increasing the skill level of teachers.* Beyond thresholds, as in item 1, the more expert teachers become, the more they will be able to accomplish. The presumption of new literacies is that we have many years ahead of bootstrapping, rising expectations, and corresponding rising accomplishments.

3. *Changing the image of products.* Current assumptions about software are that it comes in large units that are so slick and complex as to require many person-years of effort to create them, usually by highly technically competent software engineers. With sufficient resources in the underlying medium, general or more specific toolkits, and open products available to modify, such assumptions will change dramatically. Several of the Boxer examples that appear later in this book were based on teacher- and student-modifiable toolkits.

4. *Changing assumptions about curriculum.* I know that sixth-grade students can learn a great deal about motion with a computational medium. The conventional wisdom, based on conventional media, is that this is impossible. Changing assumptions about what is possible to learn may be especially difficult for teachers. We would be asking them to teach more than they now know. Learning the subject might be more difficult for teachers because they may resist playing with the ideas and programs the way children will.

5. *Revising community affiliations and work groups.* One main problem teachers have currently is not so much lack of creativity or insufficient numbers in a population of teacher-developers. Instead, it is a matter of sparseness in geographical distribution. It's unlikely that a threshold number of compatible people with similar goals work in close proximity to one another. As telecommunications becomes an integral part of computational media, as they are for Boxer, teacher colleagues will be able to work together no matter where they live. The Internet and World Wide Web demonstrate that both collaboration and product distribution can, in principle, be free and easy.

As I have suggested and will continue to illustrate, most Boxer teachers with whom we have worked have at least modified existing materials, and several have been autonomously creative in developing new materials. All it takes is one creative teacher and a small audience of collegial experimenters to offer help and criticism to begin a collaborative project. Little projects can grow gradually as their products are refined and judged worthwhile by a growing network community. Don't forget, also, that we are still in "prehistoric" times with respect to computational literacies. Dozens of excellent teacher creators could easily become thousands.

But suppose that it takes a university research project to initiate a toolset. (Indeed, one would hope collaborative development communities would cross traditional boundaries of expertise and affiliation.) Still, programming a toolset is just the beginning. An incredibly important niche in which teachers can be especially effective is the creation and documentation of productive activities for students. It is fortunately easy in Boxer to create tutorials or interactive work sheets to teach the basics of vector algebra, for example, or scaffold a student project. Yet another important service is to feed student work back to the community to refine materials, improve other teachers' preparation for the difficulties and successes experienced by students, and generally advance community know-how. (Again, see the discussion of the infinity course and the infinity box in chapter 3.) Collecting good examples of student work can be directly helpful to future students not only for ideas, but as models and even as starter kits and tools for their own projects.

Let me close this section by clarifying what I am and am not advocating here and what aspects of it are more or less certain. First, I want to share my personal enthusiasm for a certain new genre of educational software.

Relatively simple educational tools can be created in fairly large numbers. These tools are open, flexible, and combinable, and will serve students *both* by introducing and exercising powerful mathematical and scientific ideas *and* by opening avenues of personal and collective involvement in what are felt by students to be directly meaningful self- and community-expressive activities. I am convinced such tools are possible and that they are based on sound learning principles. We have had many, many experiences in working with students and Boxer to suggest that these possibilities are technically and educationally realistic and that they can be powerful. In the remainder of this book, I highlight some.

The teacher side of the critical social niches issues is more hypothetical. I have less doubt than many that there is a sufficient population of creative, energetic, and potentially technically competent teachers who may engage each other in collaboratively fashioning such tools. The telecommunity aspect of this scenario is already feasible. For reasons treated mostly later, I believe requisite technical skills in using Boxer or some future computational medium are attainable. The more difficult challenge is managing all the practical and cultural issues of the implied new social webs. Communities like this will likely have to arise out of a concerted effort to break current teacher isolation and out of confidence and commitment that teachers want to and can take charge of aspects of education that have not been their purview. These changes may well be best viewed as political issues of teacher professionalization. Can teachers, with help from some other groups, take hold of educational reform from within their group? Can they turn some very nontraditional opportunities offered by technology to their communal ends?

Finally, I do not offer the possibility of an educational culture of tool builders and sharers—teachers and students alike—as a prescription or panacea. Instead, it is one among many possibilities that should be considered. Like the best possibilities, it has deep and complex technological and social roots that I hope it will be our privilege to cultivate and come to understand.

3

Snapshots: A Day in the Life

Chapter 1 was a big bite. You might have felt it was a difficult climb up to get a broad view, but I wanted to introduce the sweep and importance of issues concerning new literacies. I also dug into some specialized possibilities, such as what algebra means for contemporary science, which are particularly relevant to science education. Chapter 2 was almost as difficult. Possible futures for education are challenging to understand partly because what exists now seems so obvious—even necessary—and partly because new educational possibilities may involve learning things that are now unfamiliar or considered difficult.

In this chapter, we can relax a little. I want to draw from some of the experiences we have had with Boxer to show you a more diverse span of images of computational media and new literacies. I want to look, however tentatively and imperfectly, at what it might feel like to participate in a society that is computationally literate. Because I rejected the notion that there is a single essence that defines the niche and power of literacy, a pastiche is not a bad way to go. This is a little like making the list in chapter 1 of the many ways literacy influences our lives each day, except that every example below is limited: it comes from things that happened at the very first stages of literacy, at best. For example, only the barest trace of a literature in this new literacy currently exists, and almost every person I describe is a neophyte, so we will be seeing only the palest shadows of what is possible. The features I pick out to emphasize, however, represent issues that I believe are characteristic and important over the long term.

Fish and Water

This example is from our work teaching physics to sixth-grade children. It is one of my favorites because it seemed so unremarkable. It was just a fleeting moment in a classroom activity, and it went essentially unnoticed by the participants. Yet it says a lot about literacy.

This moment took place while the class was engaging in an exercise thinking about relative motion. The problem was to imagine a person gliding along smoothly on a skateboard, carrying a small ball, perhaps a baseball. What happens if that person simply drops the ball from a few inches in front of his chest? The class was divided into several groups, and each group was to take a distinct point of view. What do you see if you are the skateboarding person? What do you see if you are standing at rest as the skateboarder rides past? What do you see if you are the skateboard itself?

The groups thought and talked separately for a few minutes, then they collected together to share their conclusions. When it came time to present for the group that was to take the point of view of the skateboard, their spokesperson got up, walked over to a computer, and pressed a key. The screen showed a small black dot that gradually expanded to fill the screen. Neither he nor anyone else spoke. They just watched the screen, considered what it showed, and—apparently all in agreement that this is what you would see from the skateboard as the ball dropped toward you—the class continued by turning to the next point of view.

This vignette is a wonderful emblem of how literacy disappears in literate communities, which I likened to the invisibility of water to fish in chapter 1. A little piece of a literacy perfectly fit this moment. The students found writing the one-line program that created the expanding disk the easiest way to answer their question. Their solution was judged by the participants to be perfectly adequate and completely unremarkable. Anyone in the room probably could have written the program.

Our eyes are all drawn to huge and spectacular accomplishments, such as great books or fantastic pieces of software, but for every great book, there are hundreds of useful "little" books. For each little book, there are dozens of papers or articles. For each paper or article, there are dozens or hundreds of notes, letters, or grocery lists. It is interesting to wonder what total value to civilization comes from each of these scales of accomplishment. Do the few great books really outweigh the hundreds of "lesser" ones, for example? That is probably an unanswerable question, but the important point is that true literacy makes critical contributions at all scales. I do not believe a computational literacy that has only a few gigantic products is worthy of the name, so the skateboard simulation stands in for thousands of unremarkable expressive moments when students and teachers find a computational medium to be exactly the right tool for the task at hand. The "law of the little" is an emblem I use to remind myself that many little things can frequently accumulate to rival big ones. If you can't feel at least a twinge of excitement in the skateboard simulation—even respecting that modesty is its defining characteristic— be aware that throughout the book I continue to exemplify and argue for the importance of the law of the little.

Ownership by Individuals and Communities

One afternoon I dropped by the first Boxer course—a lively sixth-grade class—because I had a special interest in what they were doing that day. They were using a little microworld I had made, and I wanted to see how it went. A *microworld* is a genre of computational document aimed at embedding important ideas in a form that students can readily explore. The best microworlds have an easy-to-understand set of operations that students can use to engage tasks of value to them, and in doing so, they come to understand powerful underlying principles. You might come to understand ecology, for example, by building your own little creatures that compete with and are dependent on each other.

Let me detour just a moment to consider my role in this class, aside from observer. I am one of those busy academics who is constantly occupied with teaching classes; participating in committees; consulting with students; writing proposals, progress reports, letters of recommendation, and memos; trying to understand budget reports from the business office; and so on. A surprisingly small fraction of my time actually goes into what I consider personally expressive and creative work. Many people involved with educational technology could be extremely happy hiring a programmer and design team, giving them some instructions, and letting them do the "boring" work of creating an artifact. I happen not to be one of those people. In the next chapter, you will see that this orientation has a long history. I enjoy many little filigrees of design—not just to have an idea, but to feel the medium bend to my wishes. Firsthand experience also happens to be important in developing good intuitions about what a system does well and where it falls short. Because I need to understand our system (Boxer) well, I have a good excuse for sometimes doing things I like.

So here is another niche: time-limited but (let us hope) creative person seeks to exercise competence with computational medium and educational design. It happens that I can almost never spare more than a day at a time to work on a programming project, and even those days come almost always on weekends or during vacations. But there is no shortage of useful Boxer creations that a technically competent person can put together in a day or so. The typical pattern for me is to take a day to make a rough draft, then another day or so, spread out over time, for improvements as I and others gain experience with the program. I am leaving unexplained, for now, how a computational medium can make usable things so easy to produce. We'll come back to this topic later in the book, after we have some other technical discussion.

The same features of a computational medium produce other advantages in other niches. For example, far less time is spent on coding, and many more members of the team can contribute to production. There's an even stronger advantage for creative individuals or teams who are not lucky enough to have the resources to hire help. When person-days are the relevant measure for a meaningful chunk of programming, rather than the current norm, team-years, a different production ecology can result. A much greater proportion of time can be devoted to exploring educational issues, such as designing and refining learning activities, and many educationally savvy but not especially technically expert people can get in on the action. Enlarging the pool of people involved in development can have broad political and cultural consequences. Think what our written-text literate world would be like if every time people wanted to write, they had to collect a team of experts and significant funding to produce anything worthwhile!

To return to my anecdote, I had spent my requisite day or so making a first draft of a learning activity/environment, and it was being tried at school. My attention was drawn to Sheena, a girl in the class who appeared engaged. When I looked over her shoulder, however, I saw that she was bored with the activity. Instead of working on it, she was busy selecting, deleting, and then pasting back arbitrary pieces of the environment. In general, Boxer doesn't protect any part of the environment. Anybody can change (or destroy) any part of the materials in which they work.

After getting over the apparent fact that this activity was not nearly as engaging as I had hoped, I asked Sheena if she was a little afraid of cutting and pasting pieces of the system. Was she worried that she might break it? She replied in unconcerned tones that she was not. These things, she reported, were not very complicated, and she was pretty sure she could put it back, whatever she did.

I am not really convinced she was right about her abilities, even if she was correct that it wasn't a complicated system, but the connection between her and this system was clearly spelled out. She was the master and certainly not intimidated. This attitude is entirely proper, but unfortunately far from most children's experience with learning technology. Even if they "master" a piece of software by school standards, it belongs to the school or to the teacher in almost every sense.

Feelings of mastering a technology translate into creative uses of it, beyond just a more positive and personal engagement. One of Sheena's brilliant creations was to see a pattern in the little speed (velocity) and acceleration tick-model programs we discussed in chapter 2. She had seen the definition of the **move** program (figure 2.3) as:

```
change position position + speed
```

This definition says that the position of an object gets increased more the more speed you have. Sheena knew that acceleration changes speed in exactly the same way (again, see figure 2.3):

```
change speed speed + acceleration
```

The program Sheena was engaged with at the time used exactly these lines as the core part of a set of activities in which students interactively controlled a moving object by adjusting speed and acceleration with their mouse. Sheena extended the program, extrapolating the pattern she saw. She added another variable, `oomft`, with the extra command line:

```
change acceleration acceleration + oomft
```

Then, she began experimenting with using `oomft` to control motion. With `oomft`, Sheena had invented and programmed a physical measure conventionally called (believe it or not!) *jerk*. Sheena saw what we had arranged the program lines to suggest: something (jerk or *oomft*) could relate to acceleration in exactly the same way that acceleration relates to speed or speed relates to position. The technical language says that speed is the derivative of position, acceleration is the derivative of speed (or the second derivative of position), and jerk is the derivative of acceleration. The reason for the name, *jerk,* I explained to Sheena, is that jerk does in fact correspond to the "jerkiness" you feel when a motion, such as a roller coaster or car, changes acceleration. If you suddenly decide you are not braking hard enough and press down much harder, that creates a high jerk. Jerk is in the transition from coasting to braking or between coasting and accelerating. If you press down on the brake of a car and hold a constant pressure, you feel a little jerk just at the point where you cease slowing down and stop. It turns out that it is extremely hard to control an object using jerk, but Sheena was persistent and relatively successful.

This example is a case of a child doing something scientifically nice because she not only *feels* in control of her learning environment, but *is* in control. Doing something as conceptually interesting as inventing and exploring jerk is rare in some ways and extremely common in others. It is rare in the sense that not a lot of children spontaneously think of jerk once they have seen speed and acceleration (although the activities and programs we designed for them deliberately invited such invention). No one should count on any particular child—still less *every* child—inventing the idea. On the other hand, it would probably be common in a class of thirty engaged students that at least one would think of this extension. In my experience, many good teachers count on at least one student coming up with particular "rare" ideas like Sheena's.

Rare ideas are common in another sense and for the same reason. Uncommon things become common, even certain, if we give them enough chances to happen. I feel it would be embarrassing if every child did not have at least one idea about as good as Sheena's *oomft* during a class using Boxer. Now that I think about it, this is an excellent, if unusual, benchmark. The central point is that computational media can foster children's having and developing their own good ideas by being open at every instant to the child's changing and extending what is there. Sheena wrote one extra line of code into a prewritten program and entered a personal, new world. Having an opportunity to be creative every instant means that every person, sooner or later, can be really creative. We need to extend the law of the little: not only do little things accumulate into big ones, but slim chances (with many people or many opportunities) accumulate into certainty.

Rare ideas are also more important than their frequency might suggest for the power they have to draw students into the game of science. If you can find a corner of science that genuinely belongs to you, it is worth dozens of more general facts or principles. We talk much more about motivation, involvement, and rare events in the next chapter.

Sheena was a charming child (even if she sometimes didn't like my microworlds). She always demonstrated her enthusiasm for her own creations, even the "nerdy" *oomft* concept, so I can't resist telling a couple of further stories about her. I recall that she created a program to draw a good-looking stop sign at one point. She walked around the room asking, "Do you need a stop sign?" to see if anyone wanted to use her creation. Pride of ownership is powerful.

One of Sheena's several personal projects during the class was a "Bouncing Babies" video game. In it, babies come flying out of a hospital window, and your job is to move a safety net under them. If you miss, the babies unceremoniously bounce on the pavement. Sheena worked hours getting her bounces just right. She was one of several students who demanded time after school to work on their projects. "Bouncing Babies" is quite an interesting, personal context for working on physics. In another project that she worked on jointly with another girl, Sheena developed a scale-model simulation in which "dangerously speeding José" (a not too subtle reference to a local baseball hero who constantly got into trouble with the police) ran down "poor innocent Sue" on the sidewalk with his Corvette. The scientific challenge here was to get Sue's walking speed and José's reckless driving speed to the same scale as the picture of the sidewalk and houses that formed the backdrop for the animation. This was to be a display in a "speed museum" that we had developed as a class project fairly early on in the course.

A computational medium can't take all the credit for the fact that these students, Sheena particularly, personalized the normally impersonal physics they were learning. Certainly the teacher gets a lot of credit, as does the design of activities that made plenty of room for both physics and children, but think how different this class was from the worlds of textual literacy that now "support" learning physics! I argued abstractly in the second chapter that putting children in the position of making and controlling motion makes a fundamental difference in how they can relate to it. Personalization is one important piece of the longer story of altered relationships between science and students.

Personalization is as important for teachers as it is for students. The teacher we worked with in this first Boxer course was exceptional, to be sure, but that does not mean she could do anything or was happy doing anything as long as it was "good for her students." Tina, in fact, became interested in Boxer because it gave her a chance to explore fractal designs on her own—not because we offered a wonderful course on motion (which did not exist at that point!). Tina made many of the materials for the course. Just as important, she changed many things we made and thus made them her own. I recall her reactions to one of our microworlds, which we had carefully put together, the day before she was going to use it. "I don't like the instructions. Just get rid of them. I prefer just to talk to my students." "The screen is too complicated. They'll never get to that, so just get rid of it." "I'd rather they start out with these puzzles. Maybe they are a little harder, but they're more interesting." With a computational medium, making all these changes was easy. The result was much better, perhaps not because the design was better for children in general, but because it was now Tina's microworld as much as it was ours.

I want to emphasize that it was not uncommon to change a microworld the day before it was used. We were forced into it because we were developing the course on the fly. Nonetheless, there is much to recommend in this mode, compared to a situation in which a whole course is developed first and then tried out. In particular, we were always reacting to how class activities were going and to the particular interests of students. If an activity did not work well, we filled in with other, related activities and microworlds. If our plans went particularly well, we tried to pattern new lessons on what succeeded. I view this only in very small degree as "getting it right" after trial and error. Much more, it is adapting to circumstances and to particular people. Computational media allow this critical adaptation to an unprecedented degree. As I suggested in chapter 2, I view ideal materials in a computational medium to be much more like an adaptable toolkit rather than a turnkey course. Literacies must fit cultures, which are always diverse and changing. Computational media facilitate best by being adaptive.

Cultures and communities own and personalize just as much as individuals such as Tina or Sheena. Tina had the wonderful idea of starting a Boxer library in the school in which children could put their finished projects. She started the library, but had children run it. Naturally it was filled with games and pretty designs more than "educational products" developed by the children, but the return value for us was amazing. Many children learned Boxer by dropping in after school to join friends in playing with programs in the library. The "never done, always changeable" aspect of a computational medium shone here. Children learned programming not so much in episodes of instruction, but more by watching the creator changing his or her program while showing it off! Going beyond what was technically feasible at that time, the World Wide Web means that communities don't have to be local anymore, and libraries like Tina's can be shared easily. Still, we need to respect the importance of community—common background sensibilities and values—without which a Web library can't accomplish what Tina's library did.

One of my staff invited me to stop by the after-school Boxer library sessions to meet two students who learned Boxer largely there. Neither was in our physics course, which was essentially the only official Boxer use at the school, but they had become true experts. Watching them work was stunning. The room had only one Boxer computer, so they worked simultaneously on the same project. One typed, and the other worked the mouse. With scarcely a word, they coordinated their actions amazingly. Typical of working with Boxer, right in the middle of showing me a checkers-like game they had constructed, they decided it wasn't quite right and started changing it.

It turned out the two had quite a lot to say about Boxer design. They were most interested in facilitating collaboration like their own. Their best idea was to have some boxes shared across machines, so people could be working on the same project but still be doing different things. The revelation to me is that they expressed this idea in exactly the same way our design group had been thinking about extending Boxer for better long-distance collaboration. (In chapter 7, you'll see Boxer ports. These sixth-grade-students wanted ports to boxes on other machines.) This episode showed not only how close to professional competence superb students can be but how a computational medium, if it is designed well, can impart a sense of itself even to young children. As text literate children can invent their own words and symbols and use them sensibly, students can see and extend the coherence of a computational medium. When we get to comprehensibility in chapters 6 and 7, the issue of how deeply people can empathize with the structure of a computational system comes to the foreground.

Let me close this section on ownership with another experience we had with a community, this time a community of teachers. We had worked on and off at one school and with a small set of teachers for an extended period. It came time for us to leave the school, and the issue was whether this community wanted to continue doing Boxer without our support. The decision was not simple. Although Boxer had some cultural resonance with the school, we also felt dissonance. In particular, some of the leaders were interested in other technologies, in some cases for obvious and good reasons. Boxer was a buggy prototype. Not every child could have a Boxer, unlike a programmable calculator.

The issue became a crisis, and it looked as though Boxer would leave the school. Even though we could no longer afford to help the school, we decided to do one last workshop to help teachers get a sense of what was possible. This was exactly the wrong plan, as one teacher let us know forcefully in the first five minutes. He said they knew *we* could do wonderful things with Boxer, but the question was what *they* could do with it. They were not even interested in appropriating and changing things we had previously done. Instead, they just wanted to start from scratch.

The story had a happy ending. We let the teachers describe just what they wanted to do and spent the rest of the workshop as peripheral coaches and aides, not as problem solvers or providers of materials. Several months later, the school had strongly reappropriated Boxer. Wonderful developments were again blooming.

This is an extreme case: only self-generated ideas were acceptable to this teacher community. I don't recommend this strategy as universal, and I don't believe computational media will always or even frequently work this way. After all, everybody is willing to read what other people have written, and most are willing to assign a textbook, even if it does not say exactly what they think. This event, however, shows again the power of ownership. A computational medium that does not let all its users create to suit their own instincts will miss probably the most powerful principle of appropriation and arguably one of the most powerful principles of learning. Owning and knowing are fraternal twins. Owning leads to knowing and vice versa.

As a footnote, true to their own feelings about how they wanted to take a new technology into their culture, these teachers did not want their students to see anything they (the students) had not built before they had achieved personal ownership of the system. The teachers had the students start by building all their own materials from scratch.

Materials That Live and Grow

Textbooks, the crown jewel of textual literacy's influence in schooling, are only minimally adaptable to local communities and cultures. You can choose a textbook from among a small number that are targeted toward some subject area at a certain level. Then you can select which parts to read and work on, and in some measure (depending on the textbook) you can select different ways of engaging the text. For example, you can have a group discussion, or you can ask individual students to write papers about it. Typical science textbooks use the model of reading and then engaging a set of not too long or difficult problems. Even the style of contemporary textbooks is remarkably similar from one to the next. They are, among other things, impersonal and generic.

A computational medium, of course, could be used in a way that is similar to textbooks, but the adaptability of the medium, as I hinted in the previous section, can allow a radical change toward diversity. Continuing the line started in the toolsets section at the end of chapter 2, I want to emphasize the long-term process of growth and change of materials in computational media as they are adapted and as they change within and between subcultures. The forces of diversity are always present. Every child is a little different from the next. Every teacher has preferred ways of doing things that are an outgrowth of his or her individual and communal personalities. Classes are different from one year to the next. The extent to which the primary medium of learning can adapt to these differences, however, is extremely dependent on the medium. I believe computational media can support unprecedented new ranges of adaptation of materials to different people, places, and times.

My first example of living, growing materials begins with one of the boys I met at the after-school Boxer library session. Mickey, as I'll call him, was not your average student. You might have to look through two or three schools to find another student with his particular strengths and interests. He was bright, to be sure, but his investment in helping other people learn stood out most for me. He was constantly explaining, and he genuinely took other students' achievements with his help as a mutual accomplishment. Once, in a context where he was clearly the leading student of a pair, when his colleague finally caught on, Mickey exclaimed with sincerity and innocence, "We are proud of ourselves!"

Mickey decided he wanted to help his fellow students learn Boxer. I do not know whether this particular project was instigated by Tina or someone else in the school, but, in any case, his taking it on was a perfect expression of his sense of self. He decided to write a tutorial that included all the interesting beginning things he had learned about Boxer. His production showed surprising sophistication in selecting and sequencing topics, and in embedding them in interesting contexts. On the other hand, his work was still easily identifiable as the product of a sixth-grade student. In some ways, he presumed more sophistication than he reasonably could expect from his audience. In particular, he made his tutees' job difficult by using many, many boxes that they would have to open and close at appropriate times in order to use the tutorial effectively.

When Mickey was done, he submitted his tutorial to the school Boxer library. Tina immediately picked up this document, modified it, and over a couple of years extended it to become her standard introduction to Boxer. In one more stage of development and appropriation for this tutorial, I picked up and modified Tina's tutorial into one of the standard tutorials that we now distribute with Boxer. I adapted the tutorial in several ways to suit my purposes. First, I eliminated essentially all the sixth-grade humor and all the extraneous boxes that Mickey had introduced because he thought it would be fun for kids to be constantly opening and closing boxes. I also developed a "pretty" presentation, with colors, buttons to click, and banners to locate the current section of the tutorial. I introduced some more advanced topics because the audience I had more in mind was teachers and developers of materials rather than children.

I expect materials in Boxer and in computational media generally to have complex paths of appropriation and development, a little like what happened to this tutorial. Books and the sorts of software that are common today simply don't work like this, and they forgo the kind of extended, grassroots development that I hint at in tracing three generations of Mickey's tutorial. Materials that can't be modified foreclose the power of people to adapt things that are close to what they want but not quite right. The extent to which people can modify what exists in computational media—instead of either starting from scratch or just taking something that may be a bad approximation to what they need—is unprecedented.

What's the next generation of Mickey's tutorial? I have to admit, from the evidence available to me, that I may have created an evolutionary dead end. For example, the teaching community I described above explicitly rejected using or adapting this tutorial for their own students. Of course, this particular community had exceptionally high standards of ownership, but I have not yet seen other adaptations in more accepting communities.

If I have managed an evolutionary dead end, I think I know some of the reasons. In making an easier, prettier, and more magical presentation,

I used mechanisms in Boxer that are a little more complicated than just opening and closing boxes. Opening and closing, which may be boring (to adults anyway), have the virtue of being among the first actions users learn in Boxer. The users have to be a fraction more sophisticated to modify and extend my version, compared to its predecessors. Here is a classic tradeoff in designing Boxer materials or materials in any medium that aims at appropriation and adaptation as fundamental modes of use. Make it pretty and slick, and you make it more difficult to understand and change, perhaps enough so that you destroy the line of adaptation. Now, the Boxer mechanisms I used in my version are really not very sophisticated. The fact that this tutorial's line of development seems to have stalled may be just because there is not a sufficient background literacy with Boxer in most current places of use. It might be that in a year or two, as Boxer gets around and we have many schools with a critical mass of expertise, the tutorial will resume its growth and adaptation. We always find thresholds like this—more than a beginner's sophistication is needed to change the tutorial—in the adoption of new media. Recall the threshold I proposed we just scraped by via Leibniz's notation, rather than Newton's, in the adoption of calculus as infrastructural in higher scientific learning. For the future of computational media, it is important to know where critical thresholds for different genres and uses of computational media are.

My next example of materials that live and grow came from a high school teacher who became a central player in the small Boxer development culture—those of us thinking about improving and extending Boxer itself. Henri's history with Boxer began when he agreed to teach a summer course on statistics that he had taught several times before, now augmented with a Boxer component. After that course, our contact initially faded because we were continuing to work with Tina on our main studies. By a remarkable chance, Tina moved from her prior school to Henri's school, across the San Francisco Bay, and because of her relocation, we moved a number of Boxer machines to the school. In those days, Boxer couldn't run on any reasonable school computer, so for our experiments we used scientific workstations that cost many thousands of dollars each.

Unknown to us, Henri designed and taught a ten-week course on infinity as an elective in his school. He collected a motley crew of students, ranging from some who clearly excelled in math to others who were much less motivated and "capable," at least by standard measures. Henri told me he had very little time to prepare the course and, in fact, did much of it on the fly, as we had done with our physics course. The mathematical component of the class was unusual and fairly sophisticated. Henri introduced iterated functions, issues of stability and instability, chaos, and fractional dimensions. To give the tiniest flavor of the content of the course for those unfamiliar with this material, let me recall for you the fantastic and beautiful fractal shapes, like the Mandelbrot set, that are a staple of chaos theory. Henri taught his students how to generate some classes of fractal shapes and how to analyze them mathematically.

Henri, like Tina, is a very good teacher, but not everything he touches turns to gold. This course, as far as I found out about it, seemed golden. The best indicator was that at the end of ten weeks every student turned in a project that was both mathematically and aesthetically interesting. To be sure, the mathematics was either clear and convincing in the most accomplished students' work or muted and muddy in some of the projects, but there wasn't a failed project in the group. The learning thresholds for programming and use of a computational medium may not be trivial, but this is a superb case: a group of completely Boxer-naive students came to own a piece of mathematical terrain within ten short weeks, via this new medium.

Figures 3.1 to 3.4 show some of the flavor and range of the products of the students' work in this course. Figure 3.2 was created by a particularly mathematically adept young man. In this project, he computed the fractal dimension of the shape created by a program that he also developed, although it was based on a famous design. Figure 3.3 was the creation of a less mathematically oriented student; it compensates for its lack of explicit mathematics by its deliberate and effective aesthetic appeal. To appreciate some of the hidden mathematics, notice that the overall shape has three-fold symmetry, but if you look in each of the three corners of that shape, you find embedded in it a four-fold symmetry. At each of the corners of that four-fold symmetry, you see five-fold symmetric shapes, and so on.

Mathematics, like physics, is dry and impersonal in textual media and standard instruction. Computation provides an unprecedented outlet for

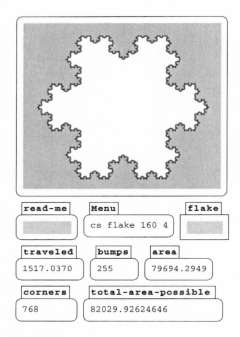

Figure 3.1
A project from the infinity class. **Flake** produced a snowflake curve, computed the total length of path (**traveled**), the number of bumps, the area, and the total area possible if the curve had an infinite number of bumps.

creativity and can be joined easily with artistic considerations. The personal investment of traditionally "mathematically oriented" students can be enhanced, and a wider range of students can be brought into the game.

Figure 3.4 (created by the same student who did figure 3.1) shows another nice property of computational media. It is easy to keep track of and organize history. This student made a box called "wrong," which shows and explains a prior attempt at producing this original fractal shape. Such historical artifacts can be marvelous resources for both teachers and researchers in understanding the usually hidden developmental paths of students' understanding and accomplishment. I believe that students' tracking their own and others' development can contribute to learning in important ways. In particular, far too many students believe their classmates are magically competent beings who learn and accom-

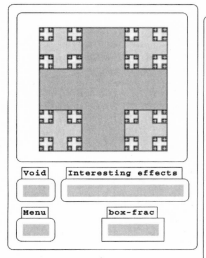

The box fractal is made up of a large square with four smaller squares at each of the box's four corners. Each of the smaller squares has a side length equal to 1/3 the length of the previous level's square. All area in the large square is "void" except for the four smaller squares. Because of this, the large square has an area equal to four times the area of a little square. So, we multiply the side length by 3 to get to the larger square, and the area by four. This allows us to set up an equation and solve for area:

$$3^x = 4$$

$$\log 3^x = \log 4$$

$$x\log 3 = \log 4$$

$$x = \log 4/\log 3$$

$$x = 1.26$$

The square is 1.26 dimensional, which makes sense since it is close to 2 dimensions, but then again, close to 1 dimension.

Figure 3.2
A project (including part of its text) that computes the fractal dimension of the shape at left.

plish without any false starts or mistakes, and many more students greatly underestimate how much they can accomplish with sustained effort. Attending to personal and others' histories can break through these misconceptions.

Yes, it is possible to have students collect and reflect on their own and others' work in other media. Yes, attending to reflection is as much a cultural accomplishment of an enlightened school community as it is a technical accomplishment. But it is also true that compared to the use of paper and pencil or other media, collecting and effectively organizing stages of your work is much easier in a computational medium like Boxer. This student's closed but accessible "wrong" box is an emblem. He put his failed efforts in a box, annotated it, and left it around for others to explore. I habitually build mechanisms into nearly every microworld I create to facilitate students' saving and presenting their history and progress.

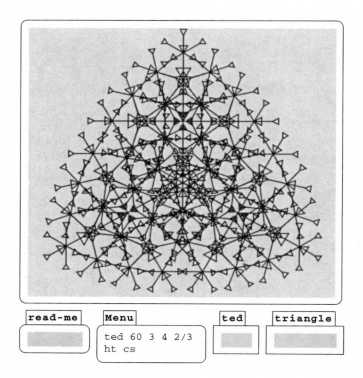

```
read-me        Menu                    ted      triangle

               ted 60 3 4 2/3
               ht cs
```

Figure 3.3
A project involving a shape with multiple symmetries.

I haven't yet got to my favorite aspect of Henri's infinity course. Henri collected all of the Boxer materials he made for his students together with commentary on how they worked—what were the tricky or easy parts. Perhaps the best thing he did, however, was to include all the students' final projects in the same "course box," which he subsequently sent to me. What a stunning artifact and aid to the next teacher who might want to duplicate or improvise on Henri's accomplishments! He included a full set of "materials," teacher commentary, and a rich, extensive database of student work as a model of what can be accomplished or as an idea book for future students. All these resources took little more than a quick cut-and-paste job by Henri, with a little thought for organization and what comments would be most helpful. The critical features of Boxer

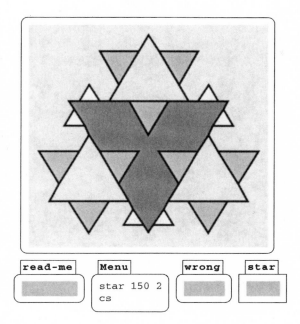

Figure 3.4
A project that shows (in **wrong**) the student's first attempts and explains why they failed.

that enabled this production are (1) its ability to organize a complex collection of things easily; (2) any part of Boxer can be annotated, for example, simply by typing in comments; and (3) everything—program, picture, text, microworld, etc.—has the same status as boxes that can be cut and pasted together to suit. Any future computational medium ought to be at least as good as Boxer in these respects.

When I discussed teachers' communities and teachers' initiatives in chapter 2, I had Henri's infinity box in mind. It beautifully sums up one energetic teacher's work, and I hope it can inspire and facilitate other teachers in a virtual community of explorers of infinity.

This chapter has overwhelmingly emphasized one basic fact: the profound integration of media into the daily lives of people and into their personal and communal concerns. I've tried to alert you to the fact that literacy tends to be invisible to literate people. We need especially to remind ourselves that simple and easy uses of a medium, not just grand accomplishments, accumulate as part of intellectual revolutions such as new literacies. Simple and easy uses are particularly important in changing students' relationships with what they are learning. A medium that gracefully accepts change and initiative opens thousands of opportunities for innovation and personalization (it's too bad there is no familiar word for communities "personalizing")—for creative engagement that productively mixes important educational goals with what makes teachers and students perk up with excitement.

I have emphasized how the process of developing genres and particular materials can take on a much more organic and extended shape with computational media. Forms will emerge here or there; they will gradually change to serve the local ends of various individuals and groups. Sometimes the forms may suddenly mutate to serve radically different ends from the ones the creator originally imagined.

Unity as well as diversity can be served. New communities can emerge as materials and cultures slowly coevolve, grow, and reinforce each other. Traditionally separated communities can discover that they can be of service to each other if the forms they exchange can be adaptively changed.

4

Foundations of Knowledge and Learning

This chapter explores some as yet unpopular perspectives on what knowledge is and how we should view its development. It serves apparently contradictory purposes. In the first instance, I want to expand the space of possibilities we consider for knowing and learning from what people commonly assume them to be. If we are to explore the possibilities that computational media afford, we must not be constrained by the prejudice of prior conceptions. Knowledge and learning are almost always viewed in forms associated with current literacies; they appear to us through the lens of a literacy. Language brings with it implicit assumptions that knowledge occurs in forms similar to those associated with language. Concepts, we are prone to think, are the meanings of words; sentences beget a belief that propositions or facts are the centerpiece, if not all, of the world of what we know.

The second purpose of the present exploration is the opposite of expanding breadth of consideration: I want to explain and argue for some particular versions of learning and knowing that I believe are important. Literacy is promiscuous. Especially if it is defined technically and materially, rather than also socially and culturally (as I advocate), a given literacy can cover an immense range of possibilities. Written language serves drug dealers, corrupt politicians, demagogues, liars, and superficial people as effectively as it serves noble ones. In a way, some of the ideas in this chapter represent value judgments on possible literacies. Which are good ones, not just effective or efficient ones?

Expanding the range of possibilities and narrowing to focus on some quite particular forms turn out not to be contradictory in this case. The particular forms of learning and knowing I advocate are sensible only in a context that goes beyond conventional assumptions.

To be just a little more specific, this chapter expands traditional views of knowledge in two ways. First, I advocate considering the power and importance of intuitive knowledge along with the more visible and sanctioned forms of knowledge. Second, I look at the fabric of activities in which a person may comfortably engage as a complementary view of resources and goals for learning. In terms of selectively focusing on "good" learning, I propose the concept of *committed learning*, where learners feel deeply connected to the activities in which they learn.

How I Became the Person I Am

I want to begin this exploration in the way I began the book, with a personal, real-world view of some of the issues. Later, I'll return with a more systematic and analytical view.

If I were asked to name the most important formative experience of my life for defining my general intellectual skills and personal style of thinking and acting, I wouldn't have to reflect for very long. From late elementary school well into high school, I was an electronics hobbyist. I built scores of devices—"studied," "experimented," and played in the way that some people get interested in reading, others love sports, and still others become involved with their friends and whatever activities friendship entails. Counting only the number of hours I spent, one would have to judge electronics my most important occupation. More than that, I can see some of the defining features of my current intellectual self growing in these activities.

Here's the problem: How do we understand the contribution of such a vast investment of time and energy to a person's development? Let me start by simply listing some of the things I did.

• I built dozens of radios of all shapes and sizes, starting with a crystal set kit I received as a present. I remember spending hours searching for the best spot on the galena crystal to place the "cat whisker" (a wire probe that one positioned manually to create the only "active" component of the radio). I wasn't really much interested in listening to programs so much as experimenting with the device. I put up a large antenna outside my window and tried my bedspring and hosts of other ersatz antennas.

A large part of the fascination of building radios for me was the challenge of making the next one better than the last. To outsiders, I'm sure the very gradual shifts in design would have made me appear almost compulsive, but those small changes marked what I considered good new ideas, innovations in fabrication technique, and so on.

One theme in my radio building was progressive miniaturization. I advanced a bit in the sophistication of the circuitry—from crystal set to three- or four-transistor radios—but more in fitting the device in a smaller case. At one point, I tried etching my own printed circuits, but I found the trouble was not worth the advantage. One of my proud accomplishments was to build a radio into a plug that I could use between the headphones and the console of the machines we used in language lab at school so that I could listen to the radio instead of language lessons. I doubt I used that device more than once or twice (actually, I loved language lessons), but the slightly subversive intention and the fact that it really might work were motivation enough.

• I built an oscilloscope from a kit after a year of planning, saving money, and doing extensive catalog searches. I didn't really need such a device for troubleshooting my electronic constructions, but I was intrigued by the idea of seeing sound as wave forms. I had fabricated a fantasy future world of exploring the shapes of all sorts of sounds. This project, as far as its outcome goes, was pretty much a bust. About the most interesting thing I learned was that I could make a near-perfect sine wave with my French horn. Most sounds were boringly complex, and I couldn't discern many interesting relationships. Constructing the oscilloscope, on the other hand, was quite a challenge, and I learned a great deal about frequency, phase, and so on in endless attempts at adjusting the thing to find something interesting about sound. I also learned, in one literally stunning instant, to be *very* careful around one thousand volts.

• I built a long streak of audio amplifiers. One line of these ended in the successful construction of a phonograph that my family used for years as our main hi-fi. This project got me seriously into woodworking to build the cabinet. I wouldn't say I ever became good at cabinetry, but I learned quite a few things, including a modicum of patience and humility in the face of others' skills. Like other academically oriented students, I had considered shop a class for others. Now, I regretted not fitting it into my schedule.

Miniaturization was a theme in amplifiers, too. My best creation was a little three-transistor job that fit into a case about twice as big as a postage stamp and about half an inch thick. I had no planned use for the finished amplifier, but the project challenged me to build in a new way something I already understood. Because I felt my devices ought to be used, I eventually concocted a scheme to spy on my sister, and I laid a "cable" of incredibly fine wire around the house into my sister's room, where I placed a microphone. I never did any spying, but the amplifier and microphone setup worked, at least in the technical sense, and my sister never discovered it!

• I built photoelectric and mechanical burglar alarms that I hooked up to my bedroom door. I made a rain alarm. Not that I thought anyone would consider ransacking my mess of a room or that I was concerned about my crops, but I loved how simple and easy it was to build devices to see and sense.

• I built a machine to shock unsuspecting friends—literally but not dangerously. During high school, I built an electronic siren that I used with some friends to chase down unsuspecting cars. Once I used a Model T ignition coil to detonate a gasoline explosion in a tin can in our kitchen. I was the one who was the unsuspecting victim in that case.

• Probably my most ambitious project was a Geiger counter that I hooked to a little "computer" I had built. Sensing invisible things—cosmic rays—was, like my various alarms, a kick! The Geiger counter was typical of my most advanced creations. It was a cut-and-paste job of designs I had found in books or magazines. My main innovation was to use a transistor amplifier rather than the tube amplifier in the original design I had found in a book. Even little innovations bring difficulties to overcome, however. The circuit that developed a high voltage for the Geiger tube blew out the first transistor of my amplifier every time I charged the tube, and every weekend I trekked to my favorite electronics store in a sleazy part of downtown Denver to buy a new transistor. No wonder the original design called for a tube amplifier. After weeks of thinking and fiddling— one idea (and one new transistor) per week—I fixed the problem with an incredible hack: I added another gang to the pushbutton that charged the Geiger tube, carefully bending the contacts so the new gang shorted out the input to the transistor amplifier before and during the high-voltage charging process (figure 4.1).

The idea of using a "computer" (it was really only an electronic counter) to count ticks from my Geiger counter was also my own creation. In contrast to my experience with the transistor amplifier, I was stunned when the computer started clicking off Geiger ticks the very first time I tried it. I got an honorable mention at the state science fair for this project, although I never took science fairs very seriously. Instead, I al-

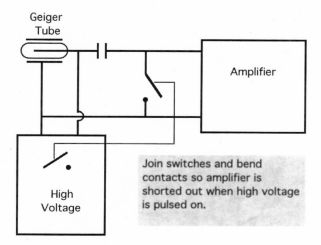

Figure 4.1
Andy's incredible hack to protect amplifier from high voltage.

most always declared something I had already done as my science project, usually wrapping some superficial "experiment" story around the device I built or adding some book research for the poster.

From a distance, all of this work has a face value. My parents were happy that I was "doing science," and I suppose they thought that the few of my constructions they saw were an indication that I was doing something profitable. If they had seen a different subset of my constructions—the siren, the shock machine, and the language-lab radio—they might have felt differently. School also approved of my work, at least superficially, yet the work I did showed up in school extremely rarely and then connected only to what were optional and unambiguously peripheral activities such as "doing a science project." Up close, my activities would probably have to be judged, minimally, inefficient. There was a huge redundancy and repetition. Surely building the same radio twice should have been enough. Occasionally, I read books about electronics, but mainly I looked for books or magazines that described interesting things to build, not science. In fact, when I infrequently tried to read explanatory texts, I found them difficult to understand and boring. Luckily, most of the "how to" magazine articles and book chapters also had a little bit of explanation, which I usually read only when something went wrong.

I almost never experimented in a scientific sense. Mostly I experimented only to find out what was going wrong in my current project or, infrequently, to see whether an idea I had for a new or improved device was technically feasible. Hypotheses were typically low level—in response to "Why doesn't this stupid thing work?" rather than about any grand principle. I remember my disbelief when I was taught "the scientific method" in school. I couldn't empathize with it. One of my few explicit attempts to explore an area scientifically, looking at sound with my oscilloscope, I judged a complete failure.

Even more, much of my investment in and enjoyment of these activities focused on "boring," menial skills. I loved soldering and working with plastic cases. I loved playing with possible layouts of parts on a circuit board. Now, that doesn't sound like good preparation for earning a Ph.D. in theoretical physics. In a nutshell, I was designing and building, not really doing science, and I was certainly not focused on the goal of learning science.

Note the profound irony in this up close look at my hobby activities. On the one hand, what I did would horrify a responsible curriculum designer. It was, in any conventional educational sense, terribly inefficient. There was no coherent curriculum with an eye toward future learning. There was no careful content analysis and no inventive curriculum materials. I was buried deep in material goals and minimally interested in learning for its own sake. Some of my social goals were either mildly subversive or intended to co-opt institutional goals by substituting what I wanted to do for what teachers thought I ought to do. I had no effective community to scaffold my learning or participation. On the other hand, I am convinced my hobby was a future-defining pattern of engagement for me. I believe it was much more important than, for example, my formal high school education.

Let me get one issue immediately out of the way. None of the details of my own experience should be taken as generally prescriptive. What I did was a perfect fit for my inclinations, interests, personal history, and family situation. I would hardly expect it to fit other people. I was simply not motivated by friends or by what my teachers or parents believed was in my best interest. This is not a common orientation or one I would argue for. My patterns of work had elements of substance and style—

for example, an insistent but both shy and modest subversiveness—that characterize very few people. We'll need to dig out the general importance of experiences like mine more slowly and carefully.

I've left you with the claim that this experience was important to my intellectual development, but I've tried to deprive you of a comfortable face validity. As I fill in the gap, I open the two main doors to different views of learning and knowing that constitute the core of this chapter.

Intuitive Knowledge

I call the first door *intuitive knowledge*. I mean by this term a whole host of ways of knowing that are beyond the stereotypes of knowledge we have culturally institutionalized in school and even in our common sense. I do not mean anything mystical by intuition, as my examples should show. I don't believe in intuitive leaps beyond scientific explanation and certainly not in paranormal sensitivity. Instead, I merely want to focus attention outside of word/concepts and facts that are prominent both in school and in other parts of our lives simply because they accord with visible aspects of current literacy.

The short version of one generalizable importance of my hobby is that, through it, I built up a rich and flexible intuition about electronic devices—what their mechanical properties in fabrication and their behaviors were, and how they worked. Here's an interesting slice of my learning: Have you ever reflectively considered what happens when you turn the radio tuning knob slowly away from a station and back to it? (For this little piece of learning, unfortunately, digital radios or radios with pushbutton tuning are of little use.) The radio seems to "stick" to the tuned station for a while, then quickly loses it entirely. Turning the knob back sometimes requires a surprisingly large motion before the station returns, and you may well have to undo some of that returning in order to find the center of the station's frequency. The same behavior is sometimes even more dramatic in adjusting the sweep frequency of an oscilloscope like the one I built. I made this kind of adjustment endless times in my failed search for meaning in sound waves. Looking at the screen, you may see a beautiful full-screen sine wave. Turning the sweep adjustment knob for a while does nothing. Then, all of a sudden, the screen is a jumble of unruly squiggles. Retreating in trying to recover your beautiful sine wave requires more than the slight twist back to where you lost sync, and, indeed, when you do regain your original, clean picture, you learn you have probably overshot the mark. The clean sine wave will be unstable, flickering in and out, unless you back up some from your retreat, thus regaining your original setting.

This behavior is called *hysteresis*. That sounds like a pretty fancy concept, and, in fact, you probably won't get it even in introductory college physics or mathematics texts. I remember encountering hysteresis in electromagnetic theory. My reaction was, "Oh, that kind of thing," while my roommate struggled with mostly irrelevant details, such as what was happening inside the magnetic material that was being subjected to a variable external magnetic field. Hysteresis really is just that pattern of "stickiness" in trying to adjust something and the corresponding need to overshoot to recover an original state.

Patterns like this happen to be an essential part of understanding change and control in any context. Let me give some other examples of such patterns. If you hook up a big capacitor (a particular electronic component) to a battery and monitor the voltage with a meter, you see that it increases rapidly at first, then slows and slows and only very gradually reaches its maximum. There's a characteristic graph for this pattern, which you can see if you use an oscilloscope instead of a meter—and I did, more times than I care to think. This is the same pattern you would see, for example, if you dropped an object from a great height (e.g., a person from an airplane) and monitored its speed. The speed increases rapidly at first, then more slowly zeros in on its ultimate value. There is a common reason for this pattern. The rate of change of the relevant quantity is less the closer it gets to its eventual value, which is the terminal velocity in the case of the dropped object and the battery voltage in the case of the capacitor.

Here's another example of patterns of change. Consider a situation where one quantity (a control or input) affects another (an output). There is a fundamental difference between a *linear* and a *nonlinear* connection between these quantities. For example, if you increase the input signal to an amplifier by a factor of two, then you really want to get an increase in output by a factor of two. Linear change like this (where a certain

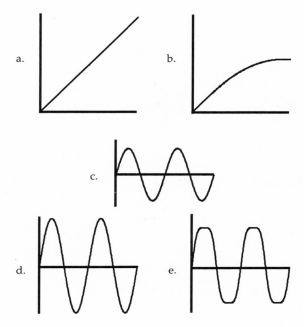

Figure 4.2
(*a*) A linear input versus output graph; a certain increase in input always leads to the same increase in output. (*b*) Nonlinear input versus output; a certain increase in input leads to decreasing increase in output. (*c*) An audio signal. (*d*) A linear amplification of (*c*), preserves "shape" (timbre). (*e*) A nonlinear amplification of (*c*), distorts "shape" (timbre).

amount of increase in input is met always with a particular corresponding change in output—figure 4.2a) is a fundamental mathematical concept. I could go on for pages describing the historical development of mathematics to handle this idea.

Anyone who has followed popular accounts of chaos theory associates the shift from linear to nonlinear with a mystical paradigm shift in mathematical understanding of the world. (Sadly, this is an unfortunate corruption of the real contributions of chaos theory.) Linearity and nonlinearity may be very subtle ideas for a high school student who has no previous associations with linear change versus other kinds of change, but if you have built an amplifier and it suddenly stops behaving linearly, you know that you can hear the difference. Your disastrously misbehaving amplifier

Figure 4.3
Left, a linear presentation of brightness. *Right,* if brightness is nonlinearly related to original, shades are distorted. Here, increases of original brightness in lighter regions result in little change in the printing brightness (saturation, clipping), resulting in lost detail.

becomes an intellectual and emotional reference point. To play this out in detail, let's say you have an amplifier that runs on twelve volts. Your amplifier cannot supply an output of more than twelve volts. If you continue to increase the input, eventually you run out of output voltage, and when that happens, the result is not subtle. It sounds horrible. This is called *saturation* or *clipping* in an amplifier. It's just a case of linear becoming nonlinear. Consult figures 4.2c, d, and e, and figure 4.3.

Linear change is usually what you want; that's a lesson I learned from electronics. In some circumstances, however, you may learn in equally dramatic fashion that you don't want linear change. You can buy volume controls with linear or nonlinear behaviors. I assumed, naturally, that linear was the correct choice and that nonlinear controls were reserved for some esoteric purpose I couldn't imagine. I was spectacularly wrong. Adjusting the linear volume control on an amplifier produced a strange phenomenon. The sound level seemed to leap up, and then the second half of the control barely seemed to do anything at all. Why? Because your ears hear sound volume based on ratios, not on repeating a constant change (linearity). A sound gets louder by the same amount if its amplitude (e.g., the voltage from an amplifier) increases by the same *factor*, not by the same *amount*. You want a control that goes 2, 4, 8, 16, 32, . . . ; you don't want the "usual" linear pattern that goes 2, 4, 6, 8, 10, . . . Comparing these two number sequences, you can see that the linear pattern starts out close to matching the nonlinear pattern, but then it falls well short, corresponding to my volume control that "stopped working" halfway up.

Anyone familiar with the important themes of science and mathematics will recognize patterns of change as a central focus of attention. Which patterns are appropriate to which circumstances and what sorts of things can cause these characteristic patterns are critical in the abstract (calculus, differential equations, system dynamics, and so on) and in every particular science. In physics, you find hysteresis in magnetic materials and in the thermodynamic Carnot Cycle; in biology, you have patterns such as population explosions and equilibrium or similar patterns in chemical reactions in cells, and so on. If authority is necessary on this issue, the American Association for the Advancement of Science, in its Science for All Americans project, lists patterns of change as one of six fundamental themes in all of science.

Even outside school contexts, patterns of change constitute part of what anyone would want to call (mathematical) literacy. I just read that we had the seventh largest point drop in the history of the stock market. Is it time to panic? No. Economic growth and retrenchment is not linear. Shrinking and expanding should almost always be measured as ratios, like a properly behaving volume control. Sure enough, the seventh largest point drop in the history of the stock market barely makes the top one hundred when measured as a ratio. Hardly worth noticing.

Similarly, every mutual fund and bank records its performance on graphs that swoop up dramatically toward the present. Surely it is time to jump on the savings bandwagon in order to catch the incredible climb we are experiencing! Or, thinking in ratios, maybe not. "2, 4, 8, 16, 32, . . ." looks dramatic, but it's a constant factor. (Can you guess why these institutions continue to use linear graphs rather than ratio-based graphs? Perhaps they wouldn't if the general population were literate enough to understand how misleading these practices are.)

What do we think of thousands or millions of tons of greenhouse gases per year? That sounds like a huge amount, but is it, proportionally? On the other hand, how long can we sustain changes of a fraction of a percent per year? One percent per year for a thousand years is not a factor of 10 (1,000 changes of .01), but 2,000 times that: a factor of 20 thousand!

What's the relationship of intuitive knowledge to schooled knowledge? I suggested above that some of the intuitive knowledge I acquired doing electronics was the sort that schooling ought to supply, but schooling is based on current literacies and on current popular prejudices about the forms of knowledge that are valuable. So even if patterns of change were taught, the lesson would likely be learned via patterns of equations. Consequently, directly recognizing patterns or their consequences in the world—as I learned in my electronics work—would be an unlikely outcome. In general, school does a remarkably bad job of preparing good intuitions. I'll speak more about this subject below. For now, though, I can speak about when the intuitive knowledge I developed in electronics finally found a home at school.

I eventually began to study some of the things for which my hobby accidentally prepared me. I took physics in high school after my hobby days were over. It wasn't that I had already learned physics. That was patently not true, but everything in class made sense in a certain way. Even when a topic didn't make immediate sense, I was still in familiar territory.

Consider this example. I remember distinctly when I learned about potential energy—that you can compute how much work is necessary to raise an object a certain distance. I found the concept simply unbelievable. Here's why. Suppose you start raising an object very quickly. Obviously it takes a greater force to do that than if you raise it slowly. Now, the work you do depends (linearly!) on force. More force, more work done. How can you wind up doing the same work if you start doing it at a different rate? Even more, how can you wind up doing the same amount of work for all possible ways you can raise an object a certain height?

The nub of what I figured out goes like this. First, you have to start lifting and end it at rest. Otherwise, you *can* do more work with one lift compared to another. You could, in principle, throw the object to the moon, giving it the huge amount of energy it would need to get there in an explosive, but spatially limited push. Second, there's a kind of balancing or compensation going on. If you start pushing an object up rapidly, then you don't have to push it with as much force near the top. In fact, you will *have* to push it with less force, or it will continue to move, rather than stop. More work early on means less later and vice versa. By thinking along these lines, I got to the point that it seemed at least possible, if still remarkable, that any method of pushing winds up doing the same amount of work.

These are the interesting points. Being surprised is a sign of relative expertise, not a sign of ignorance. If you don't know anything about a situation, how can you know what is unusual? I had enough intuitive sense that I knew I should think about this funny phenomenon of potential energy. To this day, I think it is quite fair to say that potential energy is a surprising phenomenon. Knowing when to think hard is at least half the battle in life. After being surprised, I could play with the situation, simulate in my head what force I'd have to use to move an object up and what would happen from that. Finally, I was comfortable enough with patterns of change that I could easily see, at least roughly, the qualitative compensation that might be going on. In contrast, I could imagine that another student might come to the section on potential energy and say "fine," wandering away with a ticking time bomb of incomprehension about what the principle actually entails.

In a nutshell:

• I did not know the physics already. Certainly I did not know the words and meanings I was being taught.

• I did have a feeling, however, for the kinds of phenomena being discussed. I could be surprised!

• I had further resources. I could simulate the situation, qualitatively, and draw well-founded conclusions. I couldn't necessarily conclude what was right, but I could consider what was sensible.

• All in all, I was intuitively ready, although that might not have shown on any school test about the concept of potential energy, for example.

From the outside, I looked "smart." I learned quickly and more deeply than most. When I got to college, I became famous, if not notorious, among my friends for having a superb intuitive feel for what we were learning in physics. I could guess answers and make good judgments about how things should turn out. "That can't be right," or "That must be right." I could look back and say, "We should have known that," or the opposite, "That is really surprising." I could think about problems in ways that weren't instructed, but it was not native intelligence alone, if at all, that accounted for my success. It was a strong intuitive foundation built in electronics play. There's an important little lesson in the midst of this narrative. Hidden knowledge, such as knowledge in forms we aren't used to recognizing, is frequently assigned to the category of "intelligence."

The Structure of Activities and "Committed Learning"

The learning that happened in my hobby, I've argued, was subtle and easy to miss (in part because it involved unusual forms of knowledge), but it was extremely important to me. Another aspect of this learning is equally important to understanding learning, and it is easier to see, even if its importance is missed in contemporary educational and cognitive theory. I call it the *structure of activities*. It is the second door to the revised conception of knowledge and learning introduced in this chapter.

Probably the most remarkable fact about my hobby was that it lasted for years. I needed no external incentives, rewards, or direct encouragement, although I gratefully acknowledge my parents for giving me the resources to do this work. I sometimes worked hard, despite frustrations. Other times I just let a project drop. Eventually, "doing electronics" merged into "being a physics major." How do we understand persistence, but also the reasons for transformations—decays of old lines of work and the emergence of really new ones? For this, we need an as yet nonexistent theory of the *structure and evolution of activities*.

Common sense provides a decent starting place. I was interested in electronics. Interest, in some form, must be an important component of understanding the shape of activities. I can't provide a theory of interest here, but I can say a few things about the directions I believe such a theory should follow. First, we have to get beyond listing topics and pretending we have understood an individual's interests when we have provided such a list: "Johnny is interested in cars. Sue is interested in dolls. Kids these days are interested in dinosaurs." Nobody's interest is unqualified, however. Under some circumstances, no matter how strong our interest is in the abstract, it will falter. Generally, a surefire way to find out that a child is not *really* interested in a subject is to make it into a school requirement. On the other hand, I have found in interviewing students that, under the right circumstances, almost everyone can be interested in physics; it is possible for them to want to talk and think about it and to find it engaging and motivating. How and when are therefore absolutely essential parts of a theory of interest. Interest is always contingent. What are the contingencies?

Next, we want to know, what does interest entail? I like to think about some things. They are comforting in some way—say, thinking about past vacations—but that kind of interest is nothing like my electronics interest, which entailed long-term, committed effort. How does interest intertwine with particular activities? Many people say they are interested in this or that, but they don't do anything about it. This is not a matter of strength of interest. I am committed to reminiscing about past vacations, but that will never go very far because there are almost no activity entailments. I was interested in subversive actions, such as my language-lab radio, yet that was a highly qualified interest that would go only so far and under particular conditions, such as the complete lack of public scrutiny.

Third, interests fall into patterns. My electronics interest was really a cluster: I was interested in sensing remote or invisible things; I was interested in soldering; I was interested in making small things; I was interested in machining plastic cases and circuit boards. These are not the same interest, but some interests form families, kinds of things that are all, more or less, similar and interesting for their similarities. Soldering and machining equipment cases both built on an attention to properties of materials and learning how to outsmart the material to get it to do what I wanted. More broadly, it was the whole constellation of families of interests that allowed me to meander from one thing to the next, all the time keeping up "an interest in electronics." Accidental, synergistic conspiracies of interests in particular activities like this are critical to understand.

Finally, interests simply don't stay the same. They have evolutionary patterns that we must also understand. How do new interests start? On what fragments of prior interests do they build? What else is needed in an activity mix to develop new interests?

This last is a critical theme that deserves a name: *generativity*. Interests, like almost all components of human intellectual capabilities, are fundamentally generative. They never stay the same, but constantly shift and rebuild themselves according to experiences and contexts. In contrast, one of the primary features of literacy as we have come to know it is the (unnatural) stability it affords to our thinking. Unlike propositions, however, both interests and intuitive knowledge are fluid—always changing and adapting. That is why understanding how they change and develop is important. I often hear it said that kids just aren't interested in this or that. Perhaps not, but that's irrelevant. *Can* they become interested in it? That's the important question.

Understanding interest is thus one fundamental part of understanding the structure of activities. The other component that I want to discuss here is competence. How do we see in various activities the competence that is built in performing them? I've already begun to make the case that human competence includes many hidden components like the intuitive knowledge I learned from electronics, and I develop and enrich this view later on.

I think of competence and interest as working together something like a roller coaster. Competence is like the motor that allows you to climb a hill (solve a problem, accomplish a task). Of course, competence is much more complicated than a motor because it gets you up certain hills and not others, so you need to think about the relation between the motor you have and the hill you propose to climb. Hills (problems, tasks) are at least as complex as motors. They are not just variably steep and high.

Interest, on the other hand, is like the speed you gain going down the far side of the hill. It propels you off to new adventures on new hills. Again, interest has a lot more texture than just faster or slower. Maybe we can accommodate this diversity by extending the image to a roller coaster that doesn't have tracks, but can move anywhere in two or three (or more) dimensions. Then the texture of interest can be analogous to the new direction in which you are thrust after you get past the peak of a hill.

Every hill changes your competence, and it thus changes the set of other hills you may be able to climb. Every hill also sets you in directions where you may encounter other hills—or not—and hills that may extend your possibilities for future hill climbing and downhill zooming—or not.

The roller-coaster image can help us imagine how subtle the structure of activities can be because of the complex relations between competence and interest. Let's start thinking about some of the many things that can go wrong. As I mentioned, your current competence allows you to climb certain hills and not others. The more competence you have, the greater possibility you have for continuing your fun ride. Certain hills might just be either too high or too steep for you at a given time. Similarly, interest can direct you toward hills you can vanquish or hills against which you have no chance to succeed. The territory you find yourself in is incredibly important. A territory that has some good hills that are low enough to start on but hills that develop good competence to climb neighboring hills will lead to a long and profitable ride. Some territories can lead to long rides, but rides that are confined to a particular type of hill. They might not prepare you for the hills you find in school or the hills you find in life after school. They're a fun ride for a while, but you'll stall eventually.

My electronics roller coaster was a truly excellent ride for me. It was a great initial match to my interests and capabilities, but didn't strain them too much in the beginning. On the other hand, it did develop both new competence and new interests. I got hooked on miniaturization and also on design. (In fact, design started a line that has continued right into my professional concerns, which have resulted in this book.) What I got from my activities both selected and energized future experiences. The emerging backlog of skills and competence that I developed had two wonderful properties. First, it allowed me to extend my electronics activity for years without stalling out for lack of interest, competence, or challenges so that I would continue to be productive. Just as important, that backlog of skills eventually provided a foundation for learning the school material that much later led to my graduate studies and Ph.D. degree.

I hope you can see how important it is to understand both competence and interest (and tasks because they host and develop competence and interest). If we didn't know about intuitive knowledge, we wouldn't have a chance of understanding how much good my experience actually did for me. We would have worried endlessly about the "curriculum," as it might not seem to be covering any well-known territory. I wasn't getting many word/concepts or equations of physics or even much of an academic understanding of electronics per se. By the same token, even if we focused on exactly the right knowledge, we might have simply removed from consideration all the interest components and the way those components combined with competence into a fabric of activity that made that enterprise really work for me.

I am enthusiastic about the possibilities of a better understanding of activities and engagement. In the history of psychology and education, competence and knowledge have been constant pursuits. Not that we have finished them, but from an educational perspective, activities in which we engage to learn are at least as important as setting a knowledge-oriented specification of our curriculum. In fact, with regard to knowledge in activity, I am sure our notions of knowledge itself will change. We will have to confront the rich pools of intuitive knowledge that make everyday competence and activity possible. What underlies everyday activity may be among the most poorly understood areas of our current views of knowledge. Interest, in contrast to some components of competence, is a poor handmaiden in educational research. Very few have pursued it seriously, and, in my opinion, even fewer foundational ideas are in place. The amalgam of interest and competence, activity, has been discovered by socially oriented thinkers, even if they have pursued only culturally normative (or at least culturally characteristic) activity, as opposed to the experiential and sometimes idiosyncratic activity that marked my electronics work.

From the perspective of a theory of activities and engagement, science itself looks different. Scientists aren't just people who know things. They are people who know how to manage a perpetual roller-coaster game that both provides them sufficient personal rewards and still climbs the right hills to make progress within the narrower view of humans as pure knowers. My own view of myself as a scientist was partly forged out of Howard Gruber's wonderful description of Darwin's network of enterprises that allowed him to move from area to area, depending on whether progress could be made in one or another at any given time. At the same time, each enterprise contributed substantially to others. Darwin's interest in geology led him to think about what happened when a species became isolated. He was a genius, one might say, because he was master of his own intellectual roller coaster.

We can do more than think about science as the result of a pattern of activities or even as something that may be enhanced by a proper organization of activities. We can think of the fabric of scientific activity as what science is, in its essence. Hence, we want to understand the possible evolutionary paths of activities just exactly as we want to understand how intuitive knowledge evolves into the scientific knowledge that appears in books. As developmental psychologists have spent many years understanding how competence accumulates, sometimes in surprising ways, so should we understand important subtleties in how activities evolve. My electronic experience, I believe, contained precursors and components of the scientific activities that now occupy my life, with very few of the formal trappings of science. I noted that I didn't really do experiments. I didn't follow any simple description of a scientific method, and I wasn't interested in the accumulation of knowledge. Yet I believe that "play" set me on the path to science as surely as any book or school learning and much more surely than practicing the scientific method might have. Smooth evolution is more important than proper form.

From the perspective of activities and engagement, my electronics hobby hints at a model of the best learning I believe we can hope for. To underscore this idea, let me give it a name. I was engaged in *committed learning*. A primary focus of committed learning is *the fabric of activities in which one learns*. Committed learning, in fact, is nothing more than particular relationship between a learner and a fabric of learning activities. A committed relationship entails a feeling of ownership, personal connection, and competence such that extended engagement in those activities is perceived to be a natural extension of ourselves. We value those activities; they are self-sustaining, and they feel coherent and connected.

Committed learning almost always happens in what I call the *regime of competence*. I don't recall a single moment when I felt "I just can't do this" during my hobby activities. More than that, I really was competent at what I chose to do. There was clearly a dynamic that kept me in my regime of competence. When I felt I was getting beyond my depth, I just turned to something else. More likely, I couldn't even formulate an action plan for something I wanted to do that was beyond me in the only way that counted—if I couldn't manage to continue working on it. That doesn't mean I didn't get stuck or frustrated. It means more that I got stuck only when I had a strong motivation to continue in a certain line, so strong that it felt like the right thing to work on despite ordinarily unpleasant feelings of frustration. Some unpleasant feelings are the happy *consequence* of motivation, and motivation cannot be the pure pursuit of pleasure or feeling good.

It is worth pointing out that learning in the regime of competence is highly counterintuitive. How can people learn when they are competent already? What's the motivation or need? Instead, at the very least (one might think), we must scaffold incompetence so that learners can get anything significant done.

These views, I believe, are persistent echoes of the times when almost everyone thought intuitive and commonsense knowledge were irrelevant or worse—the opposite of what needs to be accomplished in school. "Scientific, rational, abstract, logical, formal" are the goals of instruction and the opposite of everyday knowledge and activity. It follows, within this perspective, that newcomers to a field are assumed to be ignorant. To put this succinctly, there is no preparation for learning science except learning science, which is by definition a process that starts from ignorance. In contrast, the perspective afforded by the regime of competence respects the fact that resources for learning don't always look just like the product of learning. My intuitive physics established a regime of competence that eventually included learning school physics. Had I not had the experiences that developed my intuition, trying to learn physics would have been unpleasant and most likely unsuccessful. Instead, I was lucky enough to build outward from an existing regime of competence, pursuing my hobby and gradually accumulating resources that eventually enfolded learning "formal" physics.

In a nutshell, people learn best in their regime of competence. If that regime doesn't encompass something to be learned, don't jump away from that regime, but build *from* it.

I think most contemporary schools are—at the risk of oversimplification—perversely designed so that nobody gets to work very long in her regime of competence. If anyone gets remotely competent at one topic, clearly it is time for him or her to move on to the next. The external controls of teachers, curriculum, and grades work against much activity in the regime of competence for most students. At least, there is little regulation in schools of the sort that kept me in my own regime of competence with electronics, and the strongly held values of progress and efficiency push out the purportedly inefficient learning that I did as a compulsive radio builder.

Committed learning is not the same thing as efficient learning, which dominates educational research and the common intuitions of the public about what schools should do for their children. We can surely never escape from the fact that we have only so much time with our children to bring them the competence that we wish for them. But there are two other critical things to remember about education and learning. First, we need to put on better glasses to see the really productive parts of an engagement. When we add intuitive knowledge and a progressing evolution in activity competence, efficiency can take on new meaning. If the ability to dedicate oneself in extended, self-sustaining, personally meaningful, and sciencelike activities is important, school as we know it is horribly inefficient, even if it succeeds by narrower measures. The second critical thing to remember is that education is not merely instrumental. It is a significant part of the lives of our children for a significant proportion of their lifetimes. I want my children to experience the kind of pleasures I did in my hobby as much as I want them to know some useful things, and I firmly believe we can make learning a better experience and get better educational results at the same time if we take committed learning seriously as a goal.

Committed learning is rarely achieved in our society, but it is achieved, I believe, by most excellent intellectuals, artists, athletes, business people, and even people toward whose accomplishments we might not feel positively disposed, such as gang members. What we need to learn is effective principles of committed learning and the design of learning environments to foster it.

Committed learning, in my view, takes a much higher precedence than almost any instrumental goals that are popularly advocated today concerning education. For example, I am not interested in the narrow vocational or pure efficiency arguments that are so often given for computers and technology in general. Instead, I am interested in technology because of its fantastic power to help us construct committed-learning environments. Computers provide tremendous possibilities to engage students, as the phenomenon of addiction to computer games, Web surfing, and "hacking" suggest. I believe we can build wonderfully self-perpetuating roller-coaster rides for our children with just the right architecture of hills to lead them on to the scientific knowledge and activity we wish for them. We can do this without assuming that children are or should be little scientists.

Similarly, I believe many fads in education will either pass or be subsumed into a properly instrumental position with respect to committed learning. Learning in groups is wonderful, especially as it contributes to personal commitment and to other aspects of committed learning, such as creating an environment of help and caring for getting up tough hills, and I absolutely don't want to create a nation of purely individualistic people. As my own experience proves to me, however, committed learning doesn't always directly involve other people. In fact, if our educational system produces people with no personal strength and ability to pursue paths on which others may not wish to join them, it will undoubtedly be as much of a failure as it would be if graduates don't know how to deal with others at all.

I've done the main work of this chapter: I've introduced the two new perspectives that I need to make my images of future computational literacies both sensible and plausibly connected to powerful learning. Intuitive knowledge can be gained from many experiences, and the right kind of intuitive knowledge is wonderfully enhancing—or even necessary—in learning science. We must reassess how students can learn science, and we can open new vistas on what is essential and productive. The kind of work I see students doing in the future with computers is revolutionary, and it demands a strong scientific rationale. Our progressive understanding of the nature of intuitive knowledge is one key to motivating difficult, long-term changes in schooling and learning, changes that follow on understanding more of what learning is really about. Without the ongoing epistemological shift that recognizes, more and more, the importance of intuitive knowledge, a computer may really be just a toy or purely an instrument of "more efficient" learning. This book is not in its essence about lowering costs or speeding up learning. It is about redefining what learning counts and, indeed, what counts beyond lists of things we believe people should learn.

Coming to understand the importance of activity gives us new vistas. Committed learning and probably its most salient characteristic, learning in the regime of competence, are both new goals and new means. We can understand that the view of learning as an evolution in a person's fabric of comfortable activities is as important as the narrower view of "developing knowledge," and we can come to new ways of looking at what our students do while learning, ways that suggest that knee-jerk, back-to-basics reactions to low test scores and the inefficiency of allowing them to engage in activities they enjoy need to be carefully rethought. At the same time, committed learning reminds us that education is not just a technical accomplishment. It is about designing the lives of our children.

5

Intuition and Activity Elaborated

The previous chapter introduced some fundamental perspectives on knowledge and learning. Through the lenses of intuitive knowledge and the structure of activities and engagement, I hope my images of future computational literacies appear both more plausible and more desirable. Intuition and activity are extraordinarily rich topics, and we continue to explore them in this chapter. Doing so will be valuable for both skeptics and for enthusiasts.

Intuition Revisited

Intuitive knowledge is not completely absent from cognitive research. In fact, much of my own research and that of a substantial bunch of colleagues has been directed toward understanding this form of knowledge. This section briefly reviews some well-developed ideas within this research and more expansively compares intuitive knowledge with some more familiar forms. I want to contrast the use of a particular form of intuitive knowledge with the use of logic and word/concepts in reasoning.

First, I have to introduce and explain what a *p-prim* is. Would you be surprised in the following situation? Suppose you were pushing an object along—say, a wheelbarrow full of grass cuttings in your yard—and you decided to get the job done more quickly. Naturally, you push harder in order to go faster, but in this case, the wheelbarrow slows down, and it slows down more the harder you push! If someone told you a story about such an event, you wouldn't believe it, or you'd say it had to be a trick, and something was peculiar about this wheelbarrow. How about the following similar scenario: you are pushing your wheelbarrow around, this time collecting rocks for a rock garden that you intend to build, but every time you put a new rock in the wheelbarrow it got easier to push!

I believe that there is a particular element of intuitive knowledge—what I call a *p-prim*—behind your surprise in these hypothetical situations. In fact, it is the first p-prim I discovered, and it turns out that it is among the more prominent and important p-prims. I call it *Ohm's p-prim*, and it works like this. Whenever you see effort being expended to accomplish a task, you expect a particular relationship between effort and result. More effort begets more result. That is the core of Ohm's p-prim. In addition, however, you know that there is always some kind of resistance involved in accomplishing a task. In pushing things around, that resistance depends on a number of things, but everyone knows that heavier things offer more resistance. That's the other part of Ohm's p-prim. More resistance begets less result (or the reverse: less resistance begets more result).

Here's my favorite example of Ohm's p-prim. Suppose you have a running vacuum cleaner, and you put your hand over the nozzle. Will the pitch of the motor (which corresponds directly to its speed) go up or down? Many people will say that it must go down. Implicitly, they are saying that if you interfere or add resistance to a situation without compensating with an increase in effort, you must get less result, so the fan in the vacuum cleaner will spin slower. The case of the vacuum cleaner is striking precisely because Ohm's p-prim doesn't work. "Increasing the resistance" by putting your hand over the nozzle actually makes the fan spin faster. The pitch of the sound goes up. Interestingly, people preserve their belief in Ohm's p-prim even in the face of exceptions. If they know or see that the pitch goes up, they say the vacuum must be "working harder" to overcome an increased resistance!

Ohm's p-prim is a powerful and very general piece of intuitive knowledge. Nobody can get along in the world without learning some version of it. It applies to all sorts of situations where you push, pull, or in any other way interact in the world to accomplish something. Ohm's p-prim is not at all subtle. You can feel resistance whenever you try to move things, and there are very few exceptions to this regularity in the world. Even more, Ohm's p-prim is not limited to physical situations. People think "metaphorically" about their interactions with other people via this p-prim. (I put *metaphorically* in quotes because it is not clear whether the physical world is a metaphor for the social world or the reverse! I suspect neither is a good description, but we simply learn in a wide range of circumstances that more effort begets more results.) We have to try harder to overcome the resistance of someone to an argument we are making. The volume of your voice goes up in an argument as if you were turning up the voltage or pressing on the accelerator to make the engine work harder to make the car go faster. What do you suppose people mean and what do they expect when they say, "we try harder"?

I gave this intuition—more effort, more result; more resistance, less result—the name *Ohm's p-prim* because it very much resembles Ohm's law in electricity. Ohm's law says that if you increase the voltage, you get more current, and if you increase the resistance in a circuit without a corresponding increase in voltage, then the current decreases. Ohm's law is easy to learn, I believe, because people see it naturally as a simple example of Ohm's p-prim.

In general, the term *p-prim* refers to a class of simple, "little" pieces of intuitive knowledge such as Ohm's p-prim. It actually stands for *phenomenological primitive.* That's a mouthful, but it is really quite descriptive. The first part, *phenomenological,* means that p-prims are evident in our experience of the world. Many aspects of our experience are precisely the recognition of the p-prim sense that the world makes. We perceive phenomena through p-prims, and those phenomena are sensible to us because of that.

The primitive part is just as important. First, it means we can't take these p-prims apart and say why they work. Why do things move faster if you push harder? There's no way to answer that question. Our attitude is "that's just the way things are." P-prims, like any knowledge, are not always correct. If they did always work, there wouldn't be any need for physics! Instead, sometimes they don't apply when we think they might. In those cases, we are surprised. But when the p-prims we see *do* work, our attitude is nonchalant—"of course."

Because p-prims are usually taken to be obvious and self-explanatory, people seldom mention them explicitly in explanations. You don't say, "Johnny got bad grades because (*a*) he slacked off, and (*b*) less effort usually means less result." Everybody knows the (*b*) part, so nobody says it. It is very difficult to put p-prims into words, even if you choose to say one.

Ohm's p-prim serves us in many ways. It helps us regulate our own actions. It tells us what to do when we want particular effects, such as more or less movement. It also focuses our attention in particular places when something is going wrong. For example, if you are driving your car and it slows down, you check possibilities for a "decreased effort"—has your foot slipped off the pedal, or is there something wrong with the engine? Or you check for an increased resistance—has the wind come up, or did you, without noticing, start moving uphill? Ohm's p-prim is also the hidden basis for many explanations we give to ourselves or to others. Why did young Johnny get bad grades (which we naturally see as accomplishing less)? Because he "slacked off"—he didn't "work hard enough."

Of these many functions, I want to emphasize one in particular: making a particular kind of judgment. Was something that happened reasonable or not? Such judgments are frequently made when a p-prim, rather than another kind of knowledge, is doing the work. In the case of a wheelbarrow that goes slower if we push harder or gets easier to push the more rocks we put in it, pretty much everyone's judgment is swift and sure: that's crazy! But in other cases, making such judgments is more difficult.

Here's a nice case where judgments may not be so easy, and people vary in the judgments they will make. Consider a yo-yo resting on a table, with the string wound around its axle and strung out as in figure 5.1.

If you pull the string very gently to the right so that the yo-yo doesn't skid, what happens? Some people judge that the yo-yo moves to the right; others believe it should move to the left; still others see both possibilities and don't know what will happen. Here are the p-prims behind these

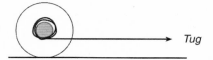

Figure 5.1
A yo-yo on a nonslip surface is pulled gently to the right. Which way does it move?

judgments. The prediction that the yo-yo goes to the right follows a basic and important p-prim that I call *force as a mover*. Basically, things move in the direction you push or pull them. How could that be wrong? Well, in a number of situations, that simply doesn't happen. In particular, if you put a pencil on a table and push it at one end, the pencil turns and does not particularly move forward. The turning pencil works by another p-prim. When you push or pull things off center, they spin in the "obvious" way. Coming back to the yo-yo, if you see it as an example of this *force as a spinner* p-prim, then you see that, in pulling the string, you are trying to spin it counterclockwise. If that happens, then the yo-yo will move to the left. This is the judgment that most people make. It happens to be exactly wrong. The first p-prim, force as mover, is correct in this case. As a consequence, the yo-yo turns clockwise and winds up the string!

People have hundreds if not thousands of p-prims. They have physical p-prims, social p-prims, even epistemological p-prims (though we won't get into that). When they make a judgment of reasonableness or unreasonableness, they are frequently summoning all the relevant p-prims and "deciding" which one or which collection of a few best matches the situation. Then what happens in the situation is reasonable if it matches the chosen p-prim or p-prims and surprising if it does not. In a trial, the jurors have to decide whether it makes sense that the defendant was jealous and committed a crime or more sensible that the evidence is accidental or the result of a conspiracy. Do they see in the accused's behavior actions that they consider (via psychological p-prims) characteristic of jealousy? Or do they see in the prosecutor's or police's behavior signs of unprofessionalism and prejudice? In the end, they work hard to summon all relevant p-prims, then do some balancing and finally render a judgment.

The contrast case to p-prims and judgments is logic using word/concepts. Take the classic example of a logical syllogism: "All men are mortal. Socrates is a man. Therefore Socrates is mortal." You could call this a judgment, but it really has a very different character. It is "hard," "crisp," and explicit. Part of these qualities come from the fact that almost all the work that is going on is carried pretty well in the language. In contrast, whether we see a particular p-prim or not is quite an iffy proposition. We just don't have words for the slew of p-prims we have, nor is it easy to "explain" why we see one in a situation and why someone else may see another. Instead, the p-prim knowledge may be carried in images or feelings. In the yo-yo situation, if you don't see force as a mover as relevant to the outcome, how do I argue you out of that judgment? In contrast, logic is universal in a certain sense. If you have the idea, you know when it applies, and there's no "maybe" about it. (I'm not saying that all cultures recognize and perform logical syllogism in the same way. It's just that when they do, it has a very different quality from a p-prim-based judgment.)

I find it very interesting that people frequently use the word *logical* for intuitive judgments rather than for real logic. Consider the following cases in which people tend to use the word logical when logic is not at issue. What seems "logical" social behavior to members of one culture is not "logical" in another. Even within the same culture, one person may see an insult and a "logical response," and someone else may be mystified. Similarly, when a juror "just knows" a witness is lying at a trial (and she might well be correct!), she is not drawing conclusions in the same way as a syllogism, and she can't convince someone else by carefully describing the situation. The fabric of intuitive sensibility is much more flexible and relative compared to the fabric of logical syllogisms.

Let me be a little more systematic in this comparison. First of all, intuitive knowledge in the form of p-prims is *rich*. As I said, there are hundreds if not thousands of p-prims that are available to us to think about the physical, social, or other domains. We interact with the physical world in thousands of subtly different ways, and we have p-prims to cover all that experience. A syllogism is powerful in that it is certain, but almost nothing about the physical or social world matches the conditions for certainty that syllogisms need. True logic accounts for very little of our everyday experiences and thought. In contrast, no p-prim is sensibly universal, certainly not by scientific standards, and there is an inescapable subtlety in knowing when one or another p-prim applies. That subtlety defines the aptness and productivity of our intuitions.

Genuine logic is not rich, but *sparse*. One good way to see this is to look in a textbook on logic. First of all, there is a curriculum that is quite teachable. In contrast, how do you think you would go about giving an alien from a different planet a good sense of our intuitive social interactional competence? That's something we learn by living through many experiences. Another way to compare logic and intuition is in terms of mathematical structure. Logic in the stricter sense (such as syllogisms) is mathematizable. In fact, the main part of logic is about as complicated as arithmetic with only two "numbers," true and false. The two-number arithmetic is called a Boolean algebra. But p-prims are essentially complex in the way that they relate to our experience: every p-prim has its own conditions of utility.

Richness also is closely connected to *generativity*. I mentioned this before as an essential feature of intuitive knowledge and of the structure of activities. P-prims are good generative devices. In coming to a new situation, you invoke your existing p-prims and adapt them to it. You meet some new people and discover that among them there are subtly different ways to be a sensible person than you assumed was true based on your experience with your family or friends. It is nonsensical to master the "right set" of p-prims in order to think about the physical or social world (although some sets may be better than others). In contrast, logic doesn't suggest new logics. It doesn't wander and change gradually as you experience new situations. There's nothing "nearby" a situation where "all P are M and S is a P." Whereas p-prims are generative, logic is *closed*.

P-prims are also *diverse*. Consider the following question. Most of us know that it is possible to have a circular orbit about a circular planet. Satellites can go in circles around the earth. What would happen if we had a square planet? Some people react that the orbit should be notably squarish, as in figure 5.2.

The expectation in figure 5.2 is not one we get from our muscles and effort, as it is with Ohm's p-prim. It doesn't involve anything like force

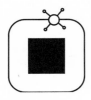

Figure 5.2
An orbit about a square planet should be sort of square?

at all. Instead, it is more like a visual gestalt. Modality like this (visual versus kinesthetic) is one dimension of diversity, and it turns out that there are many other kinds of diversity in the intuitive knowledge system. Patterns of control, such as linear and nonlinear, or the phenomenon of hysteresis have some similarities with phenomena like Ohm's law, but they are more mathematical and abstract as well. A pattern of effort isn't necessarily relevant to hysteresis. Specifically, mathematical p-prims (people do have intuitions about numbers!) and social p-prims have different characters, too. In contrast, logic is fairly homogeneous. Every form of syllogism works the same as any other. Syllogisms concern classes of entities that have unambiguous properties, such as being human. (If it is questionable that Socrates is human, then we don't have a logical issue any more. We have to negotiate our "humanness" p-prims or enter a still different game of agreeing on a verbal definition.)

As I mentioned before, p-prims and other intuitive knowledge like them are problematically related to language. P-prims are encoded visually and kinesthetically. No familiar words refer unambiguously to them. We can't base arguments with our friends about the yo-yo on p-prims. (P-prims are certainly relevant, but we can't talk explicitly about them under ordinary circumstances.) P-prims can exhibit difficulties beyond issues of language; they can be unstable. You shift your attention, and suddenly you see things in a different way. Sometimes you can't even retrieve your original way of seeing the situation. In contrast, we are pretty good at remembering words. In a conversation, I can be definite that my friend just told me we should meet at 5:00 P.M. I can remember, if I put my mind to it, that I said, literally, "OK." How do I remember how a subtle p-primish situation seemed to me? Why did I get the impression that my friend didn't really want to meet at all? We all have the experience of suddenly thinking about a situation differently and not knowing why or how to retrieve our earlier take on it.

To sum up, p-prims are *rich* and *diverse;* they constitute a fundamentally *fragmented* knowledge system. In contrast, logic is *sparse* and *homogeneous* in the structure of situations with which it deals. It is even mathematically systematizable—coherent in a sense p-prims can never be. P-prims are *generative* and *flexible;* logic is *closed* and "stiff." Finally, although logic and language can go hand in hand, p-prims don't connect very well with language. You can say, perhaps, how you feel about a situation, but it is difficult or impossible to name your reason for feeling that way. Poetry and p-prims are evocative; their power is not explicit. As for learning new p-prims, words cannot convey in any direct way the feeling of "rightness" you can have when you see a situation as governed by a p-prim, nor can words easily convey the range of circumstances in which a p-prim should work. Logic is *articulate;* p-prims are not.

I can't resist a historical note on what psychologists and educators said on discovering the existence of intuitive knowledge such as p-prims. This note makes the point that we are frequently prisoners of words and cultural assumptions about many things, including knowledge. First, intuitive knowledge was noticed only when people expressed *wrong* ideas. The ideas were called "misconceptions," and for a long time people acted as if they could not be productive at all. Later, some research showed that if teachers are very, very careful, they can make productive use of students' "alternate conceptions." This supposed lack of productivity is very different from the value my electronics p-prims had for me in learning physics.

It is natural, in a way, that researchers at first saw only "wrong" intuitive knowledge. It is more noticeable when people say things that differ from what is taught in school. Saying wrong things seems to require an explanation, but how people know all the effective things they do about dealing with the world—just getting by, moving around and moving objects around (not to mention interacting effectively with people)—seems to need no explanation. Just as with our physical p-prims, we simply don't inquire about how and why people have the competence we see in their everyday accomplishments.

To tell the truth, I strongly suspect there is another reason why researchers were so fixed on intuitive knowledge as wrong. It is great sport to make fun of students and to ridicule them for not knowing what we do. It also makes a great story that schools are failing by showing that (wrong) intuitions are not affected by instruction.

Intuitive ideas are frequently effective, if not "correct." In fact, in most usual circumstances, they work perfectly well. If they didn't, we'd probably have learned different p-prims. In contrast, researchers failed to acknowledge that their subjects were sensible in what they said. Just as bad, these intuitive ideas were described using words we have lying around to cover different knowledge types. They are (supposedly) faulty "concepts" or even deeply entrenched "theories." These descriptions of intuitive judgments completely overlook the fact that it is incredibly easy to change most situations a little bit and get people to say different things about them, and that people do adjust their p-prims to new experiences all the time. The power of conventional assumptions about knowledge overrides what is really quite easy to see. The richness and generativity of intuitive knowledge has still not propagated into general awareness. Time and time again research reports note that people said other things in addition to or even in contrast to the expected "misconception," but the meaning of those "little" exceptions is still not widely recognized.

So what are the implications of the existence and quality of intuitive knowledge, of p-prims, for computational media and new literacies? Consider this a pop quiz, as you should now be able to fill in at least some of the blanks.

Above all, recall the idea of learning in the regime of competence. Understanding that intuitive knowledge is a vast repository of capabilities that we can tap means we should have a much easier time building learning environments that capitalize on that competence. Recall also the examples of intuitive knowledge that I acquired in electronics experimenting, which eventually served me in constructing more standard, schooled knowledge, such as being able to think about and come to a reasonable equilibrium with respect to the concept of potential energy. I seemed "smart," but I was just intuitively ready for physics instruction. Understanding the role of intuitive knowledge as a basis for learning means that we can understand "smart" in substantially new ways. We can even cultivate certain versions (if not all versions) of being smart.

The fact of intuitive knowledge is critical, but understanding its nature provides another, equally important change in how we think about learning. As I pointed out, we need to reevaluate efficiency in learning. If a learning experience doesn't engage or develop intuitive knowledge, it doesn't begin to be efficient with respect to important classes of learning. Letting kids just play around is no educational program, but keeping kids from playing around probably irresponsibly restricts how they can interact with the subject matter they need to learn.

Culturally, we have a long way to go to specify the intuitive curriculum, but as we progress, we can be sure of a few things. First, language is only part of the necessary experience of learning. Direct involvement with environments designed to provide excellent (if inarticulate) contact with scientific concepts, for example, will grow in importance and prominence as we move from static literacy toward effectively using computational media. Computers as they now exist don't provide a perfect or complete experiential environment for students. Never mistake my enthusiasm for the overlooked potential of computers for advocacy of the removal of people and noncomputational things from the learning environment. Not withstanding the contribution of people and other things, computers— even by themselves—do move us dramatically away from the near-zero involvement of direct experience that is the hallmark of learning science only by reading books or even by talking with teachers and peers.

Activities Revisited

Whether or not I have been sufficiently clear and compelling to convince you about the importance of intuitive knowledge, there is much background research and critical examination to compensate. Your stance toward this section, on activity, ought to be a little different. Explore with me some new and promising ways of thinking, but realize we're just starting out.

When our sons were nine and twelve years old, my wife and I had the privilege of observing a remarkable little activity. Over a period of two days, our boys produced a marvelous collection of about twenty dinosaur cartoons. Several appear in figure 5.3. All followed a common model. The standard name of the dinosaur was corrupted into a suggestive near cognate, which was then illustrated in a drawing. For example, one of my favorites was a dime-meter-odon, a corruption of dimetrodon, a finned-back dinosaur of the Permian period. The dime-meter-odon had a coin slot for a mouth (insert ten cents!) and a meter pointer on its sail. Similarly, the broccoli-o-saurus (brachiosaurus) had a suggestively branching neck with floweret-shaped appendages, including one that constituted a head. The straight-a-saurus (stegosaurus) had the sequence A, K, Q, J, 10, 9 on its spine plates.

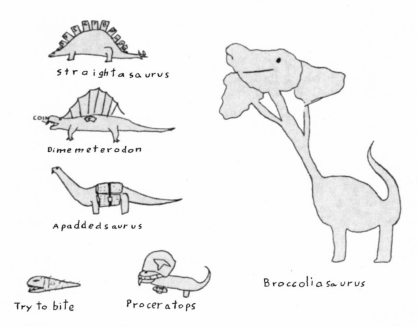

Figure 5.3
Dinosaur cartoons. Straight-asaurus (stegosaurus); Dime-meter-odon (dimetrodon); A-padded-saurus (apatosaurus); Try-to-bite (trilobite); Pro-ceratops (protoceratops); Broccoli-asaurus (brachiosaurus).

Let's jump to the heart of an activity-theoretic view of my sons' cartoons and ask the core developmental question: Where did this activity come from?

To begin, neither my wife nor I had any direct input into the design of the activity. In fact, we found out about it after it had already finished. Furthermore, I can't recall any other activity in our children's history that was substantially like it. Evidently, they must have created it for themselves.

Nothing comes from nothing, so we must persist in asking where this activity came from. In retrospect, I think I can provide some good suggestions out of the history of our family, which illustrate some things about activities until someone develops an excellent theory of activities. In the first instance, the topic, dinosaurs, should not come as a surprise to any U.S. parent, especially parents of boys. (Dinosaurs are not new! This activity took place many years before *Jurassic Park,* the famous motion picture, and before public television's amazingly successful Barney, the purple dinosaur.) Dinosaurs are impressive to almost anyone—big and fantastic—and yet they are close enough to a child's reality that one can imagine children making up "monsters" like these to fear. A part of dinosaur interest, for some children, must be mastering childhood fears. Dinosaurs also make excellent props for personal fantasies of adventure and challenge. Some people say there is a genetic component to fear of snakes, and if so, who is to say there is no genetic component to dinosaur interest? Then there is the issue of cultural resonance. Surely, Saturday morning cartoons and what one sees in toy stores cannot be irrelevant. Cultural resonance is another phenomenon we must understand in order to understand activities.

In our house, other components supported dinosaur interests. Middle-class parents know that children are interested in dinosaurs (whether or not it is always true or true without "help"), so they are certain to tempt dinosaur interest with trips to the museum, invitations to watch television programs, and books. Doing these things amounts to, at least with some children, a self-fulfilling expectation of interest. We certainly walked around museums with our children, telling them stories designed to be attractive about what was there, including dinosaurs. Once they have stimulated interest, academically oriented parents will use the dinosaur hook to introduce some science.

Feedback loops abound. Children show a hint of interest, relatives recognize it, and toys and more books appear. It doesn't take long for children to figure out they will get attention from a father trained in science if they bring interesting dinosaur tidbits to him. I was treated to many.

I see three other critical factors in the development of the dinosaur cartoons activity. Word games were a constant danger in our household. I say "danger" because this was by no means a high-brow activity. Instead, it was more an embarrassing side effect of parents who thought a lot about words and couldn't restrain the impulse to play with them. There was probably a time when we, as parents, were appropriating as many of our sons' baby words as they were learning correct English words from us. Many of these words remained in our vocabulary for years and still occasionally pop out. Along similar lines, our cat acquired so many names that even family members were sometimes confused about who or what was being referred to. Everyday objects' names acquired extra letters and syllables or lost some, as if doing so were a house rule. Whereas most people in Berkeley experience fog, we frequently have "frog" at our house. We "snurf" the Internet, cross the Golden Gate "Brrdge," and sometimes have "poisonberry" (boysenberry) syrup with pancakes.

Two activity precursors down (dinosaurs and word play) and two to go. One of our sons developed an interest in drawing and art. There's another interesting story here, but I'll cut this one short. Nicholas loved to draw, and he would certainly have seized the opportunity to draw stylized dinosaurs, however the opportunity originated.

Finally, Nicholas and Kurt were very fond of each other, and all of us know how complicated are the reasons for and consequences of brotherly love. Entertaining each other must have given our boys great pleasure. The fact that Kurt was "Mr. Science" in our household and Nick was "Mr. Art" could have led to an especially attractive synergy.

The microstructure of activities, pace and flow, should be a wonderful study, but we don't know whether, for example, funny dinosaurs came in a flurry, took a lot of care and time to invent, or popped up randomly.

What about outcomes and futures? We actually know quite a bit about what our children came to know about dinosaurs, partly because a student of mine involved them in a study of child dinosaur experts. For example, they just plain knew a lot of dinosaurs, usually including which geologic period they lived in, where they lived, and what they ate. They knew about different classes of dinosaurs, morphological indicators of predation, and environmental characteristics (big teeth suggest meat eating; two-leggedness suggests speed, which suggests predation; long necks and huge bodies both suggest plant eaters and possibly aquatic support). They learned something about professional science and were especially pleased to explain to me, for example, why the apatosaurus and brontosaurus turn out to be the same dinosaur (because of a mistaken paleontological reconstruction). They knew the most recent discoveries from the newspaper, so they understood that this science wasn't dead. They also told many causal stories, some of which were clearly of their own invention, about how dinosaurs "worked" ("the fin might have been for cooling") and how they related to their ecological context.

The dinosaur cartoon activity was just a tiny piece of a larger fabric. "Doing dinosaurs" took many forms. In making their cartoons, our boys probably learned a few new names and images from each other, and they developed some excellent mnemonics for both names and images. They were also probably learning, if they didn't already know, that science can sometimes be fun and that it can be personalized. Indeed, the larger fabric, as with my electronics hobby, is a better focus for what they learned; we can't say exactly what they learned from dinosaur cartoons, and it probably wasn't much, after all. It's just that the larger fabric does not hold together or even exist without many little pieces like this activity.

What important things does this story tell us about activities? It illustrates some general points I've already made and introduces some new complexities. I want to use it to begin to think about implications for educational design.

Dinosaur cartoons tell us children's activity capabilities are generative. The form of this activity was almost certainly new and unique. We can't expect to understand activities unless we understand their generativity. Children don't do just what they've done before. In educational design, we therefore have an easier time because we have a more open book of possibilities. We also have a more difficult time, however, because we need other principles—besides what happened before—to help us understand what is possible and what is not.

Activities are probably always multiply determined. The history of any activity will almost certainly reach into diverse corners of participants' experience.

Activities fit social and material niches. The nature of our household cannot be ignored, as if the generality "children are interested in dinosaurs" could explain Nicholas and Kurt's dinosaur game. Frequently, the relevant history may seem trivial and low-brow. Corrupting words is not particularly elevated, but it was developmentally critical to this activity. Understanding cultures and social context for educational design tends to get abstracted to supposedly educationally relevant factors, such as interest in education and home teaching, but some of the most important activity seeds will be invisible from this perspective. Because of generativity, different cultures may be much more alike than we have come to expect.

The larger fabric of activities again shows itself clearly with dinosaur cartoons. I emphasized that my electronic hobby days were, one by one, apparently inefficient and many times educationally barren. Dinosaur cartoons supply another impetus toward rethinking an educational efficiency that writes out the possibility of extended, personally driven activities. Kurt and Nick's spontaneous creation of and enthusiastic engagement with this activity emphasize both how much teachers and curriculum developers have to gain and how open the book is on excellent activity frameworks for school subjects.

Some people will just dismiss an idiosyncratic activity as educationally irrelevant—"It just couldn't happen again"—but dismissal won't do. Idiosyncratic activities should have special relevance for education because personal ownership and fit with a child's life bring great power to learning. One of the main reasons literacies that support invention and creation—not just absorption—are so important is that they give children a toehold for their own initiative.

Pretending that we can survive educationally without making room for idiosyncrasy is bound to fail to achieve anything more than boring (to us and to students) mediocrity. This is clearly an issue for modern times, especially because U.S. schools serve more and more diverse populations, but it is also an issue for all times. In even the most homogeneous classrooms, I see children making very different things out of their own participation. We must understand these constructions to understand engagement, to understand and foster learning.

I like to talk about designing for rare events. This doesn't mean *making sure* everyone creates dinosaur cartoons. Instead, it means making it more likely that all children can experience some particular activities that are like dinosaur cartoons in the relevant dimensions. That is, all children deserve to have some educational experiences that are coherent with their deepest personal interests and competencies. Indeed, all of us deserve to have our educationally relevant interests fostered and to have them nested in activities that fit into a larger fabric of long-term commitment. Everyone should experience committed learning.

Providing an environment that encourages engaged learning is a very different proposition from a curriculum that specifies only what is to be learned and nothing about how it should feel to learn it. A more subtle agenda incorporates many spaces and times for children to be themselves, to learn in their regime of competence. Fostering committed learning means fundamentally counting on natural variation and multiple opportunities rather than on lockstep approaches to guaranteed outcomes. It also means recognizing that there should be variation in testing and that it is much more important for a child to experience one or two tremendous intellectual accomplishments than a host of small and regulated progressions. Of course, each child must take baby steps. Giant steps don't come without baby steps first, and we need to help with both, but only if little things accumulate into substantial, probably idiosyncratic and unlikely events should we feel comfortable with ourselves as teachers.

I think of making dinosaur cartoons as, marginally, a giant step event. At least it's close and of the right type. How many events like this will change a life? It won't take many. (Seven, plus or minus six, is my personal estimate. I can be serious about this estimate because even a modest giant step such as creating dinosaur cartoons manifests a well-developed regime of competence.) Without any events like this, how many children will have a satisfying intellectual life within the subjects we teach? (Probably also about seven out of the millions in school!)

Rare events will not take care of themselves. It is too easy to squash them, to push them out of class. I felt, and I believe I was correct, that my electronics work had no place in school. We have a major practical and cultural chore to open school curriculum to rare events. Designing for rare events is an excellent heuristic for educational developers who want to design in the way I am advocating. Here are some others.

Always keep in mind that, whatever you think you are designing, children's activities will be the ultimate test for the validity of your work. To take a not very incidental example, although you may think you are designing a computer system, you are really designing *mediated activities*. That is, you are designing the material context that supports particular activities.

Design for continuity of activity as well as worrying about that familiar old admonition to sequence ideas properly. Think of certain activity types also as goals of instruction, not just as means. Think of how to get from where students are to where they might be without dragging them away from themselves.

The path from our culture's usual preoccupation with concepts to a genuine focus on activities is not easy. Here is one of my favorite tricks to help us make our way on this path. An *enrichment frame* is a reconceptualization of a topic that highlights a sensible activity context for it. An enrichment frame turns a topic into a sustainable roller coaster, to return to my earlier metaphor. As a handy example—even if it is unique—suppose you want some students to learn some more dinosaur names. You might consider having them design dinosaur cartoons.

Having students design is almost always a good enrichment frame. (I illustrate it and present other enrichment frames in chapter 8.) I spent time earlier talking about intuitive ideas in science and how they were labeled "misconceptions." The implied enrichment frame (if we demean the term to denote by it any activity setting for dealing with a curricular focus) has predominantly been to get students to articulate these intuitive ideas, then to confront them with contrary evidence or argument. A truer and more valuable enrichment frame begins by having students consider the many ways any "misconception" situation may actually be conceptualized, comparing and contrasting along with eliciting evidence and argument in students' own terms. Asking students to "do a project" is a step toward an enrichment frame, provided we understand and cultivate the students' roller-coaster landscape rather than just tell them to "do something interesting."

Enrichment frames always change what is learned and how it is learned. It will not do to assume that old topics that fit so well into an abstract sequence of prerequisites will also fit an orientation toward committed learning. Instead, we need to enlist our best sense of what is powerful to learn while we consider moves toward enriched activity structures.

In this and the previous chapter, we have circled from knowledge to activity and back several times. Actually, we did not make a true circle, for these topics are really two sides of the same coin—understanding the best development of human intellectual potential. Knowledge seems distinct from activity only in old epistemologies that deny status to what drives everyday sense and action. Also, there is a core unity between a revised notion of competence, which includes things such as p-prims, and a focus on the fabric of activity, on activities that participants feel are coherent and sensible. P-prims and intuitive knowledge are everyone's basis for judging whether or not things make sense. As surely as they are resources and targets for learning, they also help define the personal sense of that learning. If we do not include them in the curriculum, students may well just "learn" the material and pass the tests, but they will feel no commitment to the ideas, and certainly they will not pursue them out of class. The most disturbing thing I uncovered in a study of bright, motivated, and successful MIT undergraduates years ago was that, although all did well in high school physics and got high marks, almost none felt they really understood the material. Those students' teachers just did not work on intuitive judgments and sense making or connect instruction with ongoing enterprises that the students could own. It is a sensible extension of the evaluation of knowing to ask whether it goes anywhere, and high school physics, for these A students, was going nowhere.

Committed learning in such an environment is dead on arrival. The optimistic side of the coin is that educational research has paid so little attention to committed learning that we surely can make much progress quickly if we turn our attention to it.

6

Explaining Things, Explainable Things

Art critics talk about "Art" and feeling; Artists talk about where to get the best turpentine.

Materials Matter

It simply is not possible to take any materials that may be close at hand and make of them the basis for a deep literacy. Rocks or bricks make good houses but not an expressive intellectual medium; they are difficult to reproduce, not very user modifiable, either too uniform or uncontrollably diverse, and too heavy to be very portable. These claims about rocks and bricks may be obvious and incontrovertible, but once we get a little beyond such primitive candidates for literacy-building materials, people's intuitions diverge wildly. In chapter 1, I talked about the shameful debasing of the term *literacy* implied in essentially all conventional uses of *computer literacy*—as if a casual familiarity with any chunk of hardware that in any sense computes might do for humankind something comparable to what the written word has done. We need to be much more accountable in saying when and how certain materials, computers among them, might convey enough intellectual power to be likened to textual literacy.

In this chapter and the next, we focus on materials. How do we assess good and bad guesses about what can constitute a computational medium capable of supporting a legitimate new literacy? Is hypertext, perhaps augmented by global connectivity of nodes via network connections, enough more than conventional literacy to warrant the trouble of converting schools to it? I personally don't think so. In any case, I argue that

fairly easy extensions of hypertext, such as Boxer, offer a disproportion-
ate gain for a tolerable extra cost. It may be that hypertext has already
passed its three-to-five-year window of novelty and public accessibility
so that it's already old hat and no longer judged a hot prospect, rightly
or wrongly. But what about multimedia, a newer darling? Does the World
Wide Web change the whole game? And what's next in technological
sizzle?

Time will tell. In fact, we know so little about how material intelligence
works, even for established forms of literacy, that the best scientifically
informed judgment must be somewhat speculative. Nevertheless, there
are many reasons to think as seriously as we can about such issues now.
Obviously, the public, advanced developers, and researchers need to
make choices about where to put their efforts. Why use Boxer and not
something else? Yet there are deeper reasons. Even if we discover Boxer
is good enough to get started and multimedia is not (or vice versa), the
development of technical and cultural literacy forms will undoubtedly be
a long evolutionary process. The better we understand what is going on,
the better we will be able to enhance and speed the process.

Understand is the critical word here. It underscores why "try it and
see" is not good enough. Among the best kept secrets of educational research is that knowing what works is almost never enough. First, "what
works" implies that there are only two relevant classes: what works and
what does not. In contrast, understanding what makes things work *better,* at any level of "working," is a more valuable way of thinking. Milk-
ing more creativity and intellectual power out of ourselves rewards us
with every drop, and only understanding can guide improvements. Second, time and time again we discover that an "it" that worked in one
circumstance just doesn't work in another. Unless we know *why* something works, we won't be able to adapt to different circumstances or
even to know when we really have different circumstances. The gradual
evolution to a computationally literate society guarantees we will experience changing circumstances that we would like to negotiate with skill.
To put these considerations in the large-scale context of this book, conventional literacy works, but only if we understand something of how
literacy works can we assess and enhance the possibilities of computationally extended literacies.

The work of considering materials takes two chapters. This chapter introduces fundamental ideas. In particular, we look at how to understand and design physical devices using the powerfully complementary ideas of function and structure. The next chapter is more specific and technical. We consider the design of complex computer systems—from calculators to computational media. The rest of this book is comprehensible without these two chapters. However, I encourage even nontechnical readers at least to peruse this short chapter and to read the section in chapter 7 called "A Structure for Cyberspace."

To begin our inquiry on materials, I discuss three principles that explain what a computational medium must do for us. All three have come up previously in this book, at least implicitly. The third, which received the least emphasis earlier, constitutes the main topic of this chapter.

The Principle of Expressiveness

A computational medium must be expressive. It must extend minds with new ways of thinking and knowing. As self-evident as this principle may seem, it has subtleties that warrant attention.

Expressiveness is frequently associated with the arts—with conveying emotion, feelings, passion. In one sense, an artistic view is insightful. In another sense, it is less relevant. The insightful aspect of artistic expressiveness is the attachment to the medium that any creator feels in using it. Poets and authors love words, sculptors appreciate marble, and so on. This attachment is born of achievement, the debt creators owe to their materials, but it is also an attachment of intimacy. A creator must become familiar with his or her medium, and deeper and deeper acquaintance creates a bond. Great sculptors and painters must certainly feel that bond, but multitudes of miniature versions of the same processes are equally important to the prospects for a computational medium. That many or most teachers find some creative outlet in a medium and that children find pleasure in small bits in using it are more important than that a few genius creators come to exist with a new medium—no matter how grateful we will be to the geniuses. In the context of literacy, millions of children who enjoy the drawing pencils they got for Christmas overbalance what Degas accomplished.

What is expressed by an artistic creation is less relevant to this book. The mind encompasses a huge diversity of styles and modes, thoughts and feelings. We need to consider at least twice what may be enhanced by possible new literacies. My central concern is learning science and mathematics. These pursuits have a certain pace, patterning, and structure, and that fact partly explains why some people love them and others don't. Explicitness and precision are central, though hardly exhaustive. The warp and woof of the best ideas in science are on a staggering scale— not an idea for here and now, but for all times, everywhere. System is supreme. Of course, scientific pursuits require creativity, intuition, and a particular aesthetic in full measure; it takes a cultivated ear to hear the ring of truth in the crude beginnings of a new idea. Intuition and creativity cannot stand alone, however, and must articulate with all the rest. Do scientific intuition and rigor "fit" in a particular medium?

Think for just a moment about an initially attractive alternative to examples I have shown in Boxer. Imagine a literacy built on holographic, 3-D immersion virtual reality (VR), like the holodeck in the *Star Trek* series. No one can doubt the attractiveness of such a technology or that, when it comes, it will be a highly visible part of our world. It may supplant film, if not literature. Yet how far will virtual reality go in science education? I couldn't convince VR enthusiasts here—and won't try—but I think there are fairly definite limits to the power of these media. Science is an articulate reexperiencing of our own reality in a different form. It is supported by technical representations such as algebra and concepts that are simply *not* the common sense either of everyday experience or even of an alternate holodeck reality.

There is a fundamental lesson we must learn here. The enthusiasm we feel toward amazing new things does not come with a caution to consider whether they are suitable for deep advancement of civilization or whether they may be just a passing "wow!" (on the scale of civilizations). Our senses and short-term sensibilities just don't report to us on such issues. Current literacy provides a stark object lesson. Text is linear; it is black and white; it doesn't zoom around the page in 3-D; it isn't intelligent by itself; in fact, in terms of immediate reaction, it is quite transparently boring. I can't imagine a single preliterate was ever wowed at the first sight of text, and yet text has been the basis of arguably the most fundamental intellectual transformation of the human species. It and subforms, such as algebra, have made science education for all a plausible goal.

Along with expressiveness, we must consider forms of participation to truly evaluate future possibilities. Who will make, for example, wow-inducing virtual realities? What Lieutenant Data does off-screen to program the simulations for the holodeck is at least as important and much more difficult to imagine than what appears as the presentation. Another one-way medium (as television has turned out to be, despite "community access") is politically and intellectually suspect. The instant someone invents a language for programming a sufficiently interesting and broad range of alternate realities, a language that is simple enough for children and teachers, I will be happy to reassess my judgment.

Half a Literacy Is Not Enough

Let me make the point about participation again, first abstractly, then with a little story. Let us classify all possible literacies into *consumer literacies,* which the vast majority of participants enjoy without producing, and *two-way literacies,* in which the average literate person makes new things or at least modifies old ones. A part of our current literacy looks like a consumer literacy—the "great ideas" part where readers consume history's best ideas and most artfully done presentations. We are inclined to call people literate if they have a deep appreciation of these great ideas, whether or not they have ever produced anything of that ilk. This may be a good use of the word *literate,* but mathematics and science are different. No one believes that having read and appreciated a famous proof or that being able to read equations is a sufficient understanding of algebra. Knowing science means you can solve new problems with it.

We don't really have much of a consumer literacy of science and mathematics; novels and even coffee-table picture books far outsell scientific publications. We would be better off if we had one, and a widespread computational medium might allow a visible scientific consumer literacy to develop, but my agenda is to use computational media to bring the power of mathematics and science truly into the grasp of more people. That, as far as I can see, means that computational literacies should be two way. When we talked about the advantages that accrued to students by using the tick model in their own creations (chapter 2) and in several of the examples in chapter 3, we were necessarily talking about a two-way literacy.

Learning by Composing in Computational Media

Almost twenty years ago, a colleague and I ran a series of summer mathematics, science, and programming institutes for bright high school students. One unit was particularly successful. We taught vector algebra in the context of generating 3-D computer images. What made this learning exciting for students were the products—genuinely 3-D displays of dancing Platonic solids (using the rather primitive technology of red and green glasses), spaceship docking, and (unfortunately) war games. I recall one episode particularly clearly. I was talking with a student who had produced a "laser wars" game, and I was praising him for the clear, modular form of his program. To make the point, I mentioned casually that all he had to do to make his simulation relativistic was to replace the dot product function with a slight variant that, as Einstein discovered, characterizes space-time. I'll never forget the awe in his eyes as he said, "Really?" After a short discussion and clarification, he turned energetically to work to see if he could actually make this alteration.

We can think about this learning experience at three levels.

1. *Interesting:* Moving, 3-D displays are exciting.
2. *Empowering:* Moving, 3-D displays constructed by students are even more exciting for students and more rewarding to teachers.
3. *Intellectually Generative:* Moving, 3-D displays constructed by students using general principles that can provide powerful leverage for advancing into new intellectual domains are the best of all.

Not all learning with media follows this same model, although encompassing these three levels, with variations, covers a surprisingly wide range of what has worked well with Boxer. Still, it is easy to become excited by new media—virtual reality, hypertext, multimedia, and possibly Boxer—without focusing on exactly what is to be learned in relation to the expressive aptness of the medium. Many attractive, entertaining things don't teach, and even more don't teach mathematics and science. We must always ask, in particular, who learns from constructions in new media (consumers or producers); how exactly do they learn; and what are the long-term consequences of that learning?

The Principle of Utility: Beyond Expressiveness

Why expressiveness is important is not a mystery. Being able to lay thoughts out concretely, in some sense capture and disseminate them, is a core function of media. The powers of expressiveness are evident even in consumer literacies. "Great ideas" literacy is not a chimera, even if it is sometimes insufficient. The loss of the great library of Alexandria and the rediscovery of the ideas of a brilliant but obscure scientist are both consequential events.

There are less obvious, if no less important, aspects of the act of expressing, however. Thinking in the presence of a medium that is manipulated to support your thought is simply different from unsupported thinking. Material intelligence conveys some especially useful properties to thinking. We discussed some of these properties in chapter 1. Because the topic is so important and because it is once again relevant, let's review some of them here.

Material intelligence is frequently about systematicity and precision. When I want to "order my thoughts," I literally write them out and move them around. Care sometimes means producing a list and scrutinizing it for gaps and inconsistencies. It is occasionally important to write down a definition or stipulation and agree on every word in it.

Every representational form also leaves its imprint on the ways we think, even when a physical manifestation is not present. We do simple versions of place value addition or (some of us) vector addition in our heads, sometimes managed by an imagined version of the spatial layout of the representation: "What number is at the top of the next column to the left?" or "Mentally drag the tip a bit to the right." Graphing-literate individuals use an imagined concave upward stroke to mediate thinking about "an increasing rate." If Boxer becomes widespread, people will come to thinking about hierarchies more easily, and "we'd better pop up a few levels" will become a more endemic metaphor to communicate the management of thought processes.

Expressiveness, as one might interpret it, secretly relies on a model wherein ideas are communicated by putting our thoughts into words or symbols, but material intelligence goes well beyond that simple model. The utilities we are discussing now are not attainable—or are attainable only at great expense and effort—in the absence of the medium and the thought patterns that build up in its use. We don't always have ideas and then express them in the medium. We have ideas *with* the medium.

Making progress in an episode of materially mediated thinking—reasoning or coming up with a new idea—happens jointly in the mind and in the medium at every stage. Moves may be either a shift in mental positioning or a shift in external presentation or both more or less simultaneously. The ties between internal and external are intricate. You think a little differently, then nudge the presentation, provoking further rethinking and re-presenting.

A nice example of the ties between internal and external is a small group of people working together on a problem in the presence of a whiteboard. The process differs greatly when the group works without the board. For example, with the board, contributions can be made in parallel, while someone else is speaking or writing. Topics are revisited or dropped by pointing or erasing. Individuals control their own conceptual focus by redirecting their gaze. Mini-notations may develop as shorthand for topics referred to too frequently to bear an extended written form. The inextricable connection between thought and presentation shows up again after the conversation is done. We want a copy of the board, and corporations expect to make money by selling us the capability to produce one. A few months later, the mutual dependence of mind and matter is highlighted again. When our mind state has faded, the picture of the board will be a useless, uninterpretable jumble.

Writing is almost always this way, too, although people persist in thinking of it almost always as "expressing." I never know exactly what I think before I write about a subject, partly because the process of writing is a form of thinking. I keep copies of papers I've written because they contain many details and fine points of argument that I can't easily regenerate. On the other hand, the sense of context and purpose for a paper is important, too, and explaining context to students is critical. Mind state and presentational state are jointly necessary both in the thinking process and in interpreting the result.

Representations and externalizations have always been part of scientific thinking. We need to pay more attention to the fact that computation has now brought the possibility of a hugely expanded repertoire of media constructions that may express scientific ideas or become part of scientific thinking. The proof of the famous four-color theorem—that any map can be colored by at most four colors (with no two bordering countries having the same color)—required a computer program. Science used to be thought of as a scientist making a discovery (possibly in the presence of some technology) and explaining his or her results to others. Science should be thought of now as a scientist coming to think differently in the presence of his or her representational technology and putting others in contact with that technology so that they may also think differently with it.

I can summarize by saying that new media can be useful in "implementing" new ideas. Implementing a new idea here does not mean merely putting that idea into material form. The latter implies the ideas exist before a metamorphosis in form. Instead, implementing means "giving necessary material adjuncts in order to exist." Knights were implemented in this sense—they came into existence—with swords, armor, and stirrups. Computer scientists are implemented with computers. Science education will change not just in getting better ("computers will help us express ideas more clearly or more efficiently"), but it will change fundamentally because *the material basis for scientific thinking is changing.* Students won't be able to think science without some reflection of that change in the physical context of their thinking.

Another important aspect of media at first appears far less grand than the considerations given above. This aspect is also a form of usefulness. *Menial utility* is simply the capacity of a medium to get things done for users in their everyday lives. Not every necessary and valuable thing is deeply intellectual or ethereally conceptual. Much of life is about just getting by, dealing with "junk" such as bills, records, correspondence, and so on. Certain media, especially computational media, can help with these sorts of things.

Menial utility is much more important than it might seem, for two reasons. First, it brings the perception of value, which can be an important factor in bringing a medium across a threshold of community use to establish a social niche for itself. Menial utility may be especially important early on when only a few understand and value a new material intelligence. Arguing for a new kind of intelligence is extremely difficult when most people have not experienced that intelligence or seen any history of its power, as they have with reading or writing. The situation is worse because scientific and popular understanding of how media work to make us smarter and better learners is so poor.

The second reason menial utility is important is what I call the *learning/ use cycle*. This is the completely obvious learning principle that we learn about things we use, and the more we learn, the more usefulness we get. Of course, there are limits to this principle, as there are to any principle. Our use of some things becomes so stereotyped that learning stalls; other things we learn to use may offer nothing of value beyond a certain point of expertise. Any medium worth its salt, however, should not suffer these limits to the learning/use cycle. If the grander expressiveness and utilities that we discussed above exist, learning/use cycles are almost guaranteed a fine, extended future.

The importance of menial utility and the learning/use cycle first dawned on me in thinking about problems I saw with Logo as it began to percolate into schools in the early eighties. Logo is a computer language for learning many things, and it is a direct predecessor of Boxer. In many ways, Logo had more success with children than with teachers. Children were almost always drawn into Logo by the possibility of making pretty and unusual pictures. Honing their skills at first on obvious things to draw, they gradually became aware of more and more possibilities. The learning/use cycle worked. Incidentally, this is a nice example of a continuity of activity structures, as we discussed in chapter 5, from "drawing pictures" to "mathematical art."

On the other hand, teachers followed a different pattern. Many couldn't get started at all. If there had been a greater menial utility to Logo—or even in its rhetoric—more teachers could have glimpsed a reason to try. For many, sadly, getting by is about as grand a goal as seems achievable. In any case, offering a way into a system by providing everyday usefulness would have been an asset.

More poignantly, many teachers who did get started with Logo seemed to run out of steam. It was as if enthusiasm for the goals of the project, eloquently expressed by its advocate, Seymour Papert, traveled only so far. Why didn't Logo loose the creativity of teachers and blossom, beyond its initial success, into a widespread, vital, and growing community?

Several hypotheses come to mind. We might think that most teachers are not very creative or smart, but I don't believe it is a matter of lack of creativity or intelligence, as I pointed out in chapter 1. A second possibility is that Logo was just too difficult to learn, and teachers couldn't easily reach the levels of competence required to liberate their individual and community creativity. There is a grain of truth in this conjecture, and I will come back to it in a moment. For now, the relevant point is that we cannot see learnability as a property of a software system by itself. Instead, we must consider the fit of the software with the existing values and activities of the people who are learning it. In particular, if we can establish a good learning/use cycle, sometimes intrinsically difficult things can be accomplished easily in bits and pieces.

In designing Boxer, we have been attentive to broad ranges of use to foster positive menial utility and consequent learning/use cycles. Indeed, I count much of my own learning of Boxer as coming from my increasing use of it in personal, everyday tasks. For example, as my sons approached and entered college, financial planning became a looming necessity. I learned a lot about organizing records in Boxer and what kind of toolset could help me think about long-term plans.

A little conundrum in a designer learning about his own creation warrants brief unraveling. In a certain sense, of course, I have nothing much to learn about Boxer; I know what every part does. A true medium must be infinitely rich, however. If I ever ran out of new things to do and new ideas about how to do them, I surely should have stopped working on Boxer. In addition, computational media are especially good at accepting changes and extensions that make them more powerful, relevant, and valued. All the little tools I have created for myself are modest but true extensions of the medium and hence of my own know-how. They implement a smarter, more capable me in the same way that, on a grander scale, the laws of a nation may implement a wiser, more just country.

The Principle of Comprehensibility

Even if we know now that learning must be contextualized—we must consider value, expressiveness, menial utility, and the learning/use cycle—the form of the medium is nevertheless relevant to learning. A computational medium must be comprehensible in its own terms. This section is about what "comprehensible in its own terms" might mean. Comprehensibility is the main topic of this chapter.

When I was about twelve years old, I had a recurrent nightmare. My old balloon-tired, second-hand bicycle had about run its course as a prized possession. I was beginning to lust after a fancy new three-speed English racing bike. The nightmare was that I got my dream bike, with a twist. Instead of an elegant 1, 2, 3 on the gear shifter, my new bike had a long series of icons showing the use to which each gear was suited: smooth pavement uphill, smooth pavement downhill, gravel, crossing railroad tracks, and others I had no way to decipher (although inscrutable icons is not the point of this example).

It is a little difficult to understand how these symbols could strike terror in the heart of a twelve-year-old boy, but my memory of my alarm is vivid. In any case, the nightmare makes a good foil to wring out some of the design considerations and aesthetics that explain why Boxer is the way it is. Although that nightmare now seems to me more bizarre than frightening, I still find many modern systems truly horrifying when they are designed according to principles like the ones used for that strange bike.

What could the designer of the nightmare bike have been thinking? It is actually not difficult to see. He (let's say) conceived of the device he was designing as accomplishing a number of tasks for its operator. He thought: one needs to go uphill or downhill, travel on paved and gravelly roads, cross railroad tracks, and so on. To this observation we add one classic maxim of design, "make form follow function," which we learn from television advertisements is the practice of the best automobile designers. The design of the gear-changing mechanism follows directly: for each function, there is a corresponding structure, a "gear" that suits that function.

It's worthwhile going through what is wrong with this design to illustrate what turn out to be quite central points about comprehensible and useful design. First, my nightmare gear shift is a mess. How would I ever know where to find the gravel position, except by memorization? How would I know if there is or should be a gear for uphill, gravelly railroad tracks? There is no sense of systematicity or completeness in the mechanism. Does this sound a little like some annoyances you've found in computer applications?

Our hypothetical designer has ignored some powerful order and simplicity that might be achieved by focusing a bit more on structure, rather than on function. Order the gears in a mathematical sequence based on increasing rate of revolution of the bike wheels per stroke of the pedal: 1, 2, 3 . . . I can hear the executive talking to the engineer who came up with such an "orderly" design at Nightmare Bikes, Inc.: "Who do you think we're designing for—an engineer? That's math; that's ratios. Customers want a job done, like going uphill or down. They want form to follow function."

Of course, the executive is mistaken, as we know from our experience with bicycles, but I can guarantee you that the scenario is being played out constantly in appliance and software companies with consequences at least as bizarre as the nightmare bike. Our home hand mixer is labeled stir, fold, blend, puddings, mix, cakes, mash, cream, frosting, beat, whip, and egg whites. It's all function, with no hint of orderly structure.

How do people manage to understand bicycle gearing if, as is no secret, ratios and gearing are not a particular strength of the general populace? Their success is not "just experience," although that is not to be ignored. Instead, learning bicycle gearing is another example of one of the grand, overarching learning principles we introduced early in the book and elaborated in chapters 4 and 5. There are great resources in people's rich store of intuitive knowledge, resources that are vastly underappreciated and underused. In this case, people know about sequence and patterns of "more or less" earlier than they learn to count. Babies pile and collect things; they have early senses of more and less and how to achieve them. Before they can talk, they know "do that *again;* I want *more.*" Possibly imperfect but powerful ideas like these, plus a few pieces of experience, make bicycle gears comprehensible. Mathematical p-prims from everyone's early experience with the world can substitute, sometimes, for a formal understanding of ratios.

Think about some learning experiences. How long will it take a young biker to realize that one direction of gear changing is more generally apt for going faster and the other direction for going slower? You don't need numbers or any concept of gearing to appreciate that. Or, "I need more strength to get up this hill; my mom said 'change gears,' and I guess that means move this little thing one way or the other. That must give me more strength." A score or fewer of such learning events probably exhausts what one needs to know.

There's a long story about learning computational systems on the basis of little pieces of experience and on the basis of intuitive, p-primlike ideas. I won't emphasize it in this book, but consider: in the case of the bike, those pieces can be completely adequate to operate the bicycle (as suggested above) whether or not they constitute a "real" understanding of gearing. Second, if we are going to plan on learning that uses such pieces, it is critical that we know how people will experience our designed artifact. The tacit world of experience is our ally as designers only if we understand something about it. Finally, the way the structural simplicity of "sequence, more and less" works here is typical. It may not need instruction; people may never understand it fully, but they need that underlying pattern so that their experiences add up to a sufficient understanding.

Let's return to designer mistakes. The icon categories in my nightmare gearshift mechanism were those of its designer (if he existed). On the other hand, they *should* be the categories in which the user thinks of her task. Getting these wrong is easy, especially if users vary in expertise. I doubt that any new biker thinks of terrain as an essential modality. Faster, slower, and personal effort are so much more salient.

Nor is terrain uniquely characteristic of the relevant gear. You might use the same one for a quick ride up a moderate hill or for a leisurely ride on flat terrain. Why pick one or the other terrain to define the gear? This particular problem is especially severe for rich, multifunctional systems such as computational media. In fact, the problem is much worse than simply labeling or learning. Designers again and again tune structures to particular uses when, with a little thought, a more generic version of a structure will fit a much broader set of functions. The result could be a simpler system that does as much or more. An example we'll come back to: spatial hierarchy in popular computing systems today is limited to document (or application) and folder structure. Within an application, either there is no available hierarchy, or it is different from the folder form, generally for no good reason. Contemporary design seems frequently blind to the elegance and power of more generic structure.

I have probably flogged the imaginary designer at Nightmare Bikes, Inc., enough. One more lash and we can leave him in peace. Tinkering and adapting are going to be fundamental aspects of computational media. Consider that every sentence I write here is adapted to my image of the reader, to the local tone—playful or angry—and to the context of concepts or words that have or have not been explained to this point. Adapting for bicycles is not as dramatic, but it is just as salient. If the gravel gear is not just right for one particular stretch of dirt road at the speed that I approach it, how do I know which neighboring gears to try? The need to make things a little different for purposes a designer perhaps couldn't guess suggests that, in these cases at least, the designer might even step back from function altogether. He should design flexible structures that the user might at least have a chance of figuring out how to use for her own purposes. The designer's lust to do everything for the user must be tempered.

Let me schematize and order the discussion a little before proceeding. Above all else, we realize that function (or use) and structure (or mechanism or form) are two fundamental perspectives that both designers and users should take. They are both ways to understand artifacts and ways in which artifacts may be simple or complex, elegant or baroque. Structure and function, in fact, are the cosmic yin and yang of design and use. One makes little sense without the other. The relationship of one to the other is infinitely rich and variable; "form follows function" is only the crudest first pass at a relationship that must constantly be scrutinized as we explore both structures and functions of a possible design. In particular, we have learned that: (1) a purely functional view of a device may hide important simplicities and systematicities, such as the sequence of power and speed experiences one perceives in "gearing ratios"; (2) structure sometimes seems forbidding, but people have surprising resources for learning it, resources developed for dealing with underlying structure in the world; (3) adapting to different circumstances may require understanding some structure, not just "normal" function.

Computational media are a class of artifacts that exquisitely intensify issues of structure and function. We know so little about either the possible structures or the necessary or available intellectual functions of such media that one almost hesitates to start. Yet the complexities are intrinsically interesting, and the promise is exalted—improving humankind's intellectual powers.

Compared to computational media, other artifacts occupy quite different regimes. One of my favorite analogies to hate I originally heard from Joseph Weizenbaum, a computer scientist turned technology critic from MIT. He said computers should be like washing machines or cars. No one expects or needs to know much about how they work. They do a job when you press a button or turn a key, and if they're broken, you call a repairman. Weizenbaum argued that programming was as irrelevant as mechanical engineering to ordinary folks. We should better teach reading and writing instead.

What irony to use the best current exemplar of material intelligence—that is, conventional literacy—to argue against having any noticeable structure beyond *on* and *off* in computers! We began this book wondering if computer media could fail to surpass reading and writing as cultural instruments of augmented intellect. Even to suggest that computers might be as little textured and simple as an off-on switch forecloses in one polemical swipe the investigations of this book.

The point of mentioning Weizenbaum's comparison (which stays the same to this day when the issue of programming comes up) is to define, by contrast, the regime of artifact design for computational media. A computational medium must be about as multifunctional as we can imagine—as unlike on-off appliances as can be—because it encompasses the full range of human imagining, thinking, and expressing. A medium's participation in thinking puts us in the range of complexity of human conceptualization and more because the point is to open new possibilities that haven't yet existed.

Multifunctionality almost defines computational media, but having many, many uses makes it all the more important to find simple but flexible core structures. Language has found a workable set of core structures in grammar, sentence structure, paragraphs, and so on, as well as a large but limited lexicon. What is the equivalent for the dynamic, interactive new possibilities of computational media? Boxer is an attempt to establish a benchmark. Over the long term, we can imagine the design process as the synthesis of a strong need for generic general structure balanced with an equally strong need for spectacular multifunctionality. The synthesis will be channeled by obvious, hidden, and as yet uncultivated human capacities. Although we may agree that a computer interface should be as simple as possible, we must answer the unavoidable question of what it is an interface to. If we want a material extension of thought, surely we can start off safely somewhere in the range of complexity of written language and explore from there.

Nightmare Bikes, Inc., introduces a number of big ideas about comprehensibility, learnability, structure, and function. The following sections elaborate these ideas, at first in simpler contexts, and gradually approach the design of a computational medium.

Structure and Function in Physical Devices

Here are two little stories of structure and function. I have never been able to remember if I am supposed to turn into or opposite a skid in an automobile. "Turn into (opposite?) a skid" is a mantra I've heard a hundred times from long before I was legally allowed to drive, but I can't seem to remember the correct phrase. Worse, which way is "into" or "opposite"?

Automobile steering is not a complex mechanism. Still, people usually learn it in a completely functional way. Turn the steering to the right, and the car turns to the right. One-to-one structure and function. Add to this principle some of those easy piece-at-a-time feedback learning mechanisms I talked about with regard to bicycle gears, and you've got an intuitively obvious, foolproof understanding—until you start to skid.

Function now needs a little structure. The car mechanism itself is easy. Turning the steering wheel to the right turns the front wheels to the right, but what converts wheel turning into car turning is a little more complex. The important fact is friction, that rubber really "prefers" not to skid across the pavement. Get a little wheel (or imagine one), hold it by its axle, and push it first in the direction it rolls. Then push the wheel sideways. In the first case, friction holds the bottom of the wheel still as the axle starts to move and, presto, the wheel turns. That's an easy job. Pushing the wheel to the side is another matter. If the wheel moves, the tire must skid across the ground. Before it starts the skid, however, friction strongly resists the skidding motion, and those forces are the ones that keep a tire "tracking" in the direction the wheels are pointing. Sideways friction is necessary to convert tire reaiming into turning.

You can probably feel the remaining important fact easily. Before the wheel starts to skid, friction can push quite hard, but once the wheel starts to skid, friction is greatly reduced, and there is scarcely any tracking force at all. Applying this theory to the case at hand, your primary job in a skid is to restore the strong tracking force by getting the tire rolling nicely again. A typical situation is depicted in figure 6.1.

You want to turn left (curved arrow), but you start skidding, and the tires actually move in the direction of the shorter, straight arrows. The front wheels skid sideways while the car plows forward. Worse, you might use the p-prim "if you're not getting enough 'effect' (enough car turning) try more 'cause' " (i.e., turn the steering wheel *more* to the left). In actuality, getting the tires rolling again means turning it right! Only then can you regain a strong tracking force and nudge the car around.

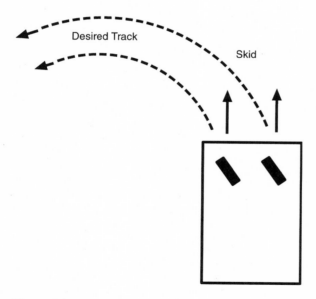

Figure 6.1
You wish to track around to the left, but instead you skid, plowing forward.

You might want to remember the rule, "if you try to turn left and you're failing because of a skid, turn right at first in order to restore rolling," but I find it much better to visualize the situation and to see which way you must turn to establish rolling and thus control. The next time you see a car skidding around a corner at high speed in a movie, notice that the front tires are turned outward (to the left if the car is turning to the right) so that the driver can maintain control. See figure 6.2.

Many excellent lessons about function, structure, and learning are here. To begin, a functional understanding is often the only understanding people have of devices, and this may be fine if nothing ever goes wrong or if you never want to do anything really new. New things might include taking a corner at high speed or extending your intelligence with a computational medium. In addition, the skid illustrates two classic understanding strategies. First, there are rules: "turn into a skid." They may be hard to remember. (This one is, for me.) They may also be difficult to interpret. (Ditto.) And they almost never explain why. Unfortunately, rules are frequently the first resort of scoundrel instructors. I have been told to "feed a cold and starve a fever" (or is it the reverse?), but I would be much better off if I knew a little about the mechanism of colds and fevers.

In contrast, the friction story and image of sideward sliding are classic structural understanding. They may be a little unfamiliar and complex at first, but at least they are sensible. You can probably regenerate the understanding by playing with a small wheel. Hands-on experimenting won't depend on opaque meanings of words, such as "*into* a skid." The image part of this understanding is also typical. Structural understanding is frequently model-like, in the sense of depending on pictures you can imagine and possibly draw. You can reason on and about these pictures in a way that is unusual with rules or purely functional understanding.

I will give one final physical example of functional and structural understanding: people think they can feel the temperature of objects they touch and, similarly, that thermometers measure the environment into which they are put. In actuality, your fingers feel only their own temperature! The nerves are embedded in your flesh, not extending outside, so heat must flow into your finger for your nerve endings to sense "hot,"

Figure 6.2
Sequence from a movie car chase (top to bottom, left to right). In frames 1–4, the car turns to its right while front wheels are neutral or even to the driver's left (viewer's right). In frames 5 and 6, notice the car continues to turn right with front wheels turned to the driver's left. (Notice the hubcap on driver's left front wheel in frame 6.) Wheels are finally "straight on" after car has turned past the viewer's line of sight in frames 7 and 8.
Source: Photographs from the motion picture *The Peacemaker.* © DreamWorks L.L.C., reprinted with permission by DreamWorks L.L.C.

or heat must flow out for you to sense "cool." The same principle applies to thermometers.

The purely functional understanding "fingers sense objects' temperature" fails much of the time for the following reasons. Insulators won't conduct heat quickly, so when you touch a cool piece of cloth, for example, it won't conduct heat away from your finger quickly. In fact, the situation may be worse than having to wait; if heat is conducted away slowly enough, the rest of your flesh and blood supply may bring enough heat in compensation for what is lost that the change in temperature at your nerve endings may be almost imperceptible. So the couch feels warm, but the coffee table feels cool, even though they are the same temperature.

Once again, the pattern is clear. People learn about many mechanisms purely by the function we ordinarily think of them as performing, but no mechanism does only and exactly what you want it to do in all circumstances. Usually, when a mechanism doesn't match our functional expectations, we think of it as a breakdown, but a good learner takes breakdowns as opportunities to learn structure, which explains breakdowns and may help to avoid them or to "patch" around them. Better, a bit of structure may open the possibility for innovative uses not originally considered. That possibility is much more salient in the case of computational media than in the example of "temperature feeling." If temperature feeling were as importantly multifunctional as computational media, then we could truly complain about Mother Nature's not making the mechanism of temperature feeling more visible!

7

Designing Computer Systems for People

Things should be made as simple as possible—but not simpler.
—A. Einstein

This chapter applies many of the ideas about function and structure introduced in chapter 6 to electronic devices. If you find the going too steep or too technical, skip ahead to the section "A Structure for Cyberspace." That section briefly explains Boxer, which helps to explain what is reported in many other sections of the book.

We begin here a gradual climb up the evolutionary ladder—and up the complexity ladder—of electronic information devices. Even at our starting point—the lowly handheld calculator—issues of structure, function, and designer choices are richly represented. The second rung of the climb is a brief look at a pocket organizer. Pausing before the last step, we consider a few issues of learning trajectory. Finally, we climb up through software applications to computational media, and I present a look at Boxer's design as a prototype medium.

Calculators

Handheld calculators are omnipresent devices in our culture. As a measure of cultural acceptance, most families have several, and many have them whether or not they use them. Without looking very hard, I found six in my own house, some bundled with more complex devices such as pocket organizers and general-purpose computers. The main example I use here is part of a Sharp pocket organizer. In what follows, you may want to play along with one or more calculators that are probably within fifty feet of where you're reading this. (Don't use the calculator that came with your Macintosh computer, for reasons I'll explain later.) Figuring out how these "simple" little devices work is almost as good as solving a Rubik's Cube puzzle!

At first blush, a calculator seems to be one of those perfectly functionally adapted and functionally defined devices. After all, every youngster knows the main functions: add, subtract, multiply, or divide a pair of numbers, and chain such operations on a sequence of numbers, prototypically adding up a list.

Indeed, almost no one needs instructions or more than a couple of minutes to figure out how to do these things. "2 + 3 =" gives you 5, then "+ 4 =" chains on to give you 9. It's almost like mind reading. Say the problem "2 + 3" pretty much as you say it to yourself or as you write it down, then say "do it" (=), and you have your answer.

Of course, calculators do not read minds. Instead, designers have successfully provided structures to meet functional needs in ways that are immediately perceived by users as relating to those functional needs.

Note that the way you say it to yourself or write it down is critical for calculators to be transparent. If we conventionally said "2 then 3 +" to specify adding two numbers, it would take you a bit longer—maybe much longer—to figure out the calculators around your house. Thus, the design of new artifacts frequently pays homage to previous technology, such as writing, by incorporating familiar structural forms, which therefore seem to relate obviously to the task at hand. Have you noticed file folders on your computer to denote document containers, telephone icons to denote telecommunication functions, and even familiar calculator shapes on computer screens? How about "tab stops"—how many people remember these were actually tabs that stopped the typewriter carriage? What about the "carriage return" key?

Technological ancestor worship is often highly effective, but it is also often limited in a few characteristic ways. First, newer technology often can do things much better, and it's a shame to be trapped by old ways. (I mention a few examples as the discussion of calculators progresses.) The second limit of technological ancestor worship is that truly obsolete technology isn't a good learning metaphor. Although file folders in the real world are not obsolete, I'll bet far more children already learn document containment functions on computers than from physical folders, so the learning advantage of this visual design is probably already past. Computational media will truly have reached "second-generation" status when the metaphors used on new systems are computational.

We can gain entry to a structural view of calculators by thinking of what is computationally necessary to perform a calculation. First, one needs memory. A calculator that forgets the numbers you enter before computing won't be much good. A calculator needs two places to store numbers—the places are called *registers*—and a place to hold the numerical operation. Then you need a way to say "do the calculation." From a structural point of view, there are many possible sequencing orders for inserting these pieces of information. Let's be deliberately contrarian. Try "2, 3, +, do it." After pressing 2, however, we immediately realize a new need—to specify that we are about to enter a second number. Otherwise, pressing 3 will result in 23. Unfortunately, there is no "enter" or "next number" on the keyboard of my calculator. This machine is a functionally adapted design—adapted to the way we usually think about arithmetic. On reflection, it seems clear that in order to follow the familiar "song" of adding, "2 + 3 =", the "specify the operation" keys must perform two actions: specify operation and "enter" (prepare for a new number). Indeed, = ("equals") must be similar. It not only does the operation but prepares for a new entry. Not being able to get at basic elements such as "enter" may be innocuous in a calculator, but it can drive you crazy if you want to tinker and adapt a computational medium. We'll come back several times to the tradeoffs of adapting to particular functionality versus making basic structure available.

Bundling structurally natural elements into functional units is a classic functional design strategy. It almost always accomplishes three things. First, it makes the usual case easy and obvious: "2 + 3 =". Second, less usual things are unnecessarily difficult. You can't get directly at the structural elements. There will always be *side effects,* other things happening that may or may not be useful. If we try to use = for an enter key, those side effects interfere; "2 = 3 + =" does nothing on my calculator. (Adding another = gives 6!)

The last thing that a strong functional move such as bundling accomplishes is that it makes the device difficult to understand. Usually, bundling subverts the simplicity of a visual model. Building a visual model is the road we started down by imagining the registers that hold operands and operators.

Let us continue to explore this calculator out of the spotlight of functions it performs so admirably well. What do you suppose will happen if you press the equals sign several times after a calculation—for example, "2 + 3 = = ="? Taking a functional view, one might guess either that this performs the same calculation again or, probably better, that the last part of it (+ 3) gets performed again on the accumulated result. Taking a structural point of view, we imagine that the result of the prior operation, "2 + 3 = 5", must fill one numerical register, so we have the other register probably filled with either 2 or 3 and likely the operation register still contains +. This is a happy occurrence because, we already decided, wanting to add on one of the addends to the accumulated result makes functional sense. Indeed, on my test calculator, successive ='s gets 5, then 8, then 11, and so on. If you press a number before you press an =, that number replaces the accumulated result, and you get the "+ 3" using that new number.

To make this clearer, let me draw a little structural model. On the left side of the model are the keystrokes, and on the right is the calculator state. The state has the three registers (two numbers and an operation). The darkened register shows what appears in the calculator window, and the arrow shows where a new number will enter if you press a number key.

2 + 3 =   ⑤ ⊞ ③
                 ↑

This sort of thing is called a *constant operation* (as in computing a constant percentage of each of a list of prices). Constant operations are instructed in many calculator handbooks. Any good designer would want to bring a new function that is easy to achieve, like this, into the fold. So far, so good, but we're about to fall off a cliff. Exploring outside the functional spotlight of the vast majority of artifacts, as I regularly do, makes it look like Nightmare Bikes designers are the norm.

The case in point is that constant calculation works differently for multiplication than for any of the other operations. For multiplication, the first rather than the second original number becomes the constant. Here is the structural model, to be contrasted with addition.

$2 \times 3 =$ ② ⨯ ⑥

Such a glaring inconsistency probably means that the designer believes users are compulsively rule-memorizing idiots who don't appreciate structural consistency or that constant operations are really not important, so they don't deserve much attention. Evidence favors designing for rule-memorizing idiots. The documentation recognizes the inconsistency as just another rule, with no comment on its inconsistency, let alone an explanation.

Here is one more escapade outside the functional focus of most calculators. Suppose we press a number, an operator, and then $=$. From a structural point of view, the calculator will have to fill in the second numerical register if it is to do anything. (In principle, the calculator could also do nothing or complain.) If the calculator fills in a number, thinking about arithmetic, really the only sensible choices are 0 or 1. Actually, 0 makes sense as the additive identity for $+$ and $-$, and 1 makes sense as the multiplicative identity for $\times$ and $\div$. Functionally, these guesses start a good pattern. Trying out "5 $-$ =" results in -5, a useful relative of 5. Evidently, though, the first operand is the 0, not the second, as you might predict by structurally extrapolating from the fact that in "5 $-$ =", it appears you've neglected the *second* operand. Well, OK, a little "hack" gets to a useful functionality. Functionally motivated devices will have many such hacks. Designers usually can't resist adding more functions and can't be bothered making them structurally simple and consistent.

Pleasantly, "5 $\div$ =" gives .2, the multiplicative inverse or reciprocal of 5. If a pattern is broken, at least it seems to be systematically replaced. In this case, the sequence "number, operator, =" seems to mean "special number (0 or 1), operator, number, =". How about "5 $\times$ ="? Structurally, it would seem that 5 is the appropriate answer (that is, 1 $\times$ 5). Although this result is useless, an occasional uselessness is frequently the price for structural simplicity. My calculator gives 25. Maybe we should have guessed this answer on the basis of the fact that structural pattern means far less than usefulness in functionally oriented artifacts. Performing a square function is useful, although remembering how you do that may require much more effort than actually typing the repeated argument to ×.

What will I get from "5 + ="? 5. Not 2 × 5 or 5 + 5. This is both useless and inconsistent with what happens with multiplication, although it fits the subtraction pattern. One wonders why the designer made an exception to find something useful to do with multiplication but not with addition.

Almost all calculators have idiosyncrasies like these. I haven't by any means presented all of them for this one calculator! A different calculator, a Casio, also bundled in a pocket organizer, makes an interesting complementary study. First, in the case of multiple equals signs, the calculator does nothing after the first =. Doing nothing represents another systematic choice: reduce complexity by closing down operations out of the central functional focus; do not even try to co-opt structural possibilities (such as funny keystroke sequences) to functional ends (such as constant calculations). This Casio calculator even gives visual help. It displays the operator on its screen when you press it, and clears it when you press =, so you have reason to expect no operation on subsequent = presses.

Now here's a good idea. Why not use a little screen space to give users help with what is going on inside the machine (perhaps showing my little structural model, above)? Besides the operator, little beyond the second number would be needed to show essentially all the calculator's state. One could then perhaps forgo closing down functionality and let users see, more or less, what is about to happen, even if it is idiosyncratic. This Casio display has plenty of room to show a second number, but it doesn't use it.

Instead of the idiosyncrasy of the Sharp, Casio designers chose to add dedicated structure for constant calculations. If you press the operator key twice, a "k" appears in the display, indicating you have activated constant calculation mode. Awkwardly, "2 − − 5 =" computes 5 − 2, and has −2 as the constant operation. At least all the constant operations use this same order, if not the obvious order, unlike the Sharp.

You may be getting the idea that Casio designers favor consistency and will close down functionality rather than allow inconsistency. Indeed, even the design of a "simple" calculator offers enough diversity for different personalities to show through (more on this point in a moment), but calculators are also complicated enough to present confusing personas. Casio does. A case in point is the omitted argument.

5 × = 25 (square)
5 ÷ = 1 (always results in 1)
5 + = 5 (no operation)
5 − = 5 (no operation)

What appears to be happening structurally is that the operation is applied to duplicated arguments in the case of multiplication and division, and with 0 as the second argument for addition and subtraction. Although these operations seem both useless and inconsistent, they are not foreclosed, nor is any visible help provided.

So Casio designers have some reasonably good strategies, including (1) foreclosing inconsistent functionality and instead providing dedicated and clean new structure for it (constant calculations), and (2) visibility to help users (showing the operation, and "k" for constant operations). Still, they apply these principles inconsistently. This is, unfortunately, the modern norm. Only one of my six available calculators comes close to thorough consistency—the one on my Macintosh computer. It consistently forecloses all functionality except the core pairwise operations and chaining. All other keystrokes, as we've investigated above for other calculators, do nothing. On the other hand, visibility is completely absent as a strategy. This is especially ironic because only a tiny bit of programming, rather than time-consuming chip design, could make this calculator do exactly what the designer chose, including having and showing a simple structural model. All the visual resources of the graphical environment are ignored. Is this a microcosm of Macintosh design personality? Make things *really* as simple as possible and don't even *allow* users to think about what is happening (along with a dash of technological ancestor worship—make sure a calculator looks like a calculator).

Besides the particular issues of how different designers handle function and structure for calculators, some important generalities are evident here. First, to the detriment of structural simplicity, functional design dominates current artifact design, which need not be the case. A number of years ago, Hewlett Packard (HP), showing an aesthetic different from any designers mentioned here, produced a line of calculators with a complete, consistent, and visualizable (if not visible) underlying model. In fact, the back of the calculator showed the model, from which you could predict the result of any sequence of keystrokes. (Incidentally, with this calculator, "2 enter 3 +" works just fine to add 2 and 3!) You can understand everything the calculator does, whether or not it is functional, and there is no functional bundling of basic structural elements, so it is easy for users to invent their own procedures for novel functionalities. You have probably never seen such a calculator, and even HP thought of it as "for engineers."

Some reasons for the dominance of functional design are evident. As we discussed early on, many designers think ordinary folks are ignorant, if not stupid, and certainly unwilling to think and learn. Moreover, even if designers view users as intelligent, more often than not they miss the nature of that intelligence. We talked in chapter 5 about how powerful experiential ideas, p-prims, were either missed or discounted as wrong. Some companies that have thought a little about comprehensibility have managed genuine advances without thinking about structure.

Finally, there's the demand side of the equation. Users have become convinced that if they are forced to think (or even allowed to think), the design is bad. The few users who have tried to understand electronic devices have been thoroughly rebuked by designs such as the ones mentioned.

Calculators are a special case. Few people ever do anything beyond adding a list of numbers. For those simple purposes, most calculators are elegant, intuitive, and well adapted. If the demands of multifunctionality are weak, why bother with structure? Yet, some artifacts, in their very essence, must be comprehensible and useful for a very wide range of applications. Purely functional design cannot succeed with computational media, as it may with calculators. Designers of media need to be concerned with simple, flexible underlying structure in a way that calculator designers evidently are not.

Beyond practicality are other issues. I believe that we should take the trouble to cultivate appropriate values and aesthetics in our culture, especially in schools. In the broader scheme of things, we need students and citizens who are not afraid to learn, who will appreciate the advantage that a little knowledge can confer, and who are insistent that what is said and given to them passes some tests of coherence and integrity. Surely calculators are a foil in this broader context, but they are just as surely indicators of where we stand culturally with respect to systems design of artifacts for committed learners.

Pocket Organizers

The next rung up the complexity and multifunctionality ladder is the personal organizer. Organizers are a good place to pause because they are familiar and still fairly simple, yet transparently encompassing in functionality compared to a calculator. Indeed, on opening the Casio organizer I use by way of example, you see four of the five main functional areas in brightly colored, prominently placed keys: telephone, memo, schedule, and calendar. The fifth functionality, a calculator, has its own brightly colored key within the number key pad. The calculator key also serves two other functions besides selecting the calculator function: clearing the calculator and reawakening the whole organizer from its sleep mode. Overloading keys or any other structure with multiple functions is a classic design move that has its own advantages and disadvantages, which I ignore for the moment.

These five separate keys are a sure sign that this device is functionally designed, but there is no reason at all to complain. These functions are familiar and relatively independent uses of the device. The immediate visibility of five functional niches will make first-time users comfortable and will not inconvenience experts much.

Take a moment to calibrate the increase in complexity and multifunctionality evident here, compared to the calculator. Functionally, we can count functional areas and guess that the Casio is about five times a calculator. This is almost certainly an underestimate, considering that areas such as schedule, telephone, and memo perform fairly rich subfunctions. In particular, in each of these areas, one can either enter new information or search old information. Each of these submodes is vaguely as rich as a calculator, so perhaps ten times a calculator is about right.

Taking a different tack, we can look at the documentation for this organizer. Amount of documentation is often not a bad measure of functionality because documentation frequently consists of little more than a list of things that can be done, followed by how to do them. There is one page of documentation for the calculator part of my organizer and sixty for the other functions. This disparity certainly represents an overestimate of relative functionality. Instruction writers undoubtedly assume users are already familiar with calculators, and furthermore there is *a lot* of redundancy in the other sixty pages, as we examine below. Overall, let's settle on a factor of ten increase in functionality, realizing this estimate may easily be off by a factor of two. I postpone an estimate of complexity increase that accompanies this tenfold functionality increase. The case study below is directly relevant to assessing complexity.

I want to look at one somewhat mysterious entry in my organizer's instructional handbook, one that makes all of the points I require concerning organizers and design. The instructional entry is boxed, so presumably it is viewed as important, and it is repeated nearly identically in three places in the handbook. Most of this entry explains how to recognize a common mistake and what to do about it. It says, in essence, if you get a "data not found" error when you're trying to enter some data, you should press a certain sequence of keys and start again. It also notes that this same information and procedure is relevant to the two other major functional areas, which correspond to the places in the handbook where the entry is repeated.

First, let me explain what is going on here. The organizer has two major modes or ways of interacting that are shared by three major functional areas. In output mode, you can inspect or search information, but that information is protected and cannot be altered. Anything you type is not altering or adding information, but only entered into a "scratch" register, which is used only to specify what you want to search for. In input mode, you may add a new item, although you must still type first into the "scratch" register, then confirm your intent to add. Input mode also allows deleting or editing old entries. Here's the problem: whether you are in input mode or output mode, you will always be entering into the scratch register, and even when you are done, you press the same key, which confirms entry in input mode and searches in output mode. So if you are in output mode (thus the machine thinks you are searching), but think you are in input mode (you intend to enter new data), you're led down a long garden path that ends, usually, with a surprise "data not found." (The garden path can get even longer if the data you are intending to enter matches with some data you already have—say, the phone number of a person with the same last name as an existing entry.)

Point number one. In retrospect, one can see this kind of error coming a mile away. Modes almost always lead to mistakes when users are accidentally in one mode but think they are in another. A common designers' fix is to make modes visually distinct. This organizer has a tiny boxed IN, which appears during input modes, but it is easy to miss. The problem is compounded by having users employ the same structure (in this case, a key) to do different things depending on mode. That's a tradeoff, and perhaps the extra cost of a dedicated key is more, in some sense, than the cost of these errors. Evidently, the person who wrote the documentation (if not the designer of the calculator) was aware of the problem and tried to compensate with three prominent warnings.

Point number two directly concerns the documentation. Once again there is a problem in an extreme functional orientation. This potential user error and how to fix it are described three separate times. Nowhere is the common structure explained. Almost no one thinks to describe structure, even if it is there and easily describable. Instead, the effects of the structure are only partially described under the topic of relevant functionality. Worse, none of these explanations really explicates the structural issues, but instead resorts to "function plus low-level prescription." In this case, you get "to correct (a mysterious) condition, press the following keys." My guess is that the procedural prescription of corrective action might be made irrelevant in this case. If users understood the issue and got the error message, they'd just say "oops, wrong mode" and start entry again.

To be fair, modes are mentioned in the documentation, but they are mentioned only as an annotation of prescriptions, "press the X key to enter Y mode." There are other suggestions of common structure—for example, the note that the same procedure works in other functional areas. Yet, although I am a pretty sophisticated device connoisseur, and although, unlike the general population, I read documentation, it took me months of using this organizer before I figured out that there was a scratch register used in two global modes and that these modes provided a common structure to three separate functional areas.

How you explain something is not a trivial part of producing a comprehensible artifact. In fact, designing an artifact *so that it can be explained* is quite a different goal from designing an artifact so that no explanation is necessary. For anything of reasonable complexity and novelty, designing so that no explanation is necessary quickly meets its limits. When one does explain, it helps to remember both function *and* structure. That's why it is so sad to see even good designs undermined at the last step—explaining the design (e.g., in a manual)—by a fixation on function.

If we look a tiny bit toward a new computational literacy, learning something general about the design and operation of computer systems should become commonplace. Understanding, for example, modes and functionally overloaded structures (such as one button that does two different things, depending on mode), as well as typical problems and solutions, is not difficult and should pay dividends whenever a user wants to learn or improve understanding of an artifact. This subject matter would be roughly the equivalent of learning about dangling participles, split infinitives, and capitalization—except it concerns computational media and not textual media.

The last point I want to make about the pocket organizer is an important one that should have been amply anticipated in prior discussion. As functionality multiplies, structural complexity does not need to increase nearly as fast, provided the designer can find common structures to serve multiple functions. For the organizer, as I've already suggested, three of the new functional areas—telephone list, memo, and schedule—are nearly identical in their structure. You enter, edit, search, and delete using the same structure and procedures, with very few exceptions that "tune" to the specific function, so, qualitatively, these three areas are close to one in added complexity. In general, dividing the number of new functions by the "savings" of how many of the new functions are served by common structures gives you net complexity increase. In this case, it looks as if three is a reasonable savings number. Functionality multiplies by ten in moving from a calculator to organizer, but complexity increases by roughly only $10 \div 3 = 3.3$. We'll come back shortly to refine and extrapolate these numbers.

Learning Trajectory

Now that we have some reasonable examples of structure and function laid out, I'd like to talk a bit about the learning process. This brief summary falls short of what the topic deserves, but we have many other topics and ideas to cover in this book. My aim is to uncover only the first layer of complexity.

Functionality is what sells designed artifacts. People want something because it does things they understand and want accomplished. In a sense, the very fact that people want an artifact implies that they know (or think they know) some things about it already. This simple fact is not inconsequential. It means designers would be foolish to design artifacts that don't show the functionality users are expecting. If you know that your user knows something directly relevant to your device, why not design so that the device is comprehensible in those terms? Showing some familiar functional aspects is a classic way of making a device initially comprehensible, no matter how new or exotic it may be.

Purely functional understanding, however, has equally classic limitations. First, almost by definition, it offers the ability to do mainly things the user already understands. New functionality, which the user may understand only vaguely or not at all, just can't be reached in this way.

Second, a purely functional understanding may leave the user mystified about how the device actually accomplishes what it does. Aside from being aesthetically unpleasant, not understanding how the device works means various levels of agony the minute one leaves the beaten path. (Remember the car skid.) What happens if you press a wrong key sequence—for example, why did you get that "data not found" message, and what can you do about it?

Third, the logic of a device's mechanism can never be exactly functional. These devices are built out of things such as registers and certain standard electronic operations. This fact is why you run into some complexities in understanding calculators, for example. Structure is also an opportunity, however. New functions, usually valuable ones, exist in any device just at the fringe of its main functional focus. For instance, constant calculations are almost trivial extensions of the minimal mechanism of a basic calculator. If the calculator shows its own structure well, users can figure some extensions out with no muss or fuss. Granted, extending to new functions is not earthshaking for calculators, but computational media are very different in this regard. Anyone starting to learn a new medium can understand only a tiny fraction of its possibilities. The consequences of *these* possibilities, however, unlike the calculator, are enormous. If we are to realize the promise of computational media in the next few generations, function will be only a beginning, and structure will be the path to new riches.

Function provides a way in. Structure follows and makes the device comprehensible in its own, probably initially unfamiliar terms, but understanding structure also makes the device flexible far beyond the way into using it.

The pattern of function bootstrapping structure bootstrapping new function seems amazingly general, if not without exception. Children learn language for its function in communicating, but as they come to understand grammar and form, they become experts and eloquent far beyond what is possible without a structural turn. Poetry, for example, makes little sense until we understand rhyme and meter, at least implicitly, but rhyme and meter are not primary functional aspects of ordinary language.

Technique is a name frequently given to structural understanding. Knowing how to place your fingers accurately and the consequences of positioning your wrists oddly is not the first concern of a learning pianist or violinist. Technique, by itself, may be uninteresting if it is not used to serve musical function, but it is a focus that can prepare the learner for wonderful new things.

Designing for a good learning trajectory is more than understanding the function/structure/function process. Earlier, I talked about some other considerations that bear repeating. Learning must be contextualized in the felt needs and activity patterns of learners. Familiar function is therefore fine, but highly valued function is better. On the other hand, even menially useful function provides better learning through repeated learning/use cycles. A motto to which a designer can aspire is "continuous incremental advantage," where a long learning trajectory can be supported by learning, bit by bit. Each bit is manageable (incremental) and confers useful advantage as perceived by the learner at that stage. The opposite is a learning plateau where a learner gets stuck either because the next structural step to better understanding is too high or because there is too little added functionality to motivate the step.

From Software Applications to Computational Media

The step from pocket organizers to a computational medium is a rather big one. To keep reasonable track of complexity and multifunctionality, let us look at an intermediate rung—a typical computer application such as a text processor or spreadsheet program. Estimates of multifunctionality and complexity compared to a pocket organizer are a little more difficult to make, mainly because the kind of unit embedding and counting that exists between a calculator and an organizer doesn't exist between an organizer and a typical application. That is, applications generally don't contain units comparable to an organizer, whereas a pocket organizer neatly contains a unit with calculator functionality (and there are several other units of comparable functionality in the organizer).

Instead, we can measure multifunctionality roughly by documentation. Again, using documentation depends on the endemic focus on functionality. If documentation were written structurally (especially if artifacts were designed with structural simplicity in mind), it might be much shorter. The average length of three text processor manuals I happen to have on my bookshelf is about four hundred pages. Correcting—somewhat gratuitously, given the general crudeness of these estimates—for the fact that these pages are significantly larger than those in my pocket organizer manual, I get about six hundred organizer-size pages, compared to the sixty pages of organizer manual. That is the same ten-to-one ratio of multifunctionality we estimated on the move from calculator to organizer. I invite you to develop other estimates.

There is also some evidence of common structure savings, although it is not particularly quantitative. The text processors have essentially one data type, text; my organizer is a bit more diverse. You can't cut and paste a complete scheduling record and move it to the telephone directory. You can't cut and paste in the calculator subfunction at all, nor can you search calculations (as you can a table of numbers in the text processors I own), even though the calculator has a mode that allows you to record long calculations. In a certain way, text processors have "discovered" a wonderfully flexible structure—text—that supports many functions.

The way I use text processing suggests generic structure with concomitant savings in complexity. I keep my "address book" in my computer in a plain text file and simply use the search function to "access records." I also keep notes to myself (memo function of the organizer) the same way. Except for portability, which is a critical independent issue, I could keep my schedule also in a text file with only a little awkwardness. I consider the pattern tentatively and crudely confirmed: we have a substantial increase in functionality, possibly again on the order of ten times, and at least some evidence of common structure savings in the transition from organizer to full-functioned application.

The next rung, finally to computational media, is a critical and uncertain one. We simply don't know if the social niches for a computational medium can come to exist, but this chapter is putting in place one piece of the argument that we can create a computational medium—the piece regarding comprehensibility, functionality, and structural complexity.

How can we estimate multifunctionality and complexity? Luckily, there are some units to count, at least as a start. I just spent a half hour doing a few chores at my computer. During that time, I used at least half a dozen applications: an electronic mail program, an Internet browser, two text editors (one on my local machine, which does formatting and printing nicely, one on a network host that offers much more control and flexibility for shuffling files of various types around the network), a network file transfer program, and a file compression and conversion program. These applications are not tiny, either. The smallest is about half a megabyte.

Two major conclusions are hinted at already. First, as for multifunctionality, the step up from an application to all the things that many or most people normally do with computers is probably at least another factor of ten. Second, the current situation with software is a mess with respect to savings using common structure across multiple functions. For example, of those six programs I just used, most were simply to get some menial chores done with plain text! The situation is therefore even worse than multiple functions not sharing common structure. Because resources come in inflexible and indivisible chunks—applications—there is even a great functional redundancy. The two text processors are the best example. Although they share 90 percent of their functionality, I am forced to use both because (1) I can't really modify either to get the extra 10 percent I need, and (2) they are indivisible—I can't use part of one text processor with the other. Before we discuss the importance of modifiability more fully, let's put my personal experience in a more general context.

Over days and weeks, as opposed to during the last half hour, I regularly use dozens of applications. Without half trying and not including small utility programs, I counted two dozen major applications that my wife and I use regularly. Now, this number may be unusual, but let's think about what most people might actually use: text processing, no doubt; some form of graphics—say, a draw or paint program; possibly a spreadsheet for personal finances and a little database system to keep track of records; network browsing and electronic mail. If we think about school and the different subject areas, it is easy to generate dozens of small-to-large applications students might well use: a graphing program, various physics simulations, a hypertext or multimedia tool for English or history presentations. Professionals like me may be a bit ahead of the curve, but less expensive and more powerful hardware will inevitably bring huge ranges of functionality within the grasp of most people in our society. Bringing more functionality to users would be easier if the tremendous cost and learning penalties now paid by purchasers of software were reduced or eliminated—costs incurred because of functional redundancy. Large, expensive chunks (applications) are essentially the only way to extend functionality; no one seems to pay attention to core multifunctional structures.

Estimating multifunctionality raises another subtle but important point. The savings factor that common structure offers for multifunctionality has an irreducibly social component. That is, looking at the savings factor that each user may perceive underestimates the real savings factor. This underestimate stems from the simple fact that different people and different groups of people will do different things with a computational medium, so the "cost" of implementing the technology is spread over more use than any one person can know. If poets had to bear the cost of building a paper and pencil industry alone, there would be no poets. If schools had to teach reading and writing only for romance novels, we wouldn't teach reading and writing. With regard to electronic technology, operating system software is inexpensive because everybody uses it, no matter what else they do.

The irreducibly social component of multifunctionality really blossoms with computational media, where we run out of familiar descriptions for "what the system does." A medium does not just calculate numbers, draw graphs, or fill any particular functional niche. The fact that a medium does so many things of such diversity that we have no familiar name for the collection—or even a good grasp of the range—means a hitch in society's learning trajectory. With no functional model, computational media will catch on only gradually as people experience their power.

To sum up, the multifunctionality of a computational medium is a dramatic increase over the application rung of our complexity ladder. A factor of ten is probably extremely conservative. For simplicity, I'll let that estimate stand.

Estimating savings via common structure, of course, demands specific cases. Different common structure will result in different savings. In the case of a computational medium, the range of function is so broad that no individual or group is in a position to perceive it; recall the irreducibly social components of multifunctionality. Trying out a structural basis for a computational medium therefore means a social experiment. No laboratory or thought experiment will do.

These remarks specify and contextualize the task of estimating common structure savings. First, I offer a case study rather than provide a general argument. Naturally, the case involves Boxer not only because it is the case I know best, but also because it is the only existing system specifically designed as a computational medium capable of supporting a popular new literacy. Second, what we can do here is only a plausibility argument. Widespread use of Boxer is yet to come, so many social niches and Boxer's fit to them must remain speculative.

A Structure for Cyberspace

Boxer is fundamentally a proposal for a unifying form for a computer user's experience. The key to its success is finding few, simple, and relatively easily mastered structures that comfortably contain almost all one might want to do—at least as a teacher or student of science and mathematics. Before looking at Boxer structure per se, I introduce three general principles that define the direction we took in designing it.

The Principle of Textuality

Many people come to Boxer expecting, perhaps naturally, an avant garde system. What they see is a system oriented in a substantial way toward text. This makes Boxer appear conservative, if not reactionary.

In a certain sense, including text as a primary surface form *is* a conservative move, but one that is carefully calculated. Text and language constitute the foremost example of a popular intellectual medium. Nontextual literacies are still mostly speculation, and, given some of our discussion earlier in this chapter about expressiveness, it seems foolhardy to jettison textual literacy. Instead, we should be encompassing; we should build outward from a strong basis. Besides, computational media can easily add important extensions to text. Easy accomplishments in an especially difficult enterprise are important.

Encompassing text brings with it a huge range of existing and plausible new social niches. The principle of textuality is not simply "doing better what we've done before," but carrying forward the scientific principles (e.g., social niches) that explain how past success has been achieved. From a learning trajectory perspective, having a prominent textual basis means people will find the medium familiar in many ways.

The Principle of Spatial Metaphor

Early and often in this book, I have referred to important and unheralded competencies people have developed in their everyday experiences. Of these competencies, the first or second I would think to mention is the ability to describe, imagine, and reason about spatial configurations. Boxer is designed explicitly to take advantage of this ability as much and as deeply as possible. Boxer's spatial metaphor means we want to allow people to think about the system as if it had a familiar spatial organization.

Using familiar things metaphorically to promote understanding is a common design strategy, but Boxer doesn't have file folders, file drawers, or windows. Instead, we use the spatial metaphor quite abstractly—

containers (boxes) contain other things, including text, pictures, and other containers. One reason motivates this move to abstractness, and another justifies its validity. Wanting as much functional diversity as possible in the uses of the same structures motivates truly generic structures. Thus, folders contain files and other folders, but documents similarly contain sections and perhaps further subsections. Programs contain subprograms, and so on. We have found that generic (box) structure can work in all these contexts and many others, but the familiar metaphors are not nearly so context independent.

What justifies this design move is that people have much more abstract knowledge than they are usually given credit for. To take a handy example, babies develop notions of containers and places to put things long before they see file folders. Indeed, people come to understand file folders when they encounter them only because they have previously mastered the spatial principles by which folders work. We can aim for structures that are familiar without their being too particular.

The Principle of Computational Structure

The principle of textuality appears to be Boxer's most conservative principle, and the principle of computational structuring may be its most controversially radical. We want to encompass programming as one of the basic uses of the system. In fact, every structure in Boxer has a computational meaning: it either computes or can be computed on or both.

The reason this principle is regarded as radical is that many people—in their experiences with languages such as BASIC, Logo, and Pascal—have concluded that programming languages are too difficult for ordinary folks to learn and also that they just don't do enough. I believe these criticisms are valid, but this was exactly the starting point for Boxer design. We set out to design a more comprehensible system and, fundamentally, one that is more immediately adapted to a broader range of uses. We have made documented advances in both these directions, so I believe the question is open whether Boxer or a future computational medium can bootstrap into a self-sustaining complex of social niches. I also believe these questions relate to one of the preeminent questions of our age—can computational media really extend our intelligence or are computers merely a matter of getting more done, faster?

Enfolding computational structure is a more basic move than adding one more area of functionality. If it were only adding on an area, the principle of computational structure would scarcely warrant mention. Instead, this is the move that turns a consumer medium into a two-way medium with respect to its best and most promising capabilities—dynamic and interactive structure. Using the term *programming*, in fact, is highly prejudicial. It evokes old systems and, more to the point, old social niches in which programming was considered difficult (because not everybody could do it) and you had to do a lot of it to get any useful effect. Of course, conventional literacy went through just such a historical stage, when it was considered for specialists only.

As an aside, note that contemporary developers continue to try to sneak programming in the sidedoor by calling it *scripting* or *macros*. Over the long haul, the central questions are about whether programming is sufficiently powerful and learnable in future social niches to be worthwhile. Games of terminology are not very telling. Society will decide, sooner or later, whether programming deserves a new name in its new forms and social contexts.

Bringing computational structure into the accessible parts of the medium enables an important new set of strategies to (1) reduce structural complexity, (2) reduce functional redundancy (as in my two text processors anecdote), and hence (3) increase simplicity and common structure savings. These strategies are modifying, combining, and extending. If the medium enfolds programming and pieces of the system supplied to users have computational structure, then anyone, in principle, can combine, modify, and extend what is supplied to meet new and different functional needs.

Figure 7.1 depicts this strategy in contrast to the current multiple applications model. In the applications model (figure 7.1a), one "covers" a range of functionality with a collection of monolithic, unmodifiable applications. Functional redundancy is evident where one may need to use two overlapping applications because each is short only a small amount of functionality. In contrast, a true computational medium allows the strategy depicted in figure 7.1b. Functionality supplied to a user (black dots) may be focused and fairly simple, but that functionality may be modified and extended by users or subcommunity programming (lighter

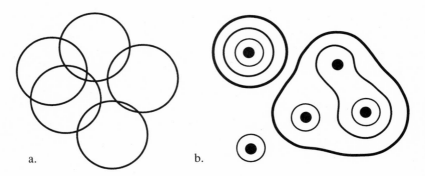

Figure 7.1
(*a*) Monolithic, nonmodifiable applications have gaps and overlaps. (*b*) A computational medium allows seeding with small but extendible tools (black dots), but these tools can be organically enriched, altered, and combined, as successive layers here show.

rings, extending outward from the dark regions). You should recognize this strategy as an essential part of the image of communities of tool builders and sharers described at the end of chapter 2.

With this preparation, let's do a little blow-by-blow description of Boxer. Figure 7.2 shows a sample document in Boxer. At this level, the document is mainly text with some pictures, although it contains subcomponents that are nested sub-boxes. Boxes provide not only a nice hierarchical way of organizing any document, but also an easy to comprehend method of flexibly browsing a document. If sub-boxes are closed (shown as small, gray boxes or a user-definable icon), you get a nice overview. Clicking on a box opens it to reveal its component pieces. If you are interested in focusing attention on one of these components (say, because it is complex and deserves your undivided attention), you can expand any box to occupy the full screen.

Notice how abstract Boxer's spatial metaphor is. Boxes are not fixed in size. Indeed, when a box is expanded, it pushes text and other boxes around to maintain the logical structuring of next to, above, below, and so on. The strict maintenance of logical structure while sizes, distances, and absolute positions change is not like real-world boxes, but we have discovered, far beyond our initial expectations, that people find this structure highly intuitive.

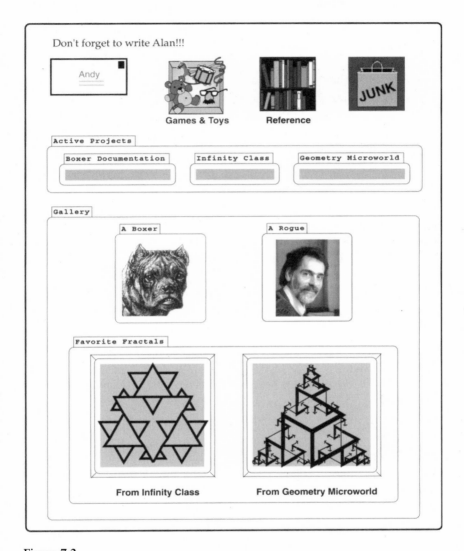

Figure 7.2
A Boxer "world" containing boxes, text, and pictures. Boxes may be full-screen (this full-world box), open (such as **gallery**), or closed (small, gray boxes, or icons like the envelope-shaped correspondence box).

I have to tell you a story. When we first designed Boxer, we realized how complex a world of boxes within boxes could become. In anticipation of users getting lost, we built a little utility that would show users a map of the "world" and where they were in it, but it turns out that no one, after a few moments with Boxer, ever gets lost. People may lose track of where they are, but it is easy to zoom out and find themselves again. Intuitive spatial knowledge is indeed abstract, flexible, and powerful.

What else can boxes do besides hierarchically organize parts of documents? Any of the subcomponents of the document in figure 7.2 could be a document in its own right, so we recognize that boxes nicely organize families of documents. In conventional computer systems, specialized structures, depicted these days as file and folder systems (files and directories), provide this functionality. Aside from being one more structure to learn, these structures limit, for example, the kind of annotations you can write on (or into) the folders (or desktop or directories). In contrast, in Boxer there's nothing to stop you from typing some notes anywhere in a box (folder) concerning the contained boxes.

Boxer does make one compromise to the limited memory of computers that means files are not exactly the same thing as boxes. Only certain boxes are "file boxes"; they are initially seen as black. These black boxes are stored on disk and take some time to read in when you click on them. In essentially every other way, however, files are boxes and boxes (can be) files.

In case it has escaped your attention, I'm sketching some of the core multifunctionalities of Boxer's box structure. We've done document structure and "file structure" so far. Figure 7.2 can also illustrate a third functionality: sharing of resources over a network and browsing or surfing the Net. Not only may some of the shrunken boxes in that figure be files or subdocuments, those boxes may even reside on a different computer, so when you click to open, the box gets read in over your network connection. Surfing is a completely transparent use of the same skills you use to navigate any Boxer structure, and, indeed, creating a document for others to browse is negligibly different from simply creating any document. All you have to learn is how to make your box accessible to other people on the network.

Because it is so important, let's look briefly at programming structure in Boxer. Programs are essentially hierarchical processes in which each process "calls" subprocesses in an appropriate order to get some work done. In Boxer, programs turn out to be hierarchically nested boxes. At each level of the hierarchy, you can choose to name a box, and then you can just use that box by name in the box in which it is defined or in any subordinate box. Variables are also boxes. In fact, variables are exactly the same kind of box that appears in figure 7.2. Programs themselves are a second kind of box—a doit (do it) box. Data boxes have rounded corners; doit boxes are rectangular.

Figure 7.3 (left panel) shows a **flower** program and the picture it draws. **Flower** uses variables such as **color, size,** and **petals,** which can be edited to change the appearance of the flower. The right panel in figure 7.3 shows **flower** when opened. It uses a subprocedure, **petal,** and **petal,** in turn, uses **side.** Each of these is defined just where it is needed in the hierarchy. The variables **size, color,** and **petals** could be enclosed inside **flower** if one didn't anticipate changing them often. In our experience, such a flexible, hierarchical organizational structure allows students to write much more complex programs much sooner in Boxer than in prior languages (I give examples in chapter 8). Of course,

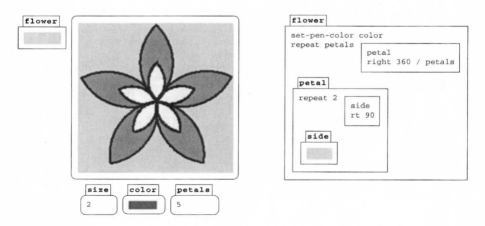

Figure 7.3
Left, a program, **flower,** and the picture it draws. *Right,* **flower** is opened to show its structure.

one uses the usual "text" editing and browsing capabilities to create the programs.

The strong visible and interactive presence of programming structure in Boxer is even more important than hierarchical organization per se. Starting with calculators, I have remarked on the learning power conveyed by having a visible model of computational structure. Variables in Boxer, for example, have a visible presence that exists in no other full programming system. If a program changes a variable, you can see the change on the screen by going to where the variable exists. The flip side of visibility is *pokability:* if you can see a variable, you can change its contents with standard text editing commands. Programs are pokable, too. You can double click your mouse to activate any program or even any line in a program, and then watch the screen for what that program or program step does internally (e.g., variables) or externally (e.g., a graphical display). Visibility and pokability together have proved critical supports for students' learning and aid students in explaining to others what they've done or in figuring out what someone else has done. Recall the student-run library described in chapter 3. Although having a rich, visible, and interactive presence is obviously a powerful learning/use principle, Boxer is the first system to incorporate it so extensively.

Let me briefly consider how we create complex data structures in Boxer. Figure 7.4 shows a couple of entries of a database. In the language of databases, each box is a record and the named subitems are fields. In most languages, records and fields are separate structures. In Boxer, they are constructible with exactly the same structures as documents, file directories, browsable networks, and programs—namely, nested and possibly named boxes. This design means you can construct, modify, and inspect databases using the things you learned in your first few hours with Boxer.

This is multifunctionality par excellence, and it comes with the attendant savings in complexity of the system and in learning. Because everything is built with the same building blocks (Lego media!), you also have extraordinary flexibility. Constructions are not locked into your initial conceptualization of them. For example, because any document is constructed of generic boxes, it can be "computed over" and even

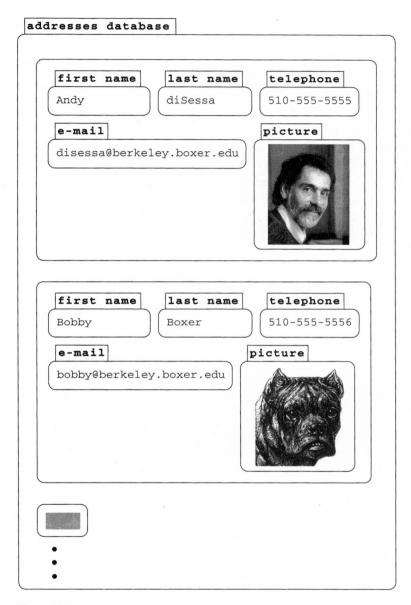

Figure 7.4
A piece of a database, built using the basic Boxer components of data and graphics boxes.

reconfigured as if it were a database or other data structure. In order to turn a document into a database, you simply think differently about it, use generic Boxer resources to operate on it, or possibly make a little tool to suit your special purpose. (I sometimes write a little program literally to reorganize a project I am working on in Boxer.) Similarly, a box becomes a file or a directory or a network "page" to browse with little more than the intent to use it in a different way.

What do you suppose hierarchy should mean in the case of graphical objects? Boxer's meaning is *part of,* in a fully functional way. For example, the left panel of figure 7.5 shows a simple graphical object. The middle panel shows the same graphics box "flipped" to reveal the hierarchical structure of the object. The man has a head and body. In the right panel, the head is opened to reveal, in addition to its own shape, a left and right eye. A command to move the man moves all his parts together. A command to move his head moves his eyes along with the head.

This graphical example uses two more of the basic types of boxes in Boxer, *graphics boxes* and *sprite boxes.* Graphics boxes are special in having a graphical presentation in addition to their logical nested box

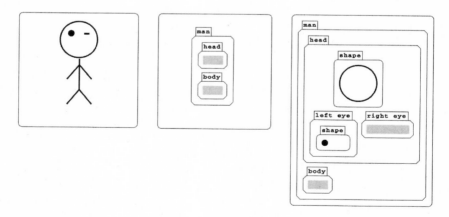

Figure 7.5
Left, a graphical object. *Middle,* his "logical" view has two parts: a head and a body. *Right,* opening his "head" reveals its shape and that it contains a left eye and a right eye.

presentation. Sprites are graphical objects that inhabit graphics boxes to represent movable, interactive parts of a picture.

Finally, mainly for completeness I would like to mention the fifth and last main type of box. (The other four are data, doit, graphics, and sprite; net boxes and file boxes are simple variations of data boxes.) *Ports* are Boxer's one and only nonhierarchical structure. They are views ("view-ports") of other boxes that may live anywhere in the Boxer hierarchy. Thus, they make excellent cross links in any Boxer document, converting text into hypertext. They also make excellent access ports to control or modify parts of a program that may be buried deep within it. From a port, you can see and modify the remote contents of the port, or you may choose to "zoom" to the target of the port to navigate to or inspect that context. Ports turn out to be extraordinarily powerful and multifunctional structures in Boxer, although many of their best uses are for relatively advanced functions.

The left panel of figure 7.6 shows a fun but fairly useless configuration of ports, all to the same box. Editing one edits them all simultaneously, so the screen changes all over as you edit even one character of one port. The right panel suggests how powerful ports can be. It shows a port that

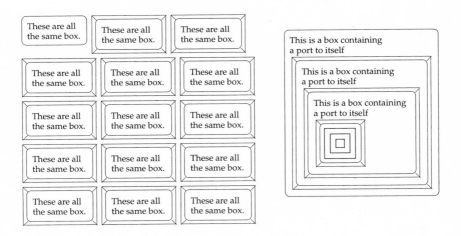

Figure 7.6
Left, ports to the same box all change simultaneously when you edit any port or the box. *Right,* a port to a box containing itself creates an infinite structure.

is targeted to the box that contains it. Part of the box (the port) contains the full complexity of the box. Mathematics tells us that an object that contains itself as a proper subpart must necessarily be infinite, and that is what we see in the figure. The abbreviated nested boxes can be successively expanded to show that the structure is, in fact, effectively infinite, with the same structure "all the way down." This example shows the power of a structurally consistent and logical system. The keystroke that made the port simultaneously touched infinity. It had to be that way, given a consistent meaning of a port. Functionally motivated and designed systems may have their own "wows," but they are seldom, if ever, of this mathematical sort.

This has been a brief view of Boxer structures and functions. Using Boxer's hierarchical boxes as an example, I have tried to suggest the huge functional range of these core ideas, from documents to file structures to network browsing to program and data structure to graphical object creation. Although we did not pursue the port examples very far, the infinitely nested structure suggests that a structurally consistent system of modest complexity will always contain surprises and possibilities for invention far from any conservative focus on functional need.

The multifunctionality of hierarchical structure and boxes in Boxer is extravagant and perhaps can't be matched by other parts of the system. On the other hand, box structure is much of Boxer, so perhaps you'll grant me a factor of three in common structure savings. All of Boxer's basic structures clearly cross boundaries of many current applications. As additional evidence, I note that the document I wrote in order to explain all the basic structural features of Boxer is about only thirty pages long. I don't mean to imply that thirty pages is a good measure of the total learning that needs to be done to master Boxer. Instead, this small document shows that there is a simple structural coherence behind the face that Boxer presents to users. Over the long haul, users will come to feel and appreciate the simplicity in the way bicycle users implicitly appreciate the simplicity of sequential gearing.

To sum up, I've argued in this chapter for the crude approximation of functional diversity and structural complexity, shown in the first two columns of the table below, as we move up the evolutionary ladder toward a computational medium. At each stage, the functionality increases by a factor of ten, but the complexity increases only by a factor of three—provided that a good design leads to common structure savings at each stage. The numbers argue that the functional advantage of a computational medium may be out of proportion to the extra complexity it entails.

The third column is a rough attempt to introduce some important learning phenomena, such as the learning/use cycle (more use implies greater opportunity to learn) and the fact that the more a community knows about something, the easier it is for each member to learn. The comparable phenomenon in language learning is that children learn language fairly easily in part because they use it every day but also because the adults around them are helpful in that they are all competent. I computed "difficulty," the third column, by dividing how much there is to learn (complexity) by the number of opportunities to learn the system (functionality). Surely it would be unfair not to note that even if a medium is more complex than an application, there would be many times more opportunity to learn.

Finally, the fourth column tries to incorporate the additional fact that even given comparable learning difficulty, learning a medium has more value for the many, many occasions in which expertise can be used *after* learning. I computed "net value" as the ratio of use (functionality) to effort (difficulty). (Perhaps uses after learning should be a different number than the multifunctionality during learning, but it is surely a big number for a medium.)

To sum up, learning a more complex device does not imply a linear increase in the necessary amount of learning (second column). Furthermore, a greater number of learning opportunities makes learning even

	functionality	complexity	difficulty	net value
calculator	1	1	1	1
organizer	10	3	.3	30
application	100	10	.1	1,000
medium	1,000	30	.03	30,000

easier. (Becoming literate involves a huge learning commitment in our society, but that learning is spread out over many years and many contexts.) Finally, the payback learners and society receive from literacy is multiplied by the tremendous range of circumstances in which the skill is useful.

Clearly these numbers are metaphorical and suggestive, at best. Nevertheless, they reflect real phenomena. There are learning economies of scale in well-designed multifunctional systems. Having more opportunities to learn clearly helps learning. The fourth column suggests why literacies overpower learning little, isolated skills. They can spread out and pervade our lives.

By the accounting given in the table, a medium is only three applications' worth of complexity. This guesstimate alone suggests that the cost of learning a computational medium is easily manageable, compared to learning several applications as happens now. Adding in the rest of the issues implied in the chart, we come to the bottom line for this chapter. By the technical measures of learnability and usefulness, there is every reason to believe an enhanced literacy via computational media is achievable and powerful. Consideration of breadth of usefulness and learnability lends theoretical sense to the empirical phenomena we exemplify in other chapters—that children can master a computational medium and become involved in using it. The analysis in this chapter stands beside other discussions and examples in this book about the importance of what may be expressed and learned with computational literacy.

Coda

The concepts of structure and function as perspectives on comprehensibility of designed artifacts have been at the core of this chapter, but the point of view presented has been the designer's point of view. It is not a trivial point that most users will not perceive systems this way, even though structural and functional organization will undoubtedly strongly influence the "feel" of a system. As a final ode to structure and function, I'd like to present an epigrammatic review of how these foundational perspectives may likely be felt by users.

Structure without function is arcane; function without structure is baroque.

Structure is powerful, limitless, surprising.

Function is easy and useful.

Structure relies on creativity; it thrives on change.

Structure is evenhanded to a fault. Its friendship must be cultivated.

Function is familiar—an old hat.

Out of its element, function withers.

Structure is crystalline and stark in its beauty—sometimes cold.

Function is comforting, immediate.

Structure is intellectual.

Function is practical.

Structure is aloof.

Function is adapted.

In the best of worlds, structure and function are friends with different personalities to be called on differently. Function is your first friend, up front and direct. Structure stands back and supports. Later, function stays home and keeps the household, while structure opens doors and builds bridges to exotic lands, but only if you understand and work with it.

8

More Snapshots: Kids Are Smart

As in chapter 3, I want to discuss what has already happened with our prototype computational medium, Boxer, in order to think about what may happen if we achieve a new, computationally enhanced literacy. We should be attentive to the goals and actions suggested in these snapshots, which can help speed and enhance the development of a new literacy.

In contrast to chapter 3, we now have a refined basis for considering examples. Chapters 4 and 5 developed improved ways to look at learning. Extending the discussion of cognitive and social pillars for new literacies in chapter 1, I emphasized different sorts of knowledge and competence to which we should attend. We should consider intuitive knowledge to be both a goal and a resource; we should also realize that embedding learning in extended activities that feel coherent and meaningful likewise constitutes both a critical subgoal of improving learning and also a goal in its own right. Chapters 6 and 7 focused on understanding how computational media work—how we can learn them and learn with them. This discussion shored up and extended our understanding of the material pillar of possible new literacies. Altogether, reading the messages in the examples in this chapter benefits significantly from the preparation in chapters 4–7.

The principal theme in this chapter is the cleverness we can find in people if we know where to look. In the chapter subtitle, "Kids Are Smart," I emphasize children, but of course teachers, curriculum developers, parents, people in general are included in my hopes and in the possibilities that are afforded by new computational literacies. I single out children partly because educational discussion usually (and appropriately) centers on students, but also because they are more vulnerable than others to being painted as incompetent. The new views of knowledge and the importance of activity I previously introduced are antidotes to an easy willingness on the part of adults to characterize kids as empty-headed, willing to do anything ("good" students), or unwilling to do anything ("bad" students). Whatever they are, children are not empty-headed, and it is as bad to think that some students are always unwilling to engage as it is to believe that others engage simply because they are willing.

An easy interpretation of some examples I present here is that they represent the discovery of new knowledge, intelligence, or competence that people already have, but which we have for some reason neglected to see. In a sense, this interpretation is reasonable, but a more powerful interpretation is that we are discovering possibilities for new intelligences based on a combined people-and-media thinking system. Material intelligence is not just an improved "pure" intelligence; it depends intimately on the properties of the medium that liberates it.

Unlike chapter 3, which started with an easy example, this chapter begins with a long and difficult one. Nevertheless, the example is particularly important. It introduces a new way to think about what computational media can afford, beyond what's offered by static media.

Metarepresentation Meets a Metamedium

In 1989, during our physics course for sixth graders, we had a remarkable experience. In about five days, our sixth-grade students seemed to invent graphing as a way of depicting and thinking about motion. Graphing, as you may recall, was actually invented by Descartes, after Galileo took the first quantitative steps toward a science of motion. This was before Newton extended algebra with calculus to complete the understanding of motion that has become known as Newtonian physics. (Yes, Galileo did his work with neither algebra nor graphing! That's one reason he gets so much credit in my book.)

Can sixth-grade children invent graphing? I have been told in public at scientific meetings that children could not possibly invent graphing because such young children are too concrete or have some other limitation. I have been told that it could not possibly happen again, even if it did happen once. The children or teacher were exceptional beyond any reasonable reality test. Nevertheless, we have the children inventing graphing on videotape; it did happen. What's more, we have repeated the activity several times since. Although it may be a bit overdramatic to say that these children "invented graphing" and hence compare them to Descartes, what happened is important to understand, and it has profound implications for the future of computational media.

The beginning of this tale takes us back to the start of our motion course. We started with a unit that taught students Boxer programming. In particular, we instructed them how to write simple programs to draw pictures on the computer screen. The first official activity about motion was an assignment to use their programming knowledge to show a few simple, real-world motions, such as what happens when you drop or toss a ball. For the dropped ball, one group developed a program that produced the picture in figure 8.1.

To most scientifically literate people, the depiction just looks wrong. It appears to show an object slowing down, but almost everybody—including this group of children—knows that objects speed up when they fall. To make matters worse, running their program reinforces the impression that something is wrong. The program takes about the same time to draw each dot and to move to the next, so as it draws the dots from top to bottom, the "ball" (graphics cursor) actually *does* slow down.

What is going on? Are these children so incompetent at programming that they can't show what they know is going on? Or have they somehow

Figure 8.1
A student depiction of a ball falling faster and faster.

forgotten what happens in the real world under the influence of the "artificial" computer context?

The resolution to this puzzle provided the first suggestion of the new intelligence we discovered in inventing graphing. It is surprisingly simple. When asked by a graduate student about the puzzling "slowing down" in the students' depiction, one of the pair who had worked on it said that they had not intended to "show it speeding up," but that they wanted to show "*that* it sped up." They believed they had done it quite well. More speed is shown as more dots.

If this representation is wrong in any sense, it is wrong only in using an unusual convention. Scientists usually pick equal time intervals as a basic method of cutting up events that unfold over time. From that point of view, the natural representation is to show where the ball is at the end of each time interval; dots get farther apart. You could, however, choose equal distances as a standard instead of equal times. Then you would want to show decreasing times to traverse the same distance. If we interpret the vertical axis as time, dots closer together toward the bottom could show decreasing intervals to move the constant distance.

These children were not so sophisticated as to be showing decreasing time intervals. We believe they really intended "more dots means more speed." Still, they showed a surprising sophistication. The students were not caught by the concrete and literal impulse to "show speeding up." Instead, they clearly intended to make a meaningful *representation* of speeding up. This distinction is exactly the transition from showing speeding up to showing *that* it sped up. That is, the students are not making a picture at all, but a representation in the true sense: a system of inscriptions with abstract rules of interpretation to show things about the world. Indeed, they invented a *new* representation, for they couldn't have learned this one at school!

Saying that these children designed a representation is not an example of a fancy description that applies to an everyday competence, like the bourgeois *gentilhomme* who discovered he had been speaking prose all his life. Instead, their design is a hint that children know a lot more about representations than we might suspect. *That* competence is consequential. Hold onto your hats as these students really get going!

Later in the course, when it came time to teach graphing as the most important standard representation we could plausibly teach sixth-grade students, I convinced my research group and Tina, the teacher, to try an unusual strategy. Instead of presenting graphing, why not ask the class to see what they could come up with to show motion? Tina was a good sport, although she said she expected this exercise would just show us a little about what they already knew about graphing; then we could move on and teach.

In the narrative of the students' exploring representations, I have to eliminate a lot of interesting detail. In particular, I show only what I consider landmark representations that the children developed. To illustrate their representations, I also depict only the first motion they were assigned to show—an object that gradually slows to a stop, pauses a while, then accelerates away. I also, in some cases, strip some pictographic detail from the students' representations: the students were presented with motions in the context of "cover stories." For example, the initial motion was presented as someone driving a car through the desert, stopping for a drink from a cactus beside the road, then resuming the trip. Students at first included elements of the story, for example, the cactus, which I won't reproduce.

Figure 8.2 shows an early representation, which the children called Dots. Note that, now, these students were using the standard scientific convention of equal time intervals, rather than their original "more dots means more speed." Shifting to a more conventional representation was probably due to the fact that, by this time, they had spent hours making realistic simulations, rather than representations, of motion on the computer. The dots representation can be produced from a simulation of the motion in question simply by making a dot after each step in the program.

The chalk representation in figure 8.3 highlights speed by showing it more explicitly in the length of lines rather than implicitly in the distance

Figure 8.2
The "dots" representation of an object slowing to a stop, pausing, then accelerating away.

Figure 8.3
The "chalk" representation.

Figure 8.4
The "sonar" representation.

Figure 8.5
The slant of the line represents how fast the object is moving.

between dots. This change is a suggestive step toward considering the task to be designing a representation rather than just drawing a related picture. That is, it seems to reignite the "showing *that*" idea evident in the representation of the dropping ball. Students were quite clear that measuring the length of the line was intended to be the method of determining the speed at which the object was moving at a particular time.

Figure 8.4 shows what may well be a critical step. Although one may say that Sonar, as the students called this representation, merely rotates each line of Chalk, its real innovation is to introduce a new representational resource into the pool students could use. The vertical dimension shows speed, independent of the "story line" horizontal dimension. This is really beginning to look like graphing. Still, we are not there yet.

Slants, figure 8.5, is a remarkable contribution. Jan carefully explained that the length of the lines in Slants doesn't represent anything. Instead, the slant of the line shows speed. Here is another representational resource, line "slantiness." Jan also explained that he meant the horizontal direction to mean "as fast as it can go" and the vertical direction to represent stop. Evidently, he didn't care which way the line slanted; the same speed in the slowing-down portion of the representation (left half of the figure) was shown with slant opposite to the speeding-up segment (right half). Another student pointed out the ambiguity, and Jan acknowledged it without changing his representation.

Figure 8.6, Ts, evidently combines the ideas of Chalk and Sonar. Ts was a response to a critical difficulty with all the representations up to this point. Tina had asked several times if one could see how long the object was stopped, from which the students recognized that no representation yet could capture this piece of information. The students understood and responded to the problem. The T representation was the result. In it, the horizontal line reverts to showing speed, and the vertical line now shows time—"how long the object stays at each speed." One of the students said explicitly, "We have two dimensions; one can mean one thing and another can mean another." One of the students even went so far as to observe that you could multiply those two numbers, speed and time, to get the distance that the object moved during each depicted segment of motion. He said you could add those numbers up to find exactly how far the object had moved. I come back to this observation shortly.

Early during the third class in this sequence, Jan introduced an improvement of his slants representation, which quickly precipitated the first unambiguous graph. He described it as an "awesome idea" that combined several previous ideas and that could get "everything we want at the same time." The essence of the idea was that his slants had used only one part of the representational richness of line segments. He had used

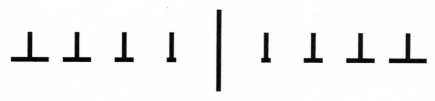

Figure 8.6
The "Ts" representation.

the slant, but the length was available to represent a second aspect of motion, either distance or time. At the board to explain his idea, he improvised: you could even connect all these slanted lines together! At every position along this newly unified line, you could see speed by attending to the slant of the line. Jan's first connected line had straight segments joined together, but successors showed a connected line that continuously changed slant as speed varied.

In order to understand what an excellent idea Jan had, you need to recall some aspects of Newton's great invention, calculus. One of the two central operations of the calculus, called the *derivative,* converts knowledge of the position of an object mechanically and perfectly into a knowledge of speed. If you imagine a graph of position versus time, it turns out that measuring the slant of the line provides the derivative; it converts from position to speed. So Jan has anticipated Newton in one crucial respect. He (and his fellow students) have learned the representational skill to look at a graph and see its slant at each point. Later in their schooling, those skills will become "seeing the derivative."

The other fundamental operation in calculus, the *integral* operation, is the opposite of the derivative. It converts speed into distance. The student observation—that with the T representation, one can multiply times and speeds and add them up to get total distance—is the equivalent of integration. See the discussion of calculus and, in particular, the discussion of the Fundamental Theorem of Calculus in the tick-model portion of chapter 2. Of course, it would be better if these children understood that the derivative is the opposite of the integral, and if they could use these operations independent of representational form, but what do you want from sixth-grade students *before instruction?*

Figure 8.7a comes from a standard calculus textbook. It depicts the derivative operation. Can you see Jan's slants? Figure 8.7b shows the integral. Rectangles substitute for Ts, but the process of adding up altitudes times widths is just the same.

Another student, Sean, extended Jan's continuous slants idea. Why don't you just place a grid over this line of changing slant? That way you could read numbers off it exactly. A grid would provide a two-dimensional ruler that measures the two aspects of motion (speed and time, or speed and distance) clearly and precisely (figure 8.8).

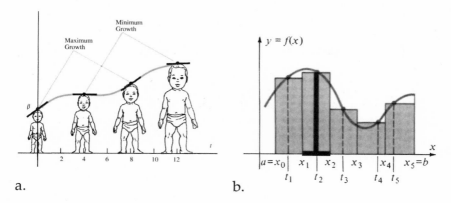

a.   b.

Figure 8.7
Illustrations from a calculus text. (*a*) Teaching students to see slant (derivative) as rate. (*b*) Integration is adding up widths times heights. A "T" is emphasized between x_1 and x_2.
Source: Figures from *Calculus* by Dennis Berkey, copyright © by Saunders College Publishing, reproduced by permission of the publisher.

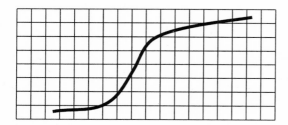

Figure 8.8
Laying a grid over a continuous line can allow precise reading off of two facets of the representation.

The students didn't seem to notice that this grid idea had transformed Jan's idea of showing speed via slant. They had returned to using vertical distance to show speed, but the image jointly produced by the students seemed to seize the floor, and it commanded attention in its own right. Although other representations were suggested, and although some students (gradually fewer and fewer) retained a preference for earlier representations, the students in the end voted nearly unanimously that what we would call "graphing speed versus time" was their best representation.

What is this inventing graphing activity about? Clearly, it is about bright children, but calling these students intelligent is another case of masking powerful, if unusual, knowledge. I believe they are actually more knowledgeable than abstractly bright. They know a lot intuitively about *representation,* the art of creating concrete, visual forms to express ideas. In the description above, I emphasized their inventive capabilities. They could see how lines, slants, and so on could represent things, and they could play effectively with putting multiple correspondences together. What I did not emphasize so much was their ability to critique representations. When any student proposed a new representation, others discussed both its advantages and disadvantages compared to other representations. We noticed at least a dozen different criteria for good representations, including:

- Transparency (The representation needs little explanation.)
- Compactness (All else being equal, representations that are smaller are better.)
- Precision (All else being equal, representations that allow more precise readout are better.)
- Completeness (You can get all the information you need from the representation.)
- Homogeneity (There are no extraneous symbols that don't relate to others.)
- Objectivity (It's better if making the representation can be automatic and strictly rule based, if it "could be done by a computer.")
- Faithfulness (For example, continuous representations show continuous speed changes better than discrete representations.)

The students made clear that they understood other aspects of the art of representation. They showed that they knew representations are for people. Alice, in particular, showed constant concern for whether a representation would be comprehensible to people outside this class. Jan, among others, showed particularly good ability to explain representations. He explained his slanted lines: "This [short line] has just the same slant as this [longer line], so they show the same speed. So we can use the length to show something else."

To put it in a nutshell, this activity shows that children have much more expertise with representations than most would give them credit for. I call this knowledge *metarepresentational* because it is *about* representation. (One standard use of *meta* is "about.") To this day, I am still a bit in awe of how much metarepresentational competence these students showed. It wasn't a fluke, however. As I mentioned before, we have watched children inventing graphing several times. We haven't always been able to count on the richness and energy of our first group, but every instance of this activity has shown substantial capabilities. I don't believe there is any question that metarepresentation names a pool of competence children have, a competence that has largely been ignored.

It's nice to find some surprising understanding in children that we didn't know about before, but what does this have to do with computational media? Indeed, this activity didn't involve computers at all. (Students did want to begin building representations on the computer, but we didn't really see at the time what this activity was about. We thought it was just about graphing, and Tina kept them from exploring computational versions, at least until after the main design was finished.)

To make my points, I need to build a bridge between metarepresentational knowledge and computational media. I'll make the bridge first on the basis of principle and then with examples.

You can probably guess the rough shape of the bridge. We have identified a native pool of intuitive resources that, it seems, children develop well and fairly early—without explicit instruction. These resources are the abilities to mold and interpret visual presentations as representations for conveying information, reasoning, and all the other purposes that inscriptions, representations, and, indeed, literacies serve. Computational media can provide a context in which these competencies can grow and transform into a qualitatively different capability. In terms I introduced in chapter 1, we want to see how computational media can *implement* a different material intelligence—a new representational intelligence—starting with representational talents people seem naturally to have.

One element of a new representational intelligence seems obvious. Computers give people unprecedented control over form and space. Words and the essentially one-dimensional run of text can give way to wonderful new structures for representing. Boxer's boxes within boxes and ports to connect distant parts of a world, like hypertext, provide a hint of what is possible. Yet at least two additional substantial stages are possible with computational media. First, representations can be dynamic as well as static. All of the power evolution has conveyed to humans to interpret change in a visual presentation can be harnessed in a way that shames what can be done with text and static pictures. I'll get to a fairly elaborate new example soon, but for now we can look back to chapter 2. The boring, inert arrows and numbers of textual vectors become dynamic on the computer screen. One can watch and interpret changing vectors and write simple programs that show the meaning of a vector in controlling motion. Indeed, this humble example also illustrates the second stage of transformation that computers allow beyond textual literacy: the dimension of interaction. Vectors succeeded with our children not only because they moved and connected with motion in illuminating ways, but because they became things that children *acted on*. From the point of view of representation, computers mean that action and reaction can enter the expressive mode. You can act on text (and standard pictures) only in the limited sense of writing it down (or drawing it), and what you thus create doesn't react at all.

This part of the story seems widely recognized, at least implicitly. Unfortunately, the larger literacy implications go unappreciated. The burgeoning representational landscape is easy to see in the educational design community, where an extraordinary number of representational forms are being developed by experts. New visual representations for important ideas, from fractions to force and beyond, are an everyday occurrence. A look at professional science alerts us to the fact that this is not just a modest innovation or one only for schools. The infrastructure of science is fundamentally changing because computationally implemented representations are blossoming like flowers after a spring rain. Graphs don't just sit there anymore. They wriggle and twist with adjustable parameters. Data are not just a long list of numbers anymore. Swarms of data points fly around in changing multidimensional "slices." Visual data analysis now virtually *means* using new techniques with computers to allow people better use of their spatial/dynamic interpretive capabilities.

The less recognized part of the story is from whom, when, and how new computational representations will emerge. Let's start with "from whom." Of course experts will make new dynamic and interactive representations, but a fundamental assumption of this book is that a mass literacy surpasses a literacy of the elite. Ordinary folks—including teachers and students—should be allowed to get in on the game. Otherwise, we'll have one of those half-a-loaf consumer literacies I discussed rather than a real two-way literacy. Can we expect ordinary folks not only to control a computational medium, but to create genuinely new representations? That's where inventing graphing surprises us. Yes, they can, and probably they do all the time, without our having noticed.

"When" people can make new representations provides as much ground for surprise as "who," I predict. As I have constantly reminded you, great people and great products attract our attention far more than the commonplace, but a true computational medium can give the law of the little its revenge. I believe that creating new representational forms can become an almost everyday event, not just an eccentric, if wonderful, aberration.

There is an important technical side of making representational invention commonplace. Way back in chapter 1, I noted that some media, some literacy substrates, can comfortably enclose subforms. Text neatly encloses algebra, for example. The computer is the protean master of this trick if we design computational systems well. Not only can independent representational forms coexist in computational media, but they can interact, evolve, and change, so an essential part of what can allow representational design to emerge as an everyday activity is that computational representations can be modified or cut apart or combined. Recall the image of organic growth of software at the end of chapter 7 (see figure 7.1). A producer computational medium is a *metamedium,* in which hundreds of microrepresentational forms can be created, combined, and extended constantly. Not every child will create a completely new representation everyday, but very often everyone can make easy extensions, combinations, and modifications; occasionally, really new things will appear. Representation will be a richly tooled, flexible, adaptive, and improvisatory activity far beyond what exists now with textual literacy.

I want to be clear on preconditions for this transformation to happen. First, we can't use just any old computer system to realize it. A consumer-only medium, for example, won't support it. Second, the range of the representational forms that are allowed will be highly constrained by the properties of the medium. If the world standardizes what is now called *multimedia* as its new literacy base, I fear new representational forms will be limited to successor variations of rock video. Naturally, I believe that vectors and hundreds of other such forms can enhance learning science and mathematics, but many current versions of computational media won't support analytic, science-relevant representation.

Finally, the emergence of representation as an explicit, valued activity—as any important component of literacy—will be a cultural accomplishment. A "literature" of representational forms must emerge, as well as an awareness of and commitment to their value. It is a plain and simple fact that technology by itself isn't enough.

I used the example of inventing graphing to argue that metarepresentation is a fundamental competence humans have. Then I argued abstractly that computational media can liberate and extend this intelligence in particular ways. Now I want to give some specific examples to put meat on these wonderful but bare bones.

Let me start with examples from some very new work. We have recently started looking specifically at student representational creativity in computational media. In particular, we taught a class of middle and high school students mainly about scientific visualization—making pictures of scientific data for visual analysis. Visualization is a part of professional scientific practice that has been radically changed by computational representations. One fairly simple but important technique is colorizing images to bring out particular detail or relations.

Instead of giving students closed scientific tools, we built some open tools in Boxer so that they could get their hands on the guts of the programs. In particular, we made it easy for them to design and construct the palettes of colors used to display images. Figure 8.9 shows an image taken from the Hubble telescope (top left), modified by one student with different palettes. The first thing Sam did was to change the color at the top of the scale, the color that showed the brightest parts of the image. In these pictures, all data that are above a certain brightness show with the color at the top of the scale. Any variation in brightness above this level just can't show in the representation; there are no more colors. In effect, Sam is showing what part of the picture has been completely washed out by the limits of the display system. He picked red for that

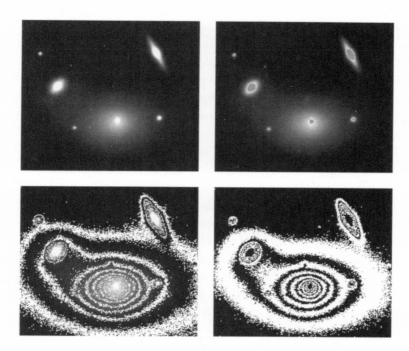

Figure 8.9
Images from the Hubble satellite telescope, modified by a student.

color, and you have to imagine the small, gray regions in the center of the bright spots (top-right image) standing out vividly. I have not seen the same idea in any professional system. Perhaps experts don't need a warning, but Sam's idea dramatically shows which parts of the picture have no detail.

The lower-left panel of figure 8.9 shows another of Sam's innovations. Again, we are limited to black-and-white printing in this book, so your imagination is important. In order to show shape and detail better, Sam built a palette that alternates a sequence of colors with a constant background color. (Successively brighter parts of the image "climb up" Sam's sequence of colors, touching base with a constant background color in between.) The result is something like a topographical map, in which contours show places of constant altitude. Here, the contours show constant brightness. The shapes of objects are much easier to see in this representation, as is how quickly light is getting brighter. (Rings that are closer together show that the image is getting brighter more quickly.) Sam's idea is better than standard contour maps in at least one respect. The color coding he put between contour lines (which were made of the constant "background color") shows brightness unambiguously. In contrast, if you use only black-and-white contour lines, you can't tell whether brightness is growing or waning; either direction results in more rings. The black-and-white contours of the last frame (lower right) can't distinguish between a "donut" nebula—which gets brighter, then darker toward its center—from a circular object that gets continuously brighter. The light gray tones near the center of the biggest galaxy in Sam's contour image (the lower-left image) make it unambiguously clear that the center of the galaxy is brighter than the surround.

What you can't see at all in these images is the spectacular impression made by the colors Sam chose. Sam was an artist, and he spent almost as much effort making things pretty as making them scientifically better. Think "committed learning," and you'll understand why his pursuing art as well as science didn't bother us at all.

One of Sam's colleagues, Mohammed, made use of the palette system for an even more personal purpose. He modified a computer game he had written so that the numerical score was not only shown but color coded. That way the game player could tell how far she had progressed without taking her eyes off the action. Besides being a nice representational idea, Mohammed's color coding the game's score both suggests the power of personalization and reminds us of the law of the little. Mohammed's creation may not be grand, but it is his. More, it suggests the thousands of little innovations awaiting students' creativity when any representational fragment that already exists in the medium can become part of their private constructions.

The final example of students' invented representations in computational media is not visually spectacular, but it is an intellectually spectacular and huge project by a high school student.

Ted got his first experience with Boxer in Henri's Boxer statistics course, which I mentioned in chapter 3. Ted, like Mickey, the young Boxer manual writer, was dedicated to helping others, and he continued working with Boxer after the course's end. He wanted to design and build

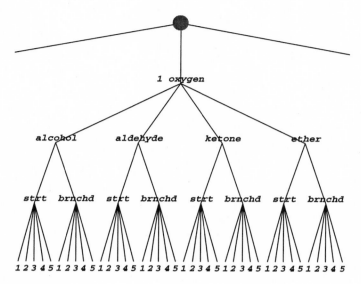

Figure 8.10
Part of a dynamic figure that illustrates an algorithm for naming molecules.

tools to help students and teachers approach particular subjects. One program he wrote, of which I'll show a tiny part, was called the *molecular toolkit,* and it provided resources for students and teachers to make interactive presentations about chemistry. Parts of the program could show pictures of molecules based on their formulas, compute such things as the weight of a molecule, and even name molecules by their formulas.

Figure 8.10 shows one-third of a representation Ted invented to show how the naming process worked. The representation is a decision tree that you work down, one branch at a time, by answering certain questions. At the top level, you need to count the number of oxygen atoms in the molecule. The portion of the tree in figure 8.10 corresponds to one oxygen molecule; zero and two oxygens are branches not shown to the left and right. At the second level, you have to decide whether the molecule is an alcohol, an aldehyde, a ketone, or an ether, and so on at lower levels. While Ted's program finds the name of a particular molecule, the ball at the top of figure 8.10 moves down the various arms of the tree, and text explains what is going on. When the ball gets to the bottom, the program spits out the scientific name of the molecule: Methane (CH_4), ethane (C_2H_6), methanol (CH_3OH), ethanol (C_2H_5OH), ethene (C_2H_4), 2-propanone (C_3H_6O, with the oxygen double bonded to the middle carbon), methylpropene. . . .

This is a wonderful dynamic representation of naming molecules. I have never seen any version of it (even a static one) in a textbook, and it almost certainly was Ted's invention. Even better, Ted clearly understood that his overall project was providing tools that others would extend and modify. As I mentioned, he explicitly considered this a toolkit to build presentations, not a "teaching program" on its own. I believe he intuitively understood the flexibility and organic growth of representations and microrepresentations in a computational medium about which I spoke earlier.

Ted's program is among the best-organized Boxer programs I have seen. His data structures are elegant. For example, he invented a new notation for organic molecules that is easy for humans both to understand and to produce, as well as computationally clean and efficient.

Figure 8.11 shows an example of Ted's Boxer code corresponding to the decision branch based on number of oxygens. The command **ifs**

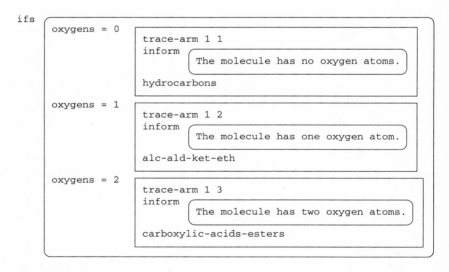

Figure 8.11
A part of Ted's program for naming molecules, displaying the algorithm for naming.

presents a number of "if" possibilities (`if oxygens = 0`, etc.) and what to do if those possibilities are realized. In each action branch, you can see the command to animate the decision tree by moving the ball down the appropriate branch (`trace-arm`), the textual information presented to the viewer (`inform`), and the next decision (e.g., `alc-ald-ket-eth` makes the decision about the second level of figure 8.10). A well-structured program is a representational achievement in its own right. Not only does such a program make it easy for others to inspect, understand, and modify the program itself, but it can even be a directly instructional representation. I am not sure that Ted's program is the best representation of the molecule-naming algorithm, but it is pretty good. It contains all the detail missing from the visual tree. On the other hand, the programs for the fractal shapes designed by the students in Henri's infinity class almost certainly *are* the best representations I know for conceiving and knowing how to build those shapes—provided, of course, you are programming literate.

The argument I am making has several parts. By this time, I hope you'll concede the first point—that the computer is the protean mother of meta-representational systems. It surpasses text and inert, noninteractive graphics as if they were baby steps and not the giant leaps of human material intelligence we know they have been.

The next point is that representations are a fundamental part of science. This part is still not at all the most difficult, although it is not a common story. Galileo invented pictorial, quantitative ways of thinking about motion that supported his investigations. Descartes invented analytic geometry and graphing. Newton and Leibniz invented the calculus and, simultaneously, ways of denoting their new ideas, ways that are conceptually suggestive and easy to manipulate and reason with. Richard Feynman invented Feynman diagrams to denote interactions of elementary particles. Lest the grand obscure the everyday, I note (again) that even grand representational accomplishments really happened gradually, in little bits and pieces, over years of use by the scientific community. Furthermore, scientists are constantly adapting and inventing, in dribs and drabs, ways of making ideas clear to others and ways to help themselves think.

Next generation students will have a bewildering array of new representational forms to master if they are to learn the science scientists are now beginning to practice. Luckily, from inventing graphing and similar experiences, we can have more confidence that students are up to the job, but here's the really difficult part of the argument that I am making: I believe we need to see putting computers and students together as liberating students' own creativity at designing representational forms, just as it has done for scientists.

The role of representational creativity in learning is just now beginning to be demonstrated scientifically. Examples can't prove the case, but look at Ted's remarkable accomplishment. He invented two marvelous new representations of the process of naming molecules. His dynamic decision tree is impressive enough, but the program that actually carries out the naming is a showstopper. Could we imagine his doing such a thing without understanding every nook and cranny of the process of naming molecules? Technical reexpression of ideas, like what Ted did, tests and improves understanding at each step in the process of construction. Success indicates a mastery that surpasses anything an ordinary school test could hope to show. (Also—although I'm getting ahead of myself—constructing representations like this is a personal accomplishment that puts typical school tests to shame in the personal value it can have for a student.)

Ted's case is too extraordinary to be convincing about the everyday future. That's the trouble with a short text in which an author is limited to a few examples—they had better be dramatic (hence, unconvincing as examples of things that will become ordinary). Sam and Mohammed's little representational achievements help, but they may also be unconvincing: it is relatively easy to imagine students doing those things, but is profound new learning at issue?

Let me sketch a pattern that may be easier to see than these examples as a new and important wrinkle in science education. Essays have been a staple of literary instruction for as long as there has been organized instruction. What happens when a student writes an essay? She needs to think hard about the subject, formulate a personal position, and systematically lay out an argument for that position. As an extra bonus, the teacher gets a great deal of insight into how the student is thinking, which would be impossible in a short test or conversation.

Essays are not nearly so popular in science or mathematics, probably because natural language is not sufficiently tuned toward the particular nuances of meaning that are important for science. Equations? They are better in some ways, perhaps, but hopelessly sparse and too impersonal to be really expressive of a student's way of understanding scientific ideas. But what about a *computational essay*? A computational essay can use text to describe and hypertext to organize. It can have diagrams, even moving diagrams, like Ted's decision tree. It can have little programs for the reader to play with, like the ones the students in Henri's infinity class created. Indeed, their final projects were nice examples of a budding genre of computational essay. A computational essay can have dynamic models. It can also include any sort of tool or computational subsystem the teacher or curriculum developer might supply to help students think and work in a particular area, modified appropriately by the student for her expressive purposes. A nice subgenre is the computational essay expressing the results of a scientific investigation, which is particularly useful to hand to other students so that they can examine the data that might be enclosed, using their own tools or models. Other students can also "borrow" tools or microrepresentations invented by their colleagues. Another subgenre already in use, at least among some researchers, is a computational essay that a student writes in order to teach another student about some subject matter. Above all else, a computational essay invites and empowers students to innovate representationally to help themselves think and to express their ideas about scientific and mathematical subjects.

We have had limited experience with computational essays as a way of learning. Sadly, exploring all the promising possibilities of computational media at once is just not feasible, especially with limited resources, but what has become fairly systematic in our work is to make each exploratory microworld also a place where students can easily collect and annotate their work to explain it to others.

One of the most exciting types of computational essays, which I call a *knowledge space,* we have only barely begun to investigate. A knowledge space explores the organization and relationships of the many parts of understanding any particular scientific topic. It's best to think of constructing a knowledge space as a culminating activity in which students or a whole class working together use a spatial metaphor to organize and show relationships they feel are critical. Of course, if they are really learning, students may already have developed intuitive mental maps of the connections between the various aspects of what they learn about photosynthesis or organic molecules or Newton's laws, but identifying the core ideas, finding an explicit and systematic external form in which to relate them to each other, linking in more peripheral ideas—pushing toward a completeness in showing and connecting things, which text or intuitive thinking cannot reach—are the distinctive activities of making a knowledge space.

An Activities Perspective on Metarepresentation

I organized my description of the inventing graphing activity as a sequence of representational ideas, which is a beautiful way to tell the story because it highlights the emergence of recognizably powerful, important knowledge out of previously unrecognized human competence. That is a central theme of this chapter. There are, however, always other ways to tell a story. In this case, my research group did not even know there would be a good knowledge story in inventing graphing when we started. It was just, after all, a curricular lark. Instead, we stood at attention and turned on the video cameras for an entirely different reason.

In simplest terms, what attracted us first to collect video data about this event was the remarkable enthusiasm and interest it engendered in the students. From the beginning, we could see that something special was going on. To put it in a different way, we could smell a good example of committed learning coming. In a larger framework, the ideas story of inventing graphing misses the critical activities perspective that we developed in chapters 4 and 5 to complement a knowledge perspective on learning. I want to redress this omission, at least briefly. I'll use inventing graphing exclusively, even though, as I hinted, the other student representational examples have interesting activity stories about them as well.

Let me start with a few vignettes and descriptions to give a sense of how we perceived the inventing graphing episode and, more importantly, how it must have felt for the participants.

Enthusiasm
The enthusiasm the students brought to this activity was extraordinary, almost from beginning to end. They were champing at the bit to get in and explain their ideas. Commitment and passion ran high. The class-

room was often bustling to the point of chaos. Many times Tina couldn't even get into the conversation, and she would repeatedly try, wait graciously if rebuffed until the students quieted down, then step in to make her points and to help direct the inquiry. One of Tina's special strengths was cultivating the personal investment of students, and she systematically tried to create situations in which she was irrelevant to the activity. At this stage of scientific study, I think clever teachers like Tina know much more about activities and how to cultivate group committed learning than researchers do.

Participation

This was not a class of super students, even if they were bright. They all had different inclinations and styles. At least two of the students were very quiet, and a couple seemed to want to dominate every activity. One unusual thing about inventing graphing was that it elicited much more even participation than other activities. Even the quietest student made critical contributions, and at various times all wanted to have the attention of the class. One of the quieter girls in the class took on the responsibility of sticking up for the poor "average person" who might walk into the classroom and find a jumble of uninterpretable squiggles on the board. How would a visitor, she kept asking, make any sense of these representations? She had the passion of a political activist defending the rights of the downtrodden.

Ownership

The "dance of ownership," as we came to call it, was amazing during inventing graphing. Students were proud of their accomplishments. Sue added a copyright notice to many of her drawings. I recall her walking past the camera at the end of one class and deliberately asking the video viewer, "Isn't my drawing nice?"

Ownership was also communal, however. Students borrowed others' ideas freely, usually with acknowledgment. Here's where the dance metaphor comes in—the ebb and flow of students' leading, following, building on each other's contributions. They could see something developing that was too big for any one of them to take credit for alone. The teacher was dancing, too. In pointing out Tina's attention to student ownership, I don't want to imply she did not want to be part of the conversation. She had ideas she wanted to share, her own ideas about "good representations," and several times I was stunned at how direct and imperious her criticisms of student ideas were, but students took the criticism with remarkable confidence. They seemed to acknowledge good points when Tina made them, and they certainly knew she could make them stick if she wanted to, but they often conveyed the sense that they were not convinced and that their conviction mattered. In retrospect, I feel Tina's skill was not either in being direct or in withdrawing, but in knowing when to act in which of these ways.

Taking It Home

We saw many signs that this activity carried on outside of class. The most vivid for me was Jan's "awesome idea," adapting slants to do "everything at once." His awesome idea came right at the beginning of class. He had to have come to class with the idea because it didn't follow any context set by the discussion to that point. Classroom barrier breaking is a fingerprint of committed learning.

Momentum

Probably the most fundamental question about any activity is whether it can continue on its own energy. Inventing graphing had plenty of such energy, but any extended activity is patterned with waves of greater and lesser intensity. The teacher's role is particularly important in the waning periods. We could almost see Tina selecting and introducing a new hill to aim toward for the class's activity roller coaster, a hill that would suit their current skills and current attention, but also one that would stress their current understanding and thus develop the ability to climb new representational hills: "Can you do this with your representation?" "Would you want to do that?" "Let's just spend some time practicing this or that representation."

An emblem of the success of this entire activity came when Tina decided it was time to quit and go on to other things. She summarized what they had accomplished and why it was important, and then she began to explain what the class would be doing next. A student raised his hand as if to ask for clarification, and Tina turned to him, but he started again asking about how they could pursue the last issue that had come up in inventing graphing! The whole class laughed at the non sequitur and the fact that Tina evidently was not succeeding in shutting down the discussion. As the bell rang, the class dispersed, and as they left, a small group discussed among themselves whether they could get a good answer to their question from NASA scientists.

Childlike

It is critically important that a good activity be continuous with the lives of the participants. Knowledge is important, of course, and in this case, inventing graphing couldn't have happened without the untutored meta-representational expertise of these students, but, just as important, this activity picked up and extended patterns of engagement. One fundamental thread was how the students attended sincerely to the contributions of their peers. School is ordinarily not like this. "Right and wrong" is always the point, and the teacher is the knighted arbiter. The teacher is even obliged to take up this role, or students will complain she is not teaching. Tina worked very hard in making students' ideas the focus for discussion. She talked to us about how difficult it was to turn students' attention away from the teacher and away from "right answers," especially in a school where teacher-centered instruction was the norm, but she succeeded in making student ideas the center of the discussion with this set of children, admitting occasional lapses.

I want to emphasize continuity by explicitly acknowledging the components of inventing graphing that were not adultlike and scientific. The participants in the activity were sixth-grade students, after all. There was plenty of teasing, complaining, and general off-task dallying. As a miniature example, when some enthusiastic exchanges broke out, one student egged his peers on with, "Let's yell at each other and stuff!" Stories about children and learning that paint them purely as little scientists leave me cold. Those stories are at best well-intentioned lies or proof that, whatever is happening, committed learning doesn't live at that address.

Final point: Inventing graphing illustrates one of the general ideas I introduced in chapter 5. An enrichment frame turns knowledge into an activity structure. Inventing graphing illustrates one of the simplest and most often successful enrichment frames: instead of showing students something, have them design it. They will surely learn more about how the thing they design serves its purpose—the function of the intended structure—and they will also learn a lot about alternatives that may be desirable in particular situations.

This painfully simple idea, "have them design it," has been a constant theme in our work. Student invention works far better with a computational medium and in tool-rich culture than with other media in other contexts. I'm sorely tempted to tell you another story about how a group of our high school students designed Newton's laws! Couldn't happen? Don't be so sure.

Did these sixth-grade students learn more about graphing than other students who might have gotten a four-day lecture and seat exercises? Perhaps. Perhaps not. But they certainly explored the space of representational possibilities more thoroughly. More directly to the activity point, they had a rollicking good time being creative around important scientific ideas.

Dynamic Representations: Intuitive Knowledge in Action

Metarepresentational competence is a lovely example of important intuitive knowledge on which computational media can build, but some readers may find it a bit too rich to wrap their heads around—like having both apple pie and cheesecake for dessert. The following example is not nearly so outer space exotic, but it makes a similar point about the adequacy of a medium for engaging natural human competence and about implementing new intelligence.

This example concerns the capacity people have for giving meaning to dynamic presentations. This is only a tiny part of what computational media can add to textual media, yet it happens to be particularly important because of how good people are at understanding moving things.

Imagine we have control of a magical railroad flatcar. It isn't *so* magical; it's just that, instead of being stuck on a one-dimensional track, it can move around in any way that we command it (except up in the air—it can't levitate). Imagine also that there is a little robot on top of the flatcar. You might think about this robot as a programmable "turtle" that you can command to move around in whatever way you want. (No

Figure 8.12
The path of a turtle moving in a circle but also being moved along in a straight line.

levitating turtles, either.) Suppose we ask the turtle to move continuously around in a circle on top of the flatcar. That's simple enough. But what if the flatcar is moving too? To start simply, let's say the flatcar is moving smoothly along in a straight line. Let's say it's going to Chicago. Now, if you were to watch the turtle from an unmoving perch, above, it would still be moving in circles, but also going along with the flatcar to Chicago at the same time. Figure 8.12 shows what you would see for the path of the turtle.

Physicists and mathematicians would call this a problem of composing motions. *Composing,* in this case, simply means putting together. The loopy path in figure 8.12 is the result of composing a circular motion with a straight line motion. Composing motions is usually introduced in high school or early in college after all sorts of mathematical preparation. I won't tire you with the details, but understanding the topic mathematically entails a number of things—for example, that the velocity of the turtle at any particular moment is the vector sum of the velocity of the flatcar plus the velocity of the turtle in its circular motion, ignoring the flatcar. How far can children come in understanding composing motions without the usual formal preparation?

I will tell this story in miniature by showing what one pair of sixth-grade students did with one fairly advanced problem. This pair of students was in a laboratory study before our full-fledged course. Let me show you just a little of what the students did before they got to the problem I want to present in some detail.

Figure 8.13a schematically represents the case where the flatcar is moving from left to right, and the turtle is also moving from left to right on top of the flatcar, at the same speed. Intuitively, this is a very simple case. Any number of p-prims can get the right prediction for the motion of the

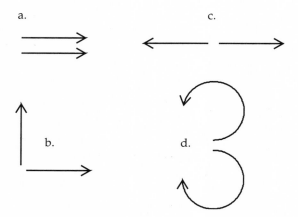

Figure 8.13
Four pairs of motions.

turtle as viewed from a fixed viewpoint. For example, you can see both motions as influences on the turtle's global motion and, in this case, they clearly "reinforce" each other. The net result should therefore be a "stronger" motion of the same sort; that is, the result should be faster motion to the right. A mathematical description of this case is colinear (in the same direction) vector addition. Children almost always guess the right magnitude, that the turtle's net motion is twice its own or the flat-car's motion.

Figure 8.13b represents a case that is still fairly easy. Here, the flatcar is moving toward the right, but the turtle is crawling in a perpendicular direction, across the flatcar (up, in figure 8.13b). Surprisingly, most children in upper elementary school also have a good sense of this case. They see the need for some kind of "compromise." The obvious compromise is a direction at 45 degrees, between the motions of the turtle itself and the flatcar. Even better, children can almost always extend this insight to the case where either the turtle or the flatcar is moving faster than the other. They guess correctly a compromise, but one oriented more toward the stronger motion. The cases of figure 8.13b with equal and unequal motion are excellent qualitative versions of vector addition in the "orthogonal" (perpendicular) case. When children do have trouble with perpendicular motions, they usually guess, for example, that the net motion will alternate small motions to the right with small motions in the perpendicular direction. Actually, alternating small motions in one direction and another is a beautiful way to think about composing motion in general, but you need to think about these little motions as being really tiny. Calculus allows you to think of them as being infinitesimally small.

The last preliminary case is where the motions are opposite, as depicted in figure 8.13c. Here the correct p-prim is *canceling*. Canceling happens to be a very compelling idea, and it usually takes little or no time for students to guess that there may be canceling in this case. Students always see canceling in retrospect, if they don't guess it. Concretizing canceling with a little mental model is helpful. Imagine walking down the up escalator at exactly the same rate as the escalator is moving up. The escalator takes you up one step length, and you take a step down. The net result is that you just don't move. Children can usually generalize this situation to the case where one motion is faster than the other: "The stronger wins."

Carol and Ming had worked through the motions described above and a few others besides using a little microworld that I had written in Boxer. The microworld allowed students to look at each of the motions individually, then I asked them to guess what would happen when we had both motions at once. Taking time to think through why whatever happens actually does happen is important, especially in cases where it is unexpected, but taking time to consider "why" is important even in the case where students first guess correctly. The microworld also has facilities to help students reflect. For example, they can slow the motions down or run them one little step at a time, or they can show the paths of each part of the motion and the path of the net motion. Seeing the path of the turtle being generated, as if it were dragging a paintbrush along as it moves on the flatcar, is especially illuminating. For the perpendicular motions, the turtle's path will be an increasingly long vertical line ("vertical" means across the flatcar) that moves with the flatcar to the right. Don't I wish you were reading this book in a computational medium so you could see the simplifying visual effect!

Now, here is the piece de resistance of child expertise. I call the motion *movie reels,* as depicted in figure 8.13d. The flatcar is moving in a circle in a clockwise direction, starting its motion toward the right. The turtle is moving similarly, but in a counterclockwise direction. Carol and Ming looked at the individual motions. Ming provided the first solution move. Wouldn't the motions cancel? After all, they are opposite, just like moving in opposite straight-line motions. Ming was casually moving his hands around in circles side by side in opposite directions.

Carol started to agree, but then she began looking at her index fingers, which she was moving more and more carefully out in front of her, each simulating one of the two movie reel motions. She noticed that the two motions start out in the same direction. "Hold it!" She described how the flatcar and robot both start moving toward the right. Then she gestured and continued, "So it's actually going to make a . . . 'cause . . . It's going to make a line!" Carol is correct. The two circles combine into a motion where the turtle simply moves back and forth in a horizontal line.

Carol made several superb moves all at the same time in leaping to the line solution. First, she followed Ming's move of considering the motions as going together abstractly, rather than trying literally to simulate the flatcar carrying the turtle. That is, she just looked at the two motions and tried to combine them. That you can do this is not at all obvious. The flatcar is carrying the turtle, not the other way around. Carol was looking at this situation as if it didn't matter who was carrying whom. Actually, this is a theorem. You can reverse the motions of the flatcar and the turtle, and you get exactly the same net result. Ming and Carol seemed to have guessed this theorem, possibly based on experience, or maybe they accidentally fell into using it implicitly. If I had asked them, though, I'm sure they could not have articulated and certainly could not have proved this theorem. In any case, Ming and Carol had a wonderful simplification that will never fail, and it will help them solve many complicated motion composition problems.

Carol did something else clever. She started looking at motion locally—that is, in short intervals of time—rather than the global consideration of opposite circles as canceling, which Ming demonstrated in his casual gesturing of opposite circles. Carol started focusing on the velocity at a particular time, at the beginning of the circular motions. She saw one of the main points of calculus, as I described in chapter 1—that whenever motion isn't uniform, you always need to say *when* in order to say anything about speed or direction. Looking at the beginning of the movie reels motion, she saw a case just like the one given in figure 8.13a, both motions going the same direction.

The final stroke of genius in Carol's analysis is that she saw canceling *in addition to* reinforcing. As became clear in asking her to explain her reasoning to Ming, Carol saw that, in the vertical dimension (again, vertical as the motions are portrayed on this page and on the computer screen), the reverse circle motions are actually mirror images. The turtle moves from the center to the top, while the flatcar moves from the center to the bottom, and so on in synchrony. Thus, in net, the circles add their motions in the horizontal direction, and their motions cancel in the vertical direction, leaving a simple back-and-forth motion in a straight line. Note that canceling does fit in this situation after all, although subtly.

What are the lessons of this example? First, some nonlessons. Ming and Carol are not "the average case." The movie reels problem is quite difficult, and not all elementary school students can master it, at least not as quickly and elegantly as these two, so I do not mean to imply that all learning can be as quick and faultless as in this example. On the other hand—and this *is* a lesson—all students with whom we have come in contact have strong intuitive resources of the same sort as Ming and Carol. That is, they can reason well about motions. Competence with motions is actually not surprising at all if you think that humans must have evolved with strong dynamic spatial visualization skills in order throw rocks and spears effectively, to block or catch moving objects, to navigate while running, and so on. Every student who used this microworld could master all of the ways of thinking about motion I talked about in preparation for the moving reels motion: canceling, reinforcing, compromise. They could even think about motions separately in vertical and horizontal components, and they could pick instants to focus on rather than using a global gestalt of motion. All of this is within the reach of essentially every late elementary school student.

On the basis of strong intuitive dynamic visual reasoning, we see where computational media can pick up from text and other static media to take us forward. This little microworld, which I programmed in about a day, turns out to be plenty of help for students to learn quite a lot. There is no magic. Just find a good source of (intuitive) knowledge, provide it some computationally enhanced experience, a few ideas and time to reflect, and quite a lot of learning happens. When it comes to learning about motion, a fine regime of competence exists, and teaching may capitalize on it.

Allow me to lay out some absolutely typical patterns of learning on the basis of intuitive knowledge. First, students don't always guess correctly. Intuitive knowledge is not reliable in the way that more systematic knowledge can be, but, critically, there is almost always a more adequate intuitive conceptualization available if the first guess fails. Students who don't see canceling or compromise at first come quickly to feel these ways of thinking are sensible after seeing what actually happens and reflecting on it. Seeing sense after the fact is just like what happened with my intuitive electronics knowledge when I got into physics class. I didn't know what was taught there, but I could think about it and integrate my intuitive knowledge appropriately.

Note how easily one could paint a negative picture of children. Without applying a little care and patience, without looking to see what resources students have available, and without giving them a situation that evokes those resources, you could find that young students don't know much about composing motions. In particular, I can guarantee that many students will think movie reels cancel the first time they see them, but you now know what we learned from students such as Carol and Ming: canceling just needs a little encouragement and help fitting into this situation. Then canceling becomes not a mistake, but part of a correct and powerful conceptualization. I don't think I can overemphasize that intuitive knowledge is not perfect, but it provides resources that designers and teachers need to know about and use.

A more subtle pattern of use of intuitive knowledge is in Ming and Carol's implicit use of the theorem that the motions of the turtle and flatcar are interchangeable with the same result. This guess happens to be brilliant because it works. On other occasions, kids will make brilliant guesses that don't work. The trick for us as educators is to collect those brilliant guesses—right or wrong—and find how we can use them productively. Even in the case where the brilliant guess has been elicited in an environment where it works, there is more learning to do. Ming and Carol couldn't articulate or justify the interchangeability theorem, so even they have an important opportunity to extend and refine what they stumbled across. The first step is to realize that the theorem might not be true. Knowledge often arises from the recognition of ignorance. This is a nice example where the more you "know" (like Carol and Ming apparently did in guessing the interchangeability theorem), the more you are in a position to learn. Recall what learning in the regime of competence means.

Another typical pattern of intuitive learning is that children initially conceptualize reinforcing, compromise, and canceling separately. They're just different phenomena. From a mathematical point of view, they are all examples of vector addition. Thus, eventually students will unify many disparate understandings under the banner of a single scientific idea. Recall the way algebra unified Galileo's six fundamental theorems about motion. I didn't show Ming and Carol getting to that level of understanding. Indeed, they did not get there; they were just subjects in a laboratory study, not students in our motion class, so it would constitute a goal for their extended learning about motion. Nonetheless, they had to learn a lot even to get to the stage they reached. Intuitive knowledge is more the basis for advancement than it is a given fact of life. Intuitive knowledge is dynamic and generative. Looking forward, what Ming and Carol did learn here will not be replaced or redone by "formal understanding." Instead, what they learned will make "formal learning" seem sensible and easy.

A final episode with Carol and Ming serves to emphasize the critical link between this particular child expertise and computational media. One of the puzzles I put to them was where the turtle goes uniformly in a straight line, but the flatcar "falls" downward. From the tick model in chapter 2, you might recall, falling is just going downward a little more each tick. (In other words, speed just increases in the simplest possible way as time marches on.) These students had an excellent science teacher at school. He had taught them about falling. When one of them asked me whether the "falling" of the flatcar was actually like gravity, like real falling, I put the question back to them. After a moment's thought, they said no. Their teacher had taught them that falling "goes like squares." (I am pretty sure what he taught them is that falling is measured by acceleration, thirty-two feet per second *squared*.) Carol was pretty sure (and correct) that the falling she saw on the screen was "just going one more each time," rather than 1, 4, 9, 16, ... How poignant that an excellent teacher with wonderful students but with the wrong medium had failed to convey a powerful, simple, and intuitively apprehensible (with the right medium!) idea. Falling is precisely "going one more each time," the pattern Carol saw easily in the microworld's falling motion. Their teacher probably never showed them a fall in slow motion, certainly never with replay and analytic facilities built into their experience, as with the composing motions microworld, and absolutely never showed them the tick model.

Prodigious Products

This final example is meant to complement the two given above. Instead of knowledge, I emphasize here some things that relate to technical aspects of a medium. In particular, I bring back issues concerning making things with computational media. These issues are in the family of modifiability, extendibility, adaptability, organic growth, cumulativity, long lines of evolutionary development for software, alternate production niches for software, communities of tool builders and sharers, and so on. In addition, I discuss some activity-relevant issues.

The main focus of attention is the product of two energetic young men in our sixth-grade motion course. This product was part of an independent project on which they worked toward the end of the course. They had many ideas and much competence on which to draw. Nonetheless, the project struck me as remarkable.

Sean and Bob had produced a huge system—a graphing adventure game. The story line, which the students had written into the introduction, starts with the fact that you are a friend of a movie star named Michael. Michael is doing commercials for the 9.3167289 Lives cat food company, and someone has written a "swear word" into the cue cards. Now, Michael is running for his life from the evil corporate bosses, and he asks you to help him. The game progresses through a long series of adventures, where at each stage a motion is described that can extricate Michael from a particular fix. You have to choose a graph that corresponded to the life-saving motion. If you do not select correctly, you and Michael die a horrible death, and the sequence of adventures starts all over again.

Here's a sample problematic situation—in fact, the very first challenge in the game. You are driving with Michael out of the parking lot and

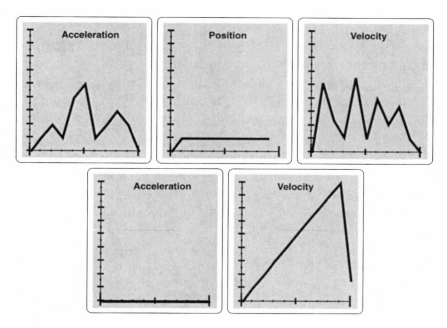

Figure 8.14
Graphs from the graphing adventure game.

need to speed past the guard post. Figure 8.14 shows your choices. The bottom row, left, is correct. It shows 0 acceleration, which is equivalent to moving at constant speed. If you choose top left, you get:

Are you sure you didn't
drink too much coffee?
Your foot is tap dancing   *long pause*   KABOOM!!
on the pedal! You swerve
into the guard post, and . . .

Notice that this text gives the player informative feedback about the selected graph. In fact, making this game educational, thus acceptable as a class project, involved a long series of negotiations with their teacher. The "educational" feedback in the text, a minor perturbation of utter sixth-grade boyishness, was one result of the negotiation. Another result was an (unfinished) tutorial about how to think about graphs, meant for players who had difficulty.

If you choose the lower-right graph in figure 8.14, you get:

| You speed through the gate, but you slow down, and get your head blown off by a surface-to-air-head missile!! | *long pause* | Die!! |

Or the top right:

| Michael gets nervous and fights for the control of the car! You crash! | *long pause* | KABLAM!! |

Later in the game, you are performing fancy motions such as accelerating while going backwards in time. You are "rewarded" with, for example:

| You speed toward the sun, but you don't slow down fast enough and are turned to . . . | *long pause* | cosmic sloppy joes SIZZLE.............. ....POP SPLAT |

In the midst of the game comes a substantial change of pace. Having gotten away, into outer space, you are attacked by space aliens and get a chance at a shoot-em-up-style video game. Even that game has four levels of difficulty.

These were the early days of working with Boxer, and I had only my prior experience with other computational systems to compare. All of the students in this class produced wonderful projects, but this one stood out for its technical accomplishments. Compared to my previous experience, it was almost unbelievable. How did they do it? In particular, how did they manage to store and reproduce all those graphs? And how had they managed the embedded video game, especially given the hurried end-of-year schedule?

I began to play detective. I knew these two students well enough to know that they were not geniuses in disguise, but the project was inescapably complex. It was larger then my own average Boxer project. I counted boxes. There were nearly five hundred in the full game and much more than one hundred in the space invaders subgame alone.

I began to inspect their code. It didn't take long to find an important clue. Right in the middle of their program boxes, I found a box that was evidently documentation for a graphing tool! It was fairly well written, hence clearly not a sixth grade construction, so part of the program had been "stolen." Later I confirmed with a graduate student that he had brought a partially constructed graphing tool into the class in order to help Sean and Bob with their project. Adaptability and combinability of the medium had helped them. A prior line of development, by others, entered into this project and became part of it.

Let's not jump too quickly past this point. It is absolutely not a trivial point that students could—and should—appropriate some previously written software seamlessly into their own product. First, they had to understand this other software much more deeply than just to be able to use it. They had to understand its "insides" enough to control it with their own code because, for example, they used none of the user interface to the prior graphing tool. Boxer's structure, pokability, and inspectability contributed here. As I have emphasized, one can count on the fact that no previously written tool ever does exactly what you want. In this case, the tool was designed to show one graph, but Bob and Sean needed to show five at once. In addition, the graphing tool was intended to be used mainly in cases where a process is producing values that will be graphed in real time. They had to make appropriate and pretty substantial changes.

When I looked to see what changes they had actually made, I was in for a surprise. They actually took very little code from the original grapher. Instead, they took *ideas*. In particular, they took the idea of representing graphs as a list of numbers, and they took the basic configuration of graphics box, sprites, and code to control them as a framework for drawing graphs. They also used the basic outline of the grapher in terms of how and when to draw the background pair of axes and labels. Most of the rest of the code was completely new, however, even if they could have reused the old grapher code. In particular, in order to "unpack" the lists of point values that they had used to store graphs, they used an inefficient collection of variables, one for each point. The code to draw the graphs themselves was an inelegant, unstructured, repetitious poster child for bad programming style, but it did exactly what they wanted, and it was their creation. What the project lacked in elegance, it excelled in showing organic growth; the grapher was not just pasted into their project, but modified and mutated in ways that matched the needs, interests, and capabilities of the current owners of the line of development.

Taking ideas instead of code is a wonderful advertisement for what a computational medium stands for. It is not simply having a computer with a lot of stuff on it, even stuff that you can reuse. Reusing is fine, but finding and *using ideas* is a much more general accomplishment. It's teaching fishing instead of handing out fish. The fact that the medium expressed ideas for how to do things well enough that sixth-grade students could take the idea, not just the code, goes well beyond my experience with prior media and presents a very hopeful sign. Surely, with a full learning culture (rather than merely the first Boxerized elementary school classroom) to create things and also powerful ideas that can fit this new medium, the scale of these students' accomplishment could be met by many if not most children.

Let me elaborate just a bit on what is happening here. One of the persistent difficulties that I and others had in trying to bootstrap computationally literate cultures was that individual constructions almost always remained individual, so, for example, what one person did in a class almost never propagated to other students. Failure to propagate happened in many, many ways. In groups of students who worked together on a project, one student almost always took over the programming, and the other students became marginal participants who frequently couldn't even effectively use the programming work created by the "group." I had certainly noticed and worried about this phenomenon, but I took it to be a cultural issue. Kids this age just don't collaborate very well, I said to myself, or the technically competent students are being isolationist, which matches our stereotypes of "nerdy" programmers.

Henri had noticed a similar phenomenon in his work. He had long been interested in the idea of computational tools for learning, but his experience was that students merely used the tools, they never took them apart, combined, extended, or modified them, even in simple ways.

Starting to use Boxer was almost like flipping a switch. All of a sudden, collaboration among students improved. It became instantly very rare that one student took over the programming in a collaborative group. To be more precise, it continued to be true that individual students often fell into the role of chief programmer, but this no longer marginalized the other students. Instead, it became the norm that all could operate a group software project. More impressive, we have videotaped exit interviews of students who seemed peripheral in the production of some software, but they turned out completely fluent with its use. They could explain how the program worked and even debug and change the program on the fly. Another surprising occurrence was that during extended group projects, when the "chief programmer" was missing, someone else almost always just sat down to fill in. We still had chief programmers, but with Boxer that role was more a convenience or an efficiency issue, not a necessity. Notice the subtlety of the change from pre- to postcomputational medium. The social phenomenon of chief programmer persisted, but its characteristics changed radically. In particular, having a chief programmer became benign and not a danger to group ownership or group learning. We learned (if we needed the lesson) that technology can have critical effects in areas that we might think are autonomously social or cultural.

Why this effect? How does Boxer facilitate collaboration? I've talked about adaptability and extendibility, but how do *they* work? I believe the core issue is visual expressiveness. The computer screen simply says much more and more effectively with Boxer than it has with Boxer's precursors. The principle of spatial metaphor has a significant role. Space is much more extensively used in Boxer to express meaning than in previous systems, which manifests itself with individuals, but also with groups. In fact, it is very nearly the same phenomenon with individuals and groups. Ted and others who managed complex systems on their own did so because they could effectively collaborate *with themselves*. That is, they could understand and extend what they had done previously in order to continue much farther than they could with a more primitive medium. In groups, this phenomenology becomes evident and explicit. Students are constantly looking at various parts of a complex system, pointing and explaining as well as poking and watching. Much more happens on the screen, and it happens via a richer, more expressive communication channel.

There are other reasons for the better collaboration effect, as well. One worth mentioning here also follows from a principle I mentioned in chapter 7: the principle of computational structuring. Compared to other systems, Boxer shows its basic structures more in the surface of applications written in it. Almost everyone uses data boxes, the ability to execute commands by clicking on them, and other similar resources in the "user interface" to their applications. It's a matter of ease and convenience. Computational structures serve interface purposes, so why construct interface structures that hide the computational structure? The advantage of using everyday Boxer as the interface to programs comes down to learning. Just by using things made in Boxer, our students keep learning about Boxer, so they naturally come to be able to understand, use, and even build and modify programs better. You can think of this process as an instance of the principle of menial utility. Just as well, we can return to the roller-coaster metaphor. In this case, almost any hill whatsoever bootstraps more competence with the medium.

I want to turn toward activity aspects of Sean and Bob's creation, although this will bring us quickly back to technical issues. I troubled to reproduce some of the text from the game in order to emphasize the personal meaning the project had for these students. If you can't imagine two preteen boys cackling and congratulating each other on coming up with an even more gruesome method of dying, I believe you have missed a not uncommon if also not terribly laudable component of young boy culture. Surely "designing death" was a significant part of establishing this project as valued and natural within their existing activity fabric. (I hate to admit it, but I kind of like the cosmic sloppy Joes idea.) What they did was also squarely within their regime of competence. You can imagine how much more teacher pleasing the project would have been without this "wasteful and off-topic" component of the activity. Imagine how much more useful the project would have been as a learning experience had they used all the time they spent inventing disgusting ways to die in order to think more carefully about how to teach graphing or to include more advanced topics, and so on. That is not a choice we have, however. We can accept continuity in the fabric of activity, we can accept off-task but personally meaningful components, or we can settle for no such project at all. Outside the regime of competence, outside a continuity in the fabric of activity, there would have been no commitment to this project.

Don't mistake this analysis for "let boys be boys" or "let children be children." Like knowledge, we should have goals and expect progress along the dimension of activity, but you cannot jump too far ahead. Their teacher, Tina, pushed and nudged this project toward educational ends, but not so hard that she destroyed it as an enthusiastic personal experience for Sean and Bob. Someday they may have enthusiastic personal experiences that mainly rather than peripherally build learning materials for others. However, that is not where they are in this snapshot. The lesson is that we negotiate, probe, try to understand, and foster possible lines of development. We don't abandon either educational goals or the essence of children.

The space invaders subgame is a relevant case in point. Sean had started this game much earlier in the year as part of another project, but Tina had thrown it out of class. Sean, at that point, could not articulate any connection at all between the game and what he was supposed to be learning in this class, so Tina requested he change topics. Typically, Sean did not abandon his space invaders game. Instead, he was one of the students in the class who requested extra time working on Boxer after school, when he finished his game as a stand-alone system. Sean managed to sneak the game back into classwork in the context of an overtly educational game—graphing adventure. I don't know what negotiation or subterfuge led to that, but it seems to me completely plausible to argue that, as motivation, space invaders served a very useful part of the graphing adventure game—even if there was no direct conceptual connection. The suppression and reentry of space invaders into the motion class represent for me the persistence of activity issues in our pursuit of intellectual advancement.

Technically, how did space invaders enter the graphing adventure game? Issues of medium are again salient. Boxer allows an incredibly simple means of joining programs. Just cut and paste one program into the middle of the other. The spatial metaphor is responsible for this easy and effective strategy. One can always manufacture more space: just insert a new box. When the new box is closed, you have, very nearly, your old world. When opened, you find a new universe in the old place. The contrast case is a typical application in which you simply cannot make any space anywhere to put a new thing without delving deep into complex and invisible processes that make things appear on the screen.

Sean and Bob, in fact, simply pasted space invaders right into the middle of the graphing adventure main box. The game was then instantly playable in the context of graphing adventure; modular, visible box-chunks are wonderfully portable. Then, step by step, they integrated the new box better and better into the game play of graphing adventure. For example, they discovered an advanced feature of Boxer that allowed them to lock the box, keeping players out until they had progressed sufficiently far with graphing puzzles. Then they added features such as having the player's score in space invaders affect the text he would see after he returned to graphing adventure. This is prototypical of organic growth. (1) There is a completely trivial principle of combining things—"paste it in"—even if it is not ideal. No threshold. (2) Then you have lots of time gradually to enhance integration. No ceiling.

Review

The message of this chapter has been a simple one: children are smart; people are smart. This simple message is not simple-minded, however. People are not perfectly smart in all possible ways, in all possible contexts. Instead, we need to be clever in order to see exactly where human intelligence lies and how to bring it out. In this chapter, we have seen that children possess a remarkable ability to design and think about representations (inventing graphing). Who would have thought that? People also possess powerful abilities to perceive and think about motion (Carol and Ming). Motion competence may seem obvious after the fact, but almost no current instruction of physics is based on exactly what students come into class capable of doing. Instead, instruction in motion is delayed a half decade or more in students' lives while we build an alternative route to understanding motion that relies on more formal means than their natural talents. Children are capable of remarkably large and complex constructions in computational media (Ted's molecular toolkit, Sean and Bob's graphing adventure), but not any computer system allows students to collaborate with others (and with themselves!) in an organic, long-term process of evolving such complex products.

These three classes of competence—metarepresentation, motion, and programming—have very special relationships with computational media. Programming, I have argued from the beginning, transforms limited consumer literacies into more powerful two-way literacies. Motion, along with an enriched spatial expressiveness and interaction, is a fundamental improvement of static media realizable with computational systems. Together, these new modes of expressiveness promise new implementations of material intelligence for humans.

Metarepresentation is the most subtle and unfamiliar of the competencies that we have seen blossom between children and computers given a sufficient computational medium, but metarepresentation may have radical and transformative implications. We may see tool-rich cultures of representational innovators in computationally literate students, teachers, and educational developers of the future. Genres such as the computational essay and the knowledge space may become commonplace in school learning of science. These genres represent not just a new possibility, but a new kind of possibility. Text has limited capabilities as a meta-medium, so that representational innovation is minimized a priori.

Although I have concentrated on knowledge, activity is a critical, complementary perspective. Indeed, I could almost as well have called this chapter "Kids Are Engaged," with the same caveats that engagement is culturally achieved—not automatic, not creatable on any ground, and not uniformly supported by any medium. Every story of accomplishment that showed surprising intelligence in this chapter is also a story of dedication and committed learning.

9

Stepping Back, Looking Forward

For an idea that is not derided as crazy when it is first proposed, there is no hope.
—A. Einstein

The Culture Gap

Prior chapters were devoted to providing a vision both of what computational literacy might mean and of what we could hope to achieve educationally through it. I needed to build appropriate ways to think about literacy in general and about computational literacy in particular. I also talked about our experiences using a prototype computational medium, Boxer, which is intended to support a deep computational literacy. Recounting those experiences was meant to enliven the abstract ideas with examples and to test their reality against what happens in the real world.

This chapter steps back to take a broader view of computational media and new literacies. In particular, I want to address macrocultural issues that have been in the background throughout this book, but now take center stage. What can we say about the processes by which larger cultures come to value new literacies and come to integrate them into their everyday fabric of activity? Until now, the broadest social issues we have considered have concerned one or another genre or social niche, such as computational essays or communities of tool builders and users, but an account of possible new literacies would be remiss without some attention to the bigger picture.

In a certain sense, this chapter is less theoretical and more concrete than much of the prior discussion. I won't offer a theory of large-scale social change (as I did in the case of intuitive knowledge) or even a beginning orientation toward such a theory (as I tried to do in the case of interest, engagement, and activity). Instead, I concentrate on how I see the current and near-future state of common culture as it impacts the development of a new, computational literacy. I supplement my observations with stories out of my own experience in the same way our experiences with Boxer, students, and teachers were meant to elaborate and illustrate other issues concerning computational media.

It should go without saying that my observations here may be less certain than some prior claims. Indeed, the work we have done with Boxer over the last decade and more has been restricted to what was accessible to us, given limited resources. We could investigate alternative designs for a new medium, technical learnability of it, expressiveness (e.g., much better means for "talking about" phenomena such as motion), and even students' engagement and interest. We simply couldn't experimentally approach—in any responsible way—broad cultural patterns and change, which is exactly the critical focus for this chapter.

Besides filling in an important perspective on computational media, the analyses of this chapter have several other purposes. Most important, I hope that thinking about these issues can make us more informed and wiser observers of what happens—and what does not—in the coming years. In particular, I want to undermine some arguments by critics and future critics of the idea of computational literacies in which they attribute implausibility to the idea on the basis of what has or hasn't happened so far. In my analyses, many of the "facts" that critics cite as demonstrating the impossibility of new literacies are either very natural components of the dynamic of change in transitions as massive as achieving a new literacy or explainable as "accidental," historically determined characteristics of present culture. Put simply, because things are the way they are is no reason to believe they couldn't be otherwise.

More optimistically, looking at macrocultural issues may put us in a position to act productively in facilitating the development of new literacies.

The pivotal and timely question that frames this chapter is: How might a society begin to believe that computational literacy is a good thing and hence dedicate itself to realizing the prospects for such a literacy? Of course, problems may appear down the line, but if getting started isn't the only big issue, it is the first big issue.

To anticipate, we are about to look at tiny funding for genuinely innovative work in education, reactionary "common sense" about what well-designed computer systems should achieve, and the broad epistemological bias against the very kinds of knowledge and activities that make computational literacies a truly transformative possibility. These all mitigate against quickly realizing the best possibilities of computational media and surreptitiously contribute to the judgment that the entire program is unrealistic. The common form of many of such arguments starts with "X is true, and therefore computational literacy is implausible." X might be "computers are too expensive," "programming is too difficult," or "people (teachers and students) aren't smart enough to do that." I argue that in many cases X is not true or at least not obvious, so the real problem is that people *assume* that X is true.

My plan is first to review and slightly extend prior discussion of practical issues such as economics. Then I'll begin the main new work of this chapter by introducing a helpful idea, *cultural resonance*. Next, I'll ease into complexity with a case study of the World Wide Web. What does the Web tell us about where we stand and how we may progress toward a new literacy? After a more extensive survey of the present cultural context in the service of understanding macrocultural change, I take a final look at the status of the idea of computational media and new literacies.

Some Practical Issues

This section briefly discusses economics and learnability. For many people, these topics are showstoppers. Computers are too expensive, and creating by means of computational media is too difficult (even if, perhaps, a consumer-only literacy may be possible). The assumed facts underlying these judgments are false, however. I discussed both of these topics before, so you may choose to skip ahead to more interesting matters.

Are computers too expensive? Already more than 10 percent of the high schools in the United States have surpassed my benchmark of one computer per three students. Superb and powerful computers—far above the threshold needed to run something like Boxer—cost about $1,000. When we started experiments with Boxer, that was far from true. A current $1,000 computer is, in fact, at least twenty-five times as powerful as the machines that worked, if imperfectly, in our first classroom Boxer trials. Prices continue to decline rapidly: every time I edit this chapter, I have had to reduce price estimates to remain up-to-date.

In addition, $1,000 is really a small number on the scale of public education. At $6,000 per pupil per year—a middling amount by today's standards—a classroom of thirty students absorbs $180,000 per year. Even bumping the rate of computer purchases to three per class per year *and* allowing $500 per machine for setup and maintenance, computer hardware would take only 2.5 percent of that $180,000. At that rate of computer purchase, it would take about three years to reach one computer per three students, even starting from scratch. Yes, many schools don't have the money to buy textbooks, but money, per se, is not the critical issue. *Priorities, political will, public and professional conviction, curriculum,* and *teacher enhancement* are the critical issues.

Let me further illustrate with a real-world example. The state of California has recently (1998) begun a drive to reduce class sizes, a multibillion dollar initiative that involves hiring eighteen thousand new teachers in K–4. Leave aside that data convince me that other uses of that money would be more cost effective; I'm discussing only economic feasibility. For the same money, politicians could have decided to do a dramatic experiment with computational literacy. Instead of reducing class size a small amount, they could use that much more than $20,000 per classroom in the first two years for ten computers (plus setup and maintenance) and at least $5,000 worth of teacher training *for every teacher*. After that, a month or two of in-service training could be supplied per year and still save significant money compared to the existing plan to reduce class size.

Furthermore, I think the scientific issue of the learnability of programming (the capability to create dynamic and interactive representations) is settled. It *is* possible for even elementary school students to learn enough programming, in a very acceptable amount of time, to serve as a critical instrument in learning important school subjects. My benchmark is sixteen hours of good learning of the computational medium. We've seen excellent things happen, without exception, when at least this much time is used wisely to teach about the medium itself. Finding sixteen hours to teach is far from solving the practical problem of achieving competence by essentially every pupil in every classroom. In particular, teachers need a good deal more experience than sixteen hours to direct learning with a computational medium, and it is even more difficult to get time from them than from students. Still, we are talking about wildly less time than is now spent with technical aspects of conventional literacy—grammar, phonics, spelling, learning about standard genres such as essays, and so on. Once things get rolling, the "cultural lever" will kick in. Positive feedback will bulldoze any problems we have in starting up. Many people will understand the medium; these people will have accumulated a lot of cultural know-how concerning teaching it; and there will be many things to do with the medium (see the discussions of menial utility and the learning/use cycle in chapter 6). In short, if computational literacy looks good enough to society so that things get going at all, then both use and learnability will snowball. People will be able to become computationally literate, most assuredly in the sense of being able to learn requisite technical parts of that literacy. To cite a different sort of benchmark, programming is both much less difficult for students to start learning and much more broadly useful compared to algebra, which has become a standard scientific subliteracy.

Cultural Resonance, Nonresonance, and Antiresonance

I have come to believe that the central practical issue in getting the ball rolling with computational literacy is not economics or learnability, but *cultural resonance*. I want to use this idea fairly extensively and just a bit more than casually, so let me start by elaborating the metaphor.

Resonance is a phenomenon that is familiar to most people. Think of an opera singer who sings a note at exactly the right pitch and with enough intensity that a wine glass shatters. Singing in the shower, you sometimes hit the resonant note, and the whole shower sings with you. You are driving a car down a washboard road, and the car starts shaking violently. If you reduce speed or—what seems less plausible—*increase* speed, the shaking subsides. In a scientific demonstration, a struck tuning fork brought near another of the same frequency starts its sibling vibrating, but if the second fork is of another frequency, nothing happens to it.

Resonance is when an action, such as vibration, is extended or even amplified into nearby objects that "recognize" a particular characteristic of the action, such as its frequency. Metaphorically, ideas may be resonant, or not, when brought to particular people or cultures. Trivial and powerful ideas alike sometimes catch on like wildfire—hula hoops or Freudian ideas such as the unconscious and suppression. Other ideas take centuries (e.g., separation of church and state) or never seem to resonate broadly. In the best of circumstances, we would hope that the idea of computational literacy is resonant with our current culture so that it might propagate and become enriched.

People are more dynamic than inanimate objects, so ideas may engender results other than resonance (effect) or nonresonance (no effect). *Antiresonance* may occur when people or a culture actively resist or attempt to suppress ideas. Foreign customs almost always seem strange and are actively rejected. Many "peculiar" ideas are initially shunted aside and only very gradually prove their value.

Resonance is a better metaphor than might be expected because intuitive judgments are really much more important than facts and reason at early stages (and maybe all stages!) of cultural change. People don't think through and decide so much as they just feel some views are sensible and others are not. Until a culture has put enough energy into an idea so that generally compelling evidence and argument may be created, gut feeling will always dominate science. I say more later about how and when feelings vanquish science.

The World Wide Web

The Internet and World Wide Web constitute a stunning social phenomenon and technological achievement. Everyone is getting on-line. The stock market is going crazy for Internet stocks, and the "WWW . . . dot com" mantra is everywhere. This is a technosocial phenomenon to reckon with, perhaps the most widely visible change in the relation between technology and ordinary people since the personal computer. What resonances lie behind this phenomenon? How have old social niches changed?

What new ones have emerged? What can this situation tell us about the emergence of new literacies?

A full analysis of the social niches of the Web would be a book-length task. However, thinking a little about the best recent example of a media-driven revolution will pay dividends in thinking about macrocultural issues concerning computational media.

I see at least four macroniches for the Web. First, it is a wonderful new means of distributing public information. Government (regulation and services), health, and even educational service and information providers are having a field day. For example, my wife and I regularly rely on Web sources for technology information (new hardware and software), financial and market information, and even—with appropriate care—medical reference. The material reasons for this niche are pretty clear: economics in production and distribution. Producing an informative document on the Web is easy, and huge numbers of people can have instant access to it.

Social resonance is transparent. People know they need all sorts of information that in the past has been difficult to find, and the threshold of work needed to access information has been reduced to a short walk to a home computer.

Clearly, literacylike synergies exist in this niche. Thousands of information providers join the same distribution mode (using the same software—Web browsers—and hardware infrastructure), and users amortize the intellectual and monetary cost of entering the game over all possible information lookups they might ever do. Once a quasi-stable niche appears, improving it snowballs. Helping information providers make things has become commercially attractive. Easy-to-use editors for Web pages followed rather than preceded the first unambiguous glimmer of widespread usefulness, and after early nonprofit Web browsers primed the pump, commercial interests jumped in with a vengeance.

On-line commerce is a second, still-developing macroniche. Again, social resonance is transparent. Producers want to sell things with minimal overhead expenses, and consumer want to buy them quickly and easily. The commercial niche has indispensable particular needs that have fed back into the technical resources available broadly. Transaction security is necessary, and that demand was strong and focused enough—and the technological know-how was available—so that Web browsers were quickly enhanced with security. A commercial battle continues over the nature of the medium and who will control it. Will we have open standards? Or will Microsoft supply the medium it chooses to supply, to maximize company profits, because everyone will use what comes with the Windows operating system?

Beyond selling per se, commercial interests have found a tremendous channel for advertisement and customer support. Advertisement, of course, is old wine in new bottles. The Web is adapted to it, but not uniquely. On the other hand, inexpensiveness and quickness of producing informational documents really have companies doing a new kind of thing in more actively supporting consumers after sales—for example, free software upgrades.

The third macroniche is personal expression. Hundreds of thousands of people now have their own Web pages, making available to the world whatever they feel they'd like the world to know. These pages range from professional self-advertisements to unabashedly personal "Here I am!" family or individual pages. The speed, ease, and lack of expense of getting into this game has made thousands of individuals and small groups widely visible in a way that far transcends the possibilities of print technology. Every scandal or other event that focuses public attention leads to an opportunity for someone to put up a Web site offering information or opinion. Consumers of information, including the traditional public information media, are adapting slowly to the consequences of easy publication. Disinformation from Web sources seems an everyday event. "If you see it in print, you can believe it" has always been problematic, but now a new level of vigilance is necessary.

Personal expression is particularly important to the enterprise of this book. The resonance driving personal expression on the Web is the power of a two-way medium, a lowered threshold for products that are personally meaningful. Almost no one can muster the time and energy to produce a book or pamphlet, but almost everyone can make a home page. Personal expression on the Web may be the first, best expression of the trend to smaller, more adapted software and to the "homegrown" tools and materials of which we spoke early and often concerning computational media.

The fourth macroniche that I see as important and distinctive is community building. Here, electronic mail and distribution lists (when people sign up to get messages from a common source) play in as strongly as the Web per se, but the main point is that many more and much smaller communities are served by Web newsletters, chat rooms, and similar forums than is possible with other media. The Web looks like a better context for the sort of community access advocates always claimed for television, but which never really blossomed.

Cultural resonance to the Internet has been stunning. The Web has certainly become "the next great thing" in education also. Networking is highly visible, if not absolutely front and center, in funding for educational research and in grassroots experimentation. Consider the phenomenon of "net days," where people and businesses donate time and materials to wire schools.

Why this resonance for education, and how far can it take us? First and fundamentally, what you get from the Web is transparently valuable: information. Information is the core commodity in schools as most people understand them: teaching and learning are transmitting and accumulating information. In addition, schools are drawn into Web use based on the irresistible conclusion that if it's useful out of school, surely we should also put it in school. Putting a wire in a school is a cheap and symbolic move to bring education along on the route to the future. "Every child should be able to log into the Internet," says President Bill Clinton. He doesn't have to explain why, as well he might. But I'm getting ahead of myself.

Ease of use seems to have a simple place in the Internet and World Wide Web story. The Internet was around for quite a long time before the Web added a layer that made it both hugely easier to produce attractive documents and also hugely easier for nontechnical people to access them. On the other hand, now that we're past the ease-of-use barrier, I am quite sure there won't be and don't need to be any more ease-of-use revolutions, at least for the niches that now exist.

The technical capabilities of the Web as a medium are undergoing a structural revolution as I write. Producing dynamic, interactive pages and even little combinable "applets" (small applications—tool components, for example) is the big draw of Java, the wildly popular Sun Microsystems

Web-enhancement technology. The resonance implied in the trend toward dynamic pages is important for the prospects of computational media in two respects. First, the trend validates that our culture appreciates (if dimly) the power of the transition to dynamic and interactive media that I identified as the core of computer-based literacies. Text and pictures alone won't make a revolution in expressiveness. A move to a dynamic medium, especially in the Java style, is encouraging because it brings programming back into the picture in a generally antiprogramming cultural scene.

The Web revolution is therefore clearly a broad revolution. It seems to provide encouraging evidence that the trends I identified as critical for new literacies have cultural resonance. Is the Web a *deep* revolution, however? Is it really a big step toward new literacies? Sadly, I think the answer is no, and why is illuminating and important.

Several perspectives bear on limits in the Web revolution. The easiest to appreciate follows directly on our discussion of Java and its innovation in dynamically enhancing Web media. Recall the important distinction between one-way literacies of the elite (where only specialists create in the medium) and true two-way mass literacies (where everyone both creates and consumes). The original Web allowed two-way literacy, but only in traditional forms of text and pictures. Java adds the ability to create dynamic and interactive documents, but only for experts. It is primitive in terms of learnability and expressiveness; it is not intended to be seen or created by ordinary mortals; and it is most certainly not designed to be directly expressive of scientific or any other ideas. We thus have a wonderful two-way medium (with wonderful economies in production and distribution) of an old form—text and pictures, but that medium is really only one-way, for experts and for the well endowed, when considered in relation to the fundamentally new expressive possibilities of computational media—dynamics and interaction.

There is a hidden epistemological issue in the producer/consumer characteristics of the Web. If the range of expressiveness of computational media did not matter, then the fact that ordinary people are shut out of the production of dynamic and interactive representations would not matter. We argued earlier and showed in the examples of student work, however, that an increase in expressiveness *does* matter. It is the most fundamental shift from a text-based literacy to a computational literacy. The fact that people don't seem to notice this about the Web or don't seem to care is the tip of a cultural and epistemological iceberg we must face and deal with. Widespread assumptions about the nature of knowledge are not resonant and may be antiresonant with the best prospects for new literacies.

The Information Illusion

I'll make the negative case here for alternative forms of knowledge. The complementary positive case was made in chapters 4 and 5.

To be direct, information is a shockingly limited form of knowledge. Unfortunately, our common culture seems insensitive to that fact. We even call the computer's influence the "information revolution." There is an information revolution, but it is not the basis for a revolution in education. As turbulent and big as the information revolution has been, I think the truly interesting (and maybe bloody) part of the revolution as regards computational literacy has yet to begin, and society is less well prepared for it. We need to dismantle some cultural common sense to let the insights of chapters 4 and 5 stand in relief.

Information is surely a valuable resource; therefore, the common intuition goes, the vast quantities of information on the Web can revolutionize learning. However, no amount of information is helpful unless it is relevant to your situation and in a form you can use.

Consider relevance. The information that you need at a particular time must be relevant to the particular problem you are facing. The problems we face are surprisingly often very special, arising out of our personal as well as local social and material context. Helping children do better at school is an excellent example. Some need to study harder; some need to study differently; some need advice about course selection; some need parents who care; some have parents who care *too much*. Without a wise diagnosis, information about how to address each of these problems is useless. (Indeed, many of these problems are information impervious. To children who don't care, the information that they should care is useless. Similarly, overbearing parents don't generally profit from being told they are overbearing.)

Now consider the form of information. People possess extremely diverse levels and sorts of competence, so they can seldom get information in exactly the form they need. Think about finding help with a computer problem. Manuals that are explicitly intended to help seem always to be either much too simplistic (and take you on a wild goose chase of procedures without letting you in on why the problem happens) or are much too sophisticated, assuming too much to be helpful. The right level is only one of many dimensions of the issue of getting information in the right form. Knowledgeable people are so much more helpful than most information sources because they instinctively tailor their help to a questioner's situation and competence.

The nub of the issue regarding both form and relevance is that people tend to assume the rest of the world is just like them. However, even the vast quantity of information available on the Web pales in comparison to the diversity of competence and situations among humans. Even the best search engine doesn't come close to solving the problem of providing learners with the right information in just the right form to substantially advance everyday learning.

Even deeper problems with information limit its role in revolutionizing education. Information, by its very nature, is a limited form of knowledge. Contrast information with know-how. Everyone understands how difficult it is to express know-how in linguistic terms—to turn know-how into information. Instructions, a most prominent form of know-how in language, are difficult to interpret and extremely fragile *unless you already know basically what you are doing.* Instructions for anything as complex as, say, a computer really only serve relative experts. What instructions or information about bicycles can help a child learn to ride?

Information is only sensible, in fact, if you have a well-oiled know-how machine into which to plug the information. If you know how to use a screw driver, if you know how tight is "secure, but not overtight," only then is it at all useful to read, "use the 4-40 bolts and nuts to fasten the fernclyde securely, taking care not to overtighten." Children do not learn arithmetic or science by teachers' describing those processes in words. Teachers do not become better teachers if we simply supply information about how excellent teachers teach. The path to better teaching requires enrichment frames—that is, good learning activities—and we need for teachers to learn to process new classes of information.

The fundamental problem of education is not lack information, but lack of the understanding that makes information useful. The big and important learning steps are made in coming to make sense of particular classes of information. Education is not a soup of ever more information.

Let me remind you about the intuitive knowledge I acquired from electronics. It was not information about physics, but it did put me in a position to process information about physics. Information that I got from my high school class about potential energy became knowledge only as I used my intuitive understanding to consider what that information meant. A child's competence at play is not well described as information. Being a member of a culture does not mean having information about a culture so much as being able to use information relevant to the culture.

The last perspective I want to introduce on the limits of information concerns its relation to and integration into activity. Here is how the "incredible possibilities" of the Web actually play out in many schools: the prototypical activity involving the Web is that students are given some topic to investigate and told to use the Web to research it themselves; students surf, find some vaguely relevant item, print it out, and hand in their "report." The frequency of this model is incredibly sad, yet the model is expectable, and the reason for it is evident. Technological possibilities can't be realized until practices involving them have reached a substantial maturity. Literacy is a social and cultural achievement, not just a technical one. That a school community has more information does not mean it can use it wisely. Instead of the availability of information, we should pay attention to culturally characteristic features such as values (e.g., critical evaluation of information), everyday practices (e.g., authentic exchange with out-of-school worlds), and new genres (e.g., the knowledge spaces or computational essays described in chapter 8). In this broader context, information availability pales in significance.

Here's my bottom line. The World Wide Web is equally encouraging and discouraging regarding the practicality of new literacies. It is a big step in economics and distribution, but a small step in form. It is two-way and reaffirms the importance of two-way media in the enthusiasm in self-expression it has engendered, but it is only one-way with respect to new expressive possibilities offered by computational media: ordinary folks are limited to text and pictures; they can't create dynamic and interactive documents.

I read in the newspapers that "the Web changes *everything*." It certainly changes a lot, and some of what it is changing, it is revolutionizing, but we have to examine whether it changes what is most important to us. The strong resonance in education to the Web is based on conventional assumptions about what knowing and knowledge are, about how important and generally useful information is. Such resonance doesn't go far toward the radical and important possibilities offered by genuine computational literacies. The Web is understood as a quick fix, an add-on, more and faster, the next great thing—not an instrument of cultural change directed toward, for example, widespread committed learning.

The Culture Gap in Detail

Beyond what we can see in the possibilities inherent in and the widespread reaction to the World Wide Web, I wish to take a broader survey of the current cultural landscape regarding computational literacies.

At the top level, the first reaction of most people to the idea of computational literacies is simply incomprehension. What could that possibly mean? How would you decide whether it could be true? Would it be a good thing even if it were possible? Computational literacies per se are generally nonresonant.

Even in the relatively rare instance that someone has a reaction to the idea of computational literacy, it is usually thin and negative—mildly antiresonant. These reactions take two forms. One is that the idea is absurd on the face of it. Literacy is about reading and writing, and it is a complete oxymoron to put computers in that picture. Or, the idea is silly because computer-based literacy is little more than word processor-enhanced textual literacy. How important could that be? The second form of antiresonance is to assume that computational literacy is the same thing as what people call "computer literacy," and we're achieving that, more or less quickly, in any case. As much as people need to use computers, they'll learn how.

The contention of this book is that the idea of a computationally enhanced literacy is neither trivial nor absurd. Computational forms extend textual forms in a substantial enough way that revolutionary material intelligence is at least a possibility we should consider. Not just any computational forms might do this, of course, but some, and I emphasize possibility—not certainty. Still, the consequences of creating a new literacy are so dramatic that the subject is worthy of considerable thought and experiment.

My position on the possibility of computational literacy is in the radical middle. I am skeptical of the reasons technofuturists usually give for the necessity of technology revolutionizing thinking and learning. I am equally skeptical of the Luddites who believe computers will pass the way of film loops or will always be as peripheral as overhead projectors. (Surely no one believes an ounce of material intelligence resides in a film loop or projector, so why is the analogy relevant? Literacy isn't the generic game of technological innovation at all. It is a very special issue.)

What I want to do in the next several sections is dig below these surface nonresonances and antiresonances to computational literacies to see if there are resonances to particular aspects of the idea, as opposed to the idea as a whole. These specific resonances could be tools for bootstrapping a better resonance overall. I want to treat separately several of the important relevant subcultures, each of which connects somewhat differently to computational media and new literacies.

Technologists
I start with a community that is not a central gatekeeper in the task of advancing computational media, but it is a community that could be a tremendous facilitator in terms of supplying resources to support experimentation with computational literacy. It is the community of technologists, including computer scientists and advanced developers—the people who design and make new computer systems.

Not surprisingly, a major difficulty here is that technologists are, by and large, not very sensitive to human affairs. Until recently, in fact, the charge of a computer scientist seemed self-evidently in caring only about machines and systems per se. Since computers have burst out of the laboratory and out of hidden infrastructure into public access and visibility, many have realized that the contributions of computers to civilization depend significantly on human-machine systems, not on machines alone. Still, human affairs—learning, psychology, sociology, and cultural studies—have not penetrated technological communities broadly or deeply.

Glitz seems so self-evidently wonderful that few in the technological community are worried about systems that might actually count as computational media capable of supporting new literacies. Even if they are concerned about such systems, they spend very little time with the people and communities that are supposed to be revolutionized by their new media. Because the value of a system such as Boxer is hidden in human affairs, few technologists have constructed competitor systems.

I wrote a paper some time ago trying to explain the idea of computational media to the technological community. The paper was rejected by the editors of the journal to which I submitted it. You have the disadvantage of not knowing how well or poorly I accomplished my task, but you may empathize with my amazement at one of the major criticisms of the paper—that there were already many such systems in existence, out there doing their jobs, that there was nothing much new in Boxer. From some technical point of view, there may not be many innovations that computer scientists appreciate in Boxer, but in intent it is clearly different. Expressively and from the point of view of learnability and supporting scientific learning, there are new things worth considering in Boxer. One reviewer cited systems that are hopelessly complex for students and teachers and have never produced an iota of evidence that they represent any expressive innovation with respect to educational goals of any sort. Even reviewers who were more sympathetic suggested I concentrate on Boxer's management of screen space (!) and so on. Overall, I couldn't get the smallest bit of resonance with the idea of computational media as developed in this book. Instead, the resonances were with the sort of "how to" and efficiency issues that dominate the technical community's concerns. The fact that software systems might serve their most important purpose in mediating human thinking, rather than in just getting things done, is a nonstarter in most technological circles.

A tremendous antilearning bias pervades contemporary systems design circles: a system is good only if it is trivial to learn, and advancement means only making things easier to learn and operate. In fact, if any learning at all is required, a system is suspect. A sidelight to this antilearning bias is that interface is all, and what the interface interfaces to comes in second or third place. *Transparency* is a buzzword; you should see through the interface directly to the problem you want to solve.

An antilearning bias is a serious problem for computational media. It is inconceivable that anything that could serve as a basis for a literacy should be trivial to learn. How could anything rich and expressive enough to reach many important and difficult corners of human understanding be trivial? Even more, the point of a computational medium is to change the thinking of humans into an enhanced, human/material system. Imagining that this change could be easy if we get the system right strikes me as looking for a knowledge or intelligence pill. Take it one day, and in the morning you wake up smarter and knowing more. I'm not investing in any intelligence pill start-up companies.

The transparency idea is also well-intentioned, but misplaced. Transparency is a form of familiarity. Anything we understand instinctively seems transparent. A hammer is transparently for hammering. Of course, we want to maximize the familiarity of a system (recall functional models) and minimize unnecessary complications, but if something is too familiar, it can't extend our thinking. We don't want to manufacture unfamiliarity, but neither can we hope to eliminate it entirely—at least if we want a computational medium.

The hidden metaphor behind transparency—that seeing is understanding—is at loggerheads with literacy. It is the opposite of how media make us smarter. Media don't present an unadulterated "picture" of the problems we want to solve, but have their fundamental advantage in providing a *different* representation, with different emphases and different operational possibilities than "seeing and directly manipulating." Words don't present the problems we want to solve as those problems usually present themselves. In fact, formulating a linguistic expression of a niggling problem is a critical first step in solving it. Formulating an insightful description is more than a first step. Writing down hypotheses and sequentially testing them, reading books, writing letters to experts, and so on are all part of an intelligent problem-solving process supported by literacy. None of these steps makes problems or solutions transparent. Instead, *literacy makes an enhanced thinking possible.* Algebra may be an equally good example. Algebra doesn't look anything like a physics problem. It is not a transparent portal onto the physical world, but it is part of our best means of representing physics problems for solution.

I can't help thinking that the breakthrough of one generation is often the albatross of the next. Making computers easier to use with graphical user interfaces—desktop metaphors, mice, and so on—was a revolution in the relation between computers and the populace. Making things simpler and easier will always be an opportunity for enhancement, but simplicity and familiarity trade off against expressiveness and many other critical features of computational media. Although we didn't ignore simplicity and learnability with Boxer—in fact, they were prime targets of our design—we kept them always in the context of expressiveness and intellectual utility. Prettiness is a similar issue, with even less face value in the context of the requirements for a deep literacy. How pretty does text have to be to support a literate culture? Sure, I want a beautifully crafted system (if I can afford it!), but when "nifty" gets in the way of "expressive and malleable," there's no thinking to be done about the choice.

Technological cultures—and maybe all cultures—build a nearly impervious common sense about what is the direction of improvement, the next great thing. In technological communities, the future tends to be an obvious extension—more, better, faster—of what currently exists. Improvement is removing the glitches in current standard operating procedures. Occasionally, the future is doing something absolutely, completely different, but something that is immediately intuitively comprehensible. Computational media are definitively off this track. They fundamentally address a tremendous possibility, a new literacy, that few have recognized. They do not address a limit that keeps current systems from doing what they advertise, and they are not even completely different, like virtual reality or artificial intelligence. Instead, they have much in common with the lowly text processor, at least as a symbol and instrument of literacy.

I have been amused by the changing resonances with Boxer and the obvious next technological frontier as it has moved. Early on, Boxer was an "integrated system." Then it was (and still is for many) "an easier programming language for children." Recently, a technologist at Apple Computer told me he liked Boxer because it is a "component-computing" system. Component computing, you see, is a software frontier that became the next great thing. Boxer is all of these things, but none of them gets unambiguously close to the heart of its intent as a prototype computational medium. The little resonances of Boxer with the "obvious" technological future have never crossed the critical threshold to recruiting the technological community as an ally in the pursuit of computational media and new literacies.

The Educational Community

One would think that computational media would resonate with the educational community because literacy is a fundamental and enduring value. Throw computers into the mix, however, and you're in trouble. In the public mind, computers are the opposite of literacy. Video games and Web surfing distract people from and perhaps make them constitutionally incapable of reading books.

C. P. Snow identified the problem of two cultures, which divides education as it does the rest of the intellectual world. On one side are the scientific, technical folks, and on the other are the literary, humanistic folks. Technical people scarcely ever talk about their own competence as literacy. Mathematical or scientific literacy, if it is mentioned at all, means only knowing enough mathematics or science to be an informed citizen. It is not taken to be a core phenomenon of learning the discipline.

The literary, humanistic folks resonate strongly with literacy, but don't care much about expressiveness in scientific or mathematical domains. Furthermore, they know so much about existing literacy that new literacies are immediately suspect as dilutions, not enhancements. I've so often heard people lamenting the loss of literacy in computer- and TV-addicted cultures; few have noticed that technology could be a tremendous enhancement.

I have also found that most literacy experts think about literacy in such particular terms that they are at a loss in trying to extend their understanding to really different media with different expressive possibilities. Literacy is about vocabulary, composition, and literature. It is about ideas that have their best expression in words, such as freedom or love. It is not about other ideas, such as symmetry or momentum, and it doesn't intersect with dynamic, interactive representations of scientific or mathematical phenomena. If only the two cultures were one, computational literacy might be much more resonant.

Education, generally, is not a fertile ground for new ideas. Pretty much everyone knows that it is an extremely conservative area. In one sense, this is natural and appropriate. Education involves a huge infrastructure and well-developed practice. Changing it is bound to be difficult. Education is also appropriately difficult to change because it involves the future of our children and hence of our civilization. If fads with hidden devastating consequences were easy to ignite, we might be in a precarious situation.

What frustrates innovators is the mindlessness of the conservatism. Getting a good conversation going about nontrivial change is difficult because people assume that conservatism as absolute. No substantial change, by definition, is worth talking about. This rhetoric of defeatism has been constantly poured on the Boxer project. As soon as people figure out we are about really big-stakes issues, we're branded pie-in-the-sky dreamers. What if some significant change might really enhance teaching and learning, however? What if we've already seen examples of similar changes (in the rise of popular literacy and even technical subliteracies such as algebra)? What if there are solid scientific grounds for believing at least in the *possibility* of this change? It would be a horrible shame if knee-jerk conservatism or awe at the scale of issues prevents new literacies from being discussed.

Scientific research has not yet been a definitive force in defeating educational conservatism. The science relevant to education is of low status—compared, for example, to biology or physics. Recently, a distinguished Nobel laureate physicist spent a year or so thinking about education. His ideas were widely circulated. Thinking about education is certainly a laudable undertaking, and good ideas from any source are worth listening to, but education's status is transparent in the authority wielded by this physicist. Could a distinguished researcher involved in education get an invitation to present a major address at the premiere research and professional conference for physics after thinking for a year about the subject?

Scientific work on education is also unfortunately fragmented. No unified voice acclaims advances or decries charlatanism. Outside scientific circles, everyone, and certainly every politician, *assumes* their own expertise in education; after all, they lived through an educational process. Scientific studies rarely enter into political debate about educational options. Although commitment to education is perennial, it is intellectually thin and tends to be sensitive only to political assumptions or personal experience. Science, of course, should transcend both politics and personal judgment, but education-relevant science has yet to conquer either.

A new literacy has to seem radical not only in principle, but in detail. Consider: a true literacy deeply affects what we can think about and how we think about it. Not only will methods be different in school, but subject matter will also change. Students will learn things that appear very different from what is in current textbooks. On one occasion, I wrote to a government funding agency about the possibilities of using Boxer to teach physics. I mentioned our work with elementary school students as an example, even though the proposal was to work at the high school level. The program director considered the fact that I mentioned vectors in the context of elementary school sufficient grounds to reject the plausibility of the work I proposed. "Vectors are not age-appropriate subject matter for elementary school students." I doubt that reading our research reports, even if he had taken the trouble, would have changed his mind. Cultural common sense has it that vectors are not sixth-grade appropriate, but this fact assumes conventional forms. As arrows whose tips one can drag around to control motion, vectors are as approachable as game interfaces young children easily master.

Vectors are, in some ways, a best-case scenario to test resonance. Nobody—and certainly not the program officer who rejected my proposal—doubts that technical education should include vectors at some point, yet the suggestion that subject matter might be approachable at earlier ages using technological support is grounds for dismissal. Creating a resonance for things that are invisible in conventional literacy, such as excellent intuitions cultivated by students' interacting with well-designed programs, is even more difficult. The problem is exacerbated by the fact that the value of intuitive knowledge is contested in research circles, even before it gets to public forums.

General conservatism, limited influence of scientific data and argument, suspicion of new forms, reactionary views of knowledge, and yet more. My convictions about the possibility of computational literacies stem in part from my constant experience of children and teachers as creative and intelligent. The conventional wisdom is that *only some* children and teachers can be intelligent and creative. For the rest, we need to dumb down the curriculum and make it teacher proof. Perhaps the problem lies in the different orientation toward people rather than in the idea of computational literacies in general. A positive view of intellectual possibilities is indispensable, however. If we fail to consider smartening up the curriculum to the level students and teachers can achieve with enhanced tools, we will surely miss the largest share of a new material intelligence. This is why I devoted two chapters to the accomplishments of children and teachers.

At the first public talk I remember giving about computational media, one of the responses afterward was shocking. A questioner asked if I really meant that teachers could add or change anything in this system. I said yes, and he spent several minutes painting a frightening picture of all the errors teachers would introduce into public education. Mistrust of teachers and students makes a two–way medium implausible as an advance to many people. Not unexpectedly, any talk that teachers may take a larger and more significant role in the development of materials, as first-class citizens in communities of tool builders and sharers, meets generally with less than enthusiastic resonance.

Doing research on something as elusive as a new literacy demands unusual and hence intuitively suspect strategies. Average accomplishments on standardized tasks is the bread and butter of educational research, but there are no standardized tasks for the really new accomplishments an innovative media supports. Worse, how do you foresee the results of a cultural accomplishment such as a new literacy before a new culture is in place? There is little if any cultural know-how concerning how to teach it. There's no literature in place expressing great ideas. (Cumulativity may be the core causal factor in the power of literacy.) Could the first readers have foreshadowed in any sense the possibility of a mass literacy?

Research on computational media requires unfamiliar strategies. For example, one must imagine a new learning trajectory or even a new goal.

Then you try to make it happen. If you succeed, you have to analyze further why it happened so that we can be better prepared to make it happen in the future and so that we can imagine other things that might work according to similar principles.

Other antiresonances breed difficulties both with the educational research community and also with consumers of educational ideas. One of these antiresonances is that in most circles, methods are the things that are tested and of value. Everyone seems to have and want to sell a wonderful new method for teaching this or that, from typing to reading, writing, and arithmetic. For a number of reasons, I am highly suspicious of methods as "goods to sell." First, clever or obstinate teachers can make any method work or fail in the most ingenious ways. Simple descriptions of what to do leave out almost all of the detail of the rich activity context in which success or failure emerges, so many people try the same method, and it works well or not at all due to many invisible factors. I feel sorry that many brilliant researchers and innovators need to hide their true intelligence behind methods—an intelligence that lies in nudging a context in many subtle ways in order to make things work. Teaching and learning are fundamentally cultural and responsive, and methods alone are too thin to provide robust guidance.

If I did believe in methods to sell, this is still the wrong time to sell them. Before people see something of value in a new literacy—and before we know much about what a literacy might really be like—selling methods to achieve and use it is doubly inappropriate.

Some History: Education Meets Computational Media

When science and reason are weak, opinion and historical tradition prevail. In the case of computational media, history is unfortunately the ally of knee-jerk antiresonance. During the early to mid-1980s, programming was a significant part of expectations concerning how computers would be used in schools. A confluence of many trends swamped this beginning, and now anyone who advocates programming—that is, anyone who advocates two-way media—is usually regarded as anachronistic, possibly fighting a battle that was lost long ago. One of the trends that swamped programming was that it was co-opted by a vocational image. Viewed vocationally, programming is only the professional practice of computer scientists or software makers. Learning it, therefore, is relevant only for people who wish to pursue such vocations. Computer science, of course, avidly promoted this idea and supported its realization. The influential testing community stepped in dramatically to sanction the movement. To measure computational accomplishment of high school students, the Educational Testing Service adopted Pascal, a computer language invented by computer scientists to teach computer science.

The vocational image of programming became a self-fulfilling prophecy. Courses were taught with no connection to any traditional subject matter; hence, computer programming became definitively marginalized with respect to learning subjects such as mathematics and science. Courses were also designed for students with computer career interests. Naturally, nontechnically oriented students found little of interest in these courses, and the courses came to be viewed as difficult as well as irrelevant for most students. To be fair, other factors besides vocationalism were involved in pushing computers out of core curricula. Traditional subject areas, as one would expect, did not welcome computers, much less programming, into their domains.

During the 1980s and into the 1990s, proponents of computational media suffered, I believe, a broad misunderstanding about the nature of the challenge. Technically, most people assumed the media that existed at the time were sufficient, with minor changes. As a consequence, few if any attempts emerged to improve the medium specifically as a literacy base (as opposed to commercial work to improve the "interface," speed, and prettiness). Cognitively, very little thinking went into understanding the new expressiveness of computational media, into finding ways of approaching old subject matter or important new subject matter that really took advantage of the medium. Finally, the large cultural scale of the issues of new literacies was all but completely ignored. People pretended, and still pretend to this day, that cultural cumulativity is irrelevant to finding out if computers are good things in education.

In the mid-1980s, especially in the United States, burgeoning interest in programming and in computers in education in general was met by a furious backlash among researchers. Consider some representative statements.

The straight line should be drawn by the child, not by the computer. . . . Turtle geometry [a programming-based approach to geometry developed by colleagues and me] ultimately usurps important activities essential for the child's development. (Arthur Zajonc)

Plato also complained that reliance on writing usurped important intellectual functions.

All a program can do is substitute one set of abstractions for another. (H. Dreyfus)

Like words, I suppose. Or maybe algebraic symbols. I wonder what abstractions are substituted when a child plays with a dynamic simulation of motion using vectors as controls, as described in chapter 2?

Computers embody a mechanized version of thinking. (John Davy)

What kind of thinking do people in interaction with computers embody?

That cognition involves a rationality much deeper and capacious than technical reason is forgotten. (Douglas Sloan)

That technical reason is powerful and not well expressed in words is also frequently ignored.

[Consider] the sheer impoverishment of simply sitting still for hours, absorbed in an artificial world. (John Davy)

Just like reading a novel. "Being absorbed" is not the worst thing I can imagine from computers.

Interestingly, one of the facts that fed the backlash against programming was an initial, strong resonance among schools and teachers to the idea. Programming advocates were among the few to hold up students as intelligent and creative, and for whom a new, computer-based expressive outlet was appropriate. Antiprogramming researchers took a self-righteous tone as if they were "saving the masses from themselves" until programming proved its value. They denigrated the optimistic hopes for new literacies with the slogan, "Programming is the new Latin." The slogan likened programming advocates' claims to much earlier claims that learning Latin disciplined the mind and made people more logical and powerful thinkers. Research is reputed to have debunked these claims about Latin, but the analogy is false. Mass literacies don't convey power by mere technical competence. Instead, the relevant question is whether a culture that values and practices a certain literacy can profit intellectually from it. The ancient Romans benefited from Latin, I feel safe in asserting. The comparable question for computational media is more difficult—certainly beyond the scale of a simple experiment done long before any culture has developed practices that capitalize on expressive possibilities of the medium.

Researchers on the literacy side of the debate retrenched, but they blurred critical issues by abandoning the word *literacy,* even for all of its antiresonances. Computer literacy returned to the resonant but vapid "casual familiarity with the real world of computation," like spreadsheets and word processors. In stark and ironic contrast to the protests against programming, I don't know of any researcher who contested the value of "casual familiarity" literacy.

The net result of these historical trends is that now if we advocate computational literacy, we have to buck many antiresonances from tales of the recent past. We have a much more difficult task than starting from scratch.

Funders and Developers

People who fund research and those who are interested in making commercial software products constitute the target communities for this section. These folks determine which ideas get support at early stages of research and development, and then later at the transition from proof of concept to viable, real-world technology. As gatekeepers, funders and commercial interests can compensate for widespread non- and antiresonance if they are wise and informed enough to transcend culturally persistent but possibly prejudicial intuitions, but they can also amplify negative resonances because they control resources, with obvious consequences.

Early development and the transition to widespread use are both critical phases for computational media. A medium is by definition a large and complex piece of software. You have to build it from scratch or make very significant changes to existing software because almost all existing software serves much narrower purposes than a computational medium. A proof of concept, even in miniature (such as in one or a few classrooms) is not a project taken on lightly. One must invent a host of new teaching approaches, targets of instruction, methods, materials, techniques, and so on—all in intimate connection with the special new properties of the new medium. In essence, you must transcend the existing literacy, developed over hundreds of years, and create a new one—at least in some very modest approximation. This takes time, people, and a lot of thought, which are impossible to manage without funding.

The transition to widespread use is similarly precarious. It is sometimes possible simply to get an excellent idea for a piece of software, implement it (without long research and development phases), and have widespread, even commercial success, but this happens usually only when the software fits existing social niches well enough that it can fall unproblematically into an existing niche or into a niche that is trivial to create, given the larger social and cultural surround. People must resonate easily with descriptions of the software so that they will be convinced to spend money on it in the short window of time that determines the success or failure of a commercial software venture. The spreadsheet is an archetypical example of these properties. It perfectly matched a social niche—financial planning for businesses. It even matched the prior material forms that served the niche, a spatial array of numerical values, and it had completely evident incremental advantage in overcoming glitches in prior standard operating procedures ("running the numbers" by hand), mainly in speed and accuracy. The World Wide Web is a similar, if more complex, instance of fitting a niche (even if some of its resonance—for example, the value of information in education—is illusory). The emergence of computational media can't work by falling into an existing niche.

A bare-bones history of Boxer's funding and development record can serve here as a prelude to further considerations of funding and development communities. When we started the Boxer project in about 1982, we were essentially unfunded. We didn't even have a programmer. Instead, we depended on undergraduates at MIT who passed through the project and were willing to implement parts of a preprototype Boxer.

I wouldn't be in a position to write this book at all if we hadn't had an excellent streak of funding from the National Science Foundation (NSF) for about six years, starting in 1985. Even during this time, however, we struggled with the scale of the project. We never succeeded in convincing the NSF that we needed more than one programmer for the size of software project we were undertaking. Given that even relatively simple commercial products have many person-years of programming, the prospect of having to make a decent prototype of a computational medium in a couple of years and demonstrate its educational viability was daunting. In addition, Boxer was too big and complex to run on then-available school computers. Our development machines cost the better part of $100,000. As I mentioned, our first school sites used machines that cost more than $10,000. Even to enter the game, we required equipment donations and funding from other sources to add to our sizable NSF grant.

A critical event, about which I say more later, was that after six years of support, the NSF terminated the funding for our project. My plan all along was basically a decade-long program. During the first third (technological level), we'd concentrate on software and get our prototype medium going. During the second third (cognitive level), we'd do small-scale experiments with individual students and single classes as a proof of concept for funders and to collect enough know-how for using a computational medium in the final stage. Then, the culminating third of the project was to be an experiment at the cultural level. We wanted to see if we could cross the threshold to self-sustaining innovation, involving one or two entire schools. Dealing with an entire school, one must confront social and cultural issues that are manageable at smaller scales by dint of external energy poured into the experiment. At the school level, the community simply has to take over substantial initiative—which must emerge from its own understanding of the possibilities of the new medium—in order for any sustained, innovative use of the medium to occur. Can the cultural lever kick in?

Our technical and cognitive stages were extremely successful. The project produced more than fifty papers documenting successes like those reported here in the "Snapshots" chapters (3 and 8). Despite these papers (and successes) and despite extensive intellectual preparation for the third stage, however, we never succeeded in getting funding to initiate study at the cultural level. In the years following, up to now (1998), we have patched together enough funding to keep the project going in some semblance, but we have had to satisfy ourselves with technological twiddling and a few minor experiments, mostly continuing cognitive-level studies.

Given this background, let me sketch some (mainly anti-) resonances with the funding and development communities.

The project's "people are smart" orientation was a problem with funders. The prejudice against ordinary folk is deep and very widespread. Its appearance in this community should not be surprising. Let me give a couple of examples. First, I discovered that any sort of data about students' producing exceptional results were dismissed. Even if we could show that every student in the class made some excellent accomplishment, funding officers and often proposal reviewers used any surprising accomplishment against us to show that we were working with very special children. They wanted every student to demonstrate the *same* excellent accomplishment.

To be fair, we set ourselves up for this reaction in early experiments by using "above average" children. I believe this decision was well justified. Given the difficulty of what we were trying to accomplish, it seemed absurd to take on all the troubles of society. I had thought *any* results showing that sixth-grade students could learn substantial high school or university physics using radically different media and methods would be notable, but the reaction was almost always like the comment we got about age appropriateness in teaching vectors: "That's manifestly too difficult to be relevant to 'real kids.' Your experiment or methods are suspect."

We received negative feedback of the same sort concerning teachers. On one of my trips to Washington, I asked Henri (the expert high school mathematics teacher who produced the infinity box mentioned earlier) to come along in order have a spokesperson from the teacher community. I have always been straightforward in saying that Henri is not "the average teacher." He is, instead, a very real exemplar of a possible future class of teacher leaders who can appropriate a new medium and show other teachers the way. I also thought funders would be interested in the insights and orientation of an articulate and thoughtful practitioner, especially one independent enough to disagree with many things our project has said and done.

After the meeting, an NSF official told me directly that bringing a smart teacher had been a significant liability. He wasn't "the average teacher," so what could he contribute? It seems educational success can come only in demonstrably raising the average only a little bit. A more nuanced message about critical niches—in this case, leader teachers—was missed. Again we see that the scale of the project, making a little progress on a civilizationwide issue, was not the frame for assessment.

Let me synthesize many of these considerations into opposing frameworks for doing innovative educational research. I believe funders, by and large, inherit as common sense the "Standard Program" outlined in the following table, and it is a large task to explain the plausibility of another approach.

A Program Appropriate for Researching New Literacies	The Standard Educational Research Program
Small steps toward big changes: You are exploring the early stages of a very large sociocultural process that could lead to a radical shift in the fundamental modes of learning.	*Absolute incrementalism:* Any change is an incremental change. Radical changes never happen.
New intelligence: If people can't become "smarter" than current expectations, the program is a failure.	*Accepting old expectations:* Have limited expectations, especially for "average" students.
Rearranged intellectual terrain: Standards are important. However, not only are new standards possible, but they are certain in this long-term, large-scale educational change. A new literacy is of no value if it doesn't expand and rearrange approachable intellectual terrain.	*Standards' stranglehold:* Improvement must be validated against existing standards.
How: Although you must very carefully document advances, they are only *similar* to what might be in store. It is much more important, therefore, to document "how" than to quantify "how much," as long as there is no doubt that radical improvement is plausible.	*How much:* Reproducibility is critical. Define your methods carefully so that others can reproduce them exactly. It is important to know exactly how much improvement was achieved. Otherwise, it is impossible to choose between this innovation and competing ones.

A Program Appropriate for Researching New Literacies	The Standard Educational Research Program
Cultural diversity: In foreshadowing a substantial sociocultural change, be aware that coordinated changes of many sorts will eventually occur. Such changes will affect different groups differently—for example, teacher leaders and other teachers. You can't model all these changes in an experimental project. Just choose the niche you investigate wisely.	*Cultural homogeneity:* If a method is to have consequences, it must work with all teachers and all students. Work with many students and average teachers; document improvement on the average. (Cultural leverage, as well as cultural diversity, is a completely invisible positive force.)
Individual diversity: Especially attend to different routes to success for different students, reflecting their natural diversity of strengths, interests, and cultural identity. New media *should* liberate a multiplicity of ways to succeed in learning mathematics and science.	*Individual homogeneity:* Make sure the same changes work for all students.
Cultural change: Dissemination is exploring and exploiting cultural resonances. It is recruiting others into building communities and literatures that manifest creativity in developing new possibilities. A move to a new literacy doesn't make sense as one run from the top down. No individual or group can make a new literacy.	*Dissemination:* Dissemination is finding a publisher, developing workshops to teach your methods, and selling your system and methods.

Resonances with the next great thing, inherited from technical communities, have shown themselves many times in Boxer's funding history. Here's one example that seems particularly poignant.

At one time, one of the prominent themes in funding circles was reusable software. This issue is especially important to computational media and new literacies. I've already discussed (e.g., in chapters 2 and 7) organic growth of software, rich and flexible toolsets that allow the coevolution of communities and the material resources they use, and even the efficiency of computational media in getting around the problem of large, monolithic, and inflexible software applications.

One of my project colleagues reported to me a conversation he had with a funding officer.

Official: Does Boxer do text processing?

Colleague: Yes.

Official: Why don't you just use Microsoft Word for that? We can't just have every software developer reinventing the wheel!

The conversation is ironic in the context of Boxer's technical intent to break the monopoly of large, nonmodifiable software units. It is ironic in the context of Boxer's ambitious goal of being an exemplar medium capable of supporting a huge range of genres and niches. It is even more ironic in view of Boxer's strategy as a prototype computational medium that can support *new* literacies. We wanted to extend text processing with fundamentally new capabilities of organization, dynamics, and interaction. How could we do that and leave text processing alone or make it a separate, stand-alone application? For example, "use Microsoft Word" rules out exploring the spatial metaphor, which critically expands expressiveness, in part by enfolding representations of process. (See chapter 7.)

Thinking that these misunderstandings of goals and means arise from maliciousness or ignorance would be a serious mistake. Instead, we penetrate the process of cultural change or cultural stability by understanding why they are so expectable and difficult to avoid.

First, what is happening here is an awkward knee-jerk antiresonance concerning technical issues. This Word advocate is taking for granted current assumptions about the architecture of computer systems (e.g., that text processing is a modular function accomplished by a separate application) in judging a piece of software that violates those assumptions. However, we violate those assumptions (in part) precisely to get past the problem that motivates this criticism. Every application should not need to implement its own form of text processing or programming, which should be universal media resources. Because Boxer addresses redundancy and reusability in a nonstandard way, it appears to be contributing to the problem rather than to the solution. The self-evident state of the art blinds people to other possibilities.

Second, and probably more important, Boxer's agenda is just plain big. I believe this officer's concerns are part of what we want to address, but they are down one or two levels of importance. Boxer has connections to reusable software that are real and significant, but I never start a discussion of our work by talking about this sort of thing; the overarching conception of computational media and new literacies is really the critical top-level entry point. Superficial antiresonances with the entry point then block deeper considerations.

How might program officers surpass superficial antiresonances? (If our project deserved termination, surely we must still understand how *some* project might come to resources that allow it to pursue big and unfamiliar agendas.) Time for thoughtful attention is the only solution I can think of. Unfortunately, time is not a luxury program officers have. Few resources are put at the disposal of these critical guides, and ever more demands are made on them. Economy in governance is laudable, but leadership with the time and the resources to do that job are prerequisite to surpassing the garden path of always only incremental change.

The larger concern is with the resources that our society puts into educational research that could lead to the sort of change envisioned in this book. There are many ways to look at this concern, and they all come to the same unfavorable conclusion. Consider, for example, that public education in the United States is about a \$300 billion a year industry. What is a reasonable fraction of such investment that should be spent on research and advanced development? Five percent may be conservative, leading to \$15 billion per year, but that is almost five times the yearly budget of the entire NSF, the only serious funder that might support research in the sorts of issues covered in this book. The division of NSF that deals with education is about one-fifth the NSF budget, and if you take out support for fellowships, infrastructural support, and so on, the real educational research budget is certainly less than half that. Arguably, the biggest and best public pocket (private foundations are dwarfed by government funding) appears, at best, to support a reinvestment ratio of about one-tenth of one percent—about 2 percent of a reasonable need.

If your salary were cut to 2 percent of a living wage, how would you get along?

There are many ways to define and cut pies, so I don't want to overstress this particular calculation. If you throw in what Department of Education counts as research, that might double the 2 percent figure. Some responsible people would claim that the amount of genuine, basic educational research funded by the U.S. government is less than $10 million per year, less than a tenth of one percent of a sensible amount. The qualitative conclusion, relative to the goals of this book, is not contestable, as far as I'm concerned. There is very little chance—bordering on none—for projects as big or unusual as the one described in this book to get and keep funding. In retrospect, it's amazing we did so well.

Big Problems

Funding is salient, but it is only a piece of what I call the "big problem problem." Understanding the scale of the problem you are dealing with is a critical part of getting it solved. If the United States limited itself to a few percent (as described above) of the effort it put into the Manhattan Project or the attempt to put a man on the moon, it would have been far better not to start either project. Some sciences are in a position to argue effectively that critical projects (1) must be done and (2) have a large threshold of investment. "You can't investigate atomic particles without a billion-dollar accelerator," or "mapping the human genome will provide the foundation for myriads of wonderful new accomplishments." Finding out how computational media can work is the biggest, most timely, and potentially most important educational problem that I know. It includes understanding certain types of cultural change, not to mention how material intelligence works. Even the modest goal of a single responsible study of the cultural context of a school innovation is much more than an illusory "validating that it works," much more than I have seen funders willing to pay. The pity is that such experiments are well within reasonable reinvestment parameters for such a large and important enterprise as education.

Education is triply lacking in the face of big problems. First, the field of education doesn't generally appreciate how difficult and large the issues it faces genuinely are. The incremental assumptions of standard educational research provide no purchase in big problems or big possibilities because they assume things will stay more or less the same. New subject matter is invalid. New standards of knowledge are suspect. Teachers will never be more professionally responsible.

Second, educators have been trained out of going after big scientific problems. A critical distinction is necessary. Society is always faced with big problems that deserve correspondingly big resources—such as equity, economic prosperity, social welfare, and the rule of law—but it is seldom true that science can make the critical contribution. Education has always been treated as one of those huge but scientifically intractable problems, so if money is spent, it's on programs, policy, and dissemination of methods. In contrast, new literacies are a scientific issue right now—not a matter of policy or dissemination. Computational media offer unprecedented promise, but we do not have ready technology and know-how. They must be developed. Educational researchers need to define a clear, long-range program; they need to learn how to coordinate and run such a program and to connect productively with demands for instant fixes to educational problems.

Finally, even if education generates a responsible commitment to the real scale of problems it faces, and even if the profession were far better prepared internally to undertake them, who would believe it? Education is so far behind in scientific status that I am quite certain resolving the status and belief issue will lag even the apparently more substantial problems. Politicians and the public need to learn to take science seriously in education and to develop stable, long-term funding commitments.

I want to close this section by taking a short look at commercial development. Commercial development is a critical stage. No academic setting can hope to produce, support, and consistently upgrade a significant piece of software. That's just not what universities are for. In our project's case, the sensible road to scientifically experimenting at the cultural level has apparently been foreclosed. If we want any data on these issues, however unscientifically prepared and collected, or if we have the faintest hope that Boxer might really support a widespread literacy, we have to go commercial technologically and grassroots intellectually.

Scale is less an issue with the community that decides commercial investment. Provided large returns can be expected, large investments are possible. Instead, the unfamiliarity with the concept of computational medium (as pursued in this book) is the most salient block.

The community that is likely to pick up and fund software development is also likely to be technologically savvy and hence educationally conservative by dint of divisions between technological and humanistic cultures. Educational and cultural issues rarely come up when I talk to members of that community. Instead, Boxer's position in the contemporary technological landscape is at issue. I am asked, "What are Boxer's software competitors?" An honest answer is that, I believe, there are none. That's an unacceptable answer. A more nuanced answer is that many pieces of software represent different aspects of Boxer's goals, even if none are serious contenders for the most central of them. That's a very complicated answer, however, and integrating the pieces of it into a sense for what computational media might achieve is not something to expect in a few meetings. What frequently happens is that one currently popular genre gets picked as a model for Boxer—say, an authoring language (for professional developers to make materials for schools)—but a computational medium just doesn't match existing social niches well enough, so a negative assessment of competitive advantage is likely.

The force of contemporary software models has been surprising to me. Getting beyond them is a serious issue. After a fairly recent talk I gave about computational media and new literacies, an intelligent and well-informed listener noted that, given our goals, it sounded as if we were dealing with a new class of software. "Maybe you shouldn't call it a programming language," he said! "Maybe it needs a new name." I was stunned, but politely (I hope) offered the term *computational medium*. Evidently he caught a glimpse of what we intended, but that was on the background assumption that Boxer was (just) a programming language. Despite how I talk, ready technological assumptions control perceptions.

Uncertainties

In this section, I want very briefly to introduce two other issues that bear on the emergence of new literacies. The economics of computational media pose an interesting paradox. On the one hand, the structure of the medium very likely should not be owned by anyone. This is just like the fact that the alphabet, grammar, syntax, and vocabulary of natural language, not to mention literary genres, are not owned by anyone. On the other hand, the standard path to commercial development is the opposite. Someone must own the resources and hence expect to get significant return on investment.

In some countries, it is remotely possible that the government could play a central role in supporting the infrastructure of computational media, as governments have taken on infrastructural responsibilities in areas such as highways and even the Internet. However, given present expectations and incomprehension of computational media, this scenario is unlikely. Without public interest and contributions to development, the only plausible path is vested commercial interest, transitioning to multiple implementations that share a core structure. It will be fascinating to watch the conflict and negotiation between diverse interests that will eventually result (one hopes) in standards or strong conventions.

The economics of materials prepared in the medium is also problematic. The goal of being open and modifiable conflicts with the profit motive. If someone has an excellent idea that anyone can copy, the economic motive for developing good ideas is undermined. I hope to see a lively community of free materials develop; this community seems a natural concomitant to making a system that almost everyone can master in production as well as in consumption, but large constructions, on the scale of books, are an important part of computational media as well. How do these constructions get supported?

Finally, let me reopen one of the working assumptions of this book, which is that we should study and support the development of a unified computational medium. The commonsense view of computer literacy is that people should know a little about all sorts of different systems or applications, or at least they should learn the commonalties of such systems—say, the interface conventions. Deep literacies cannot follow from superficial structures, however. In order to be sufficiently expressive, a computational medium must make choices and, in particular, make a choice about how users will produce and consume dynamic, interactive entities. The average application (much less the common form of all applications) has no such structure at all. Multiplying media forgoes the immense power of synergy, which we spent so much time discussing, particularly in chapters 1 and 7. In multiplying media, we forgo the powerful incremental learning in menial utility and in everyday learning/use cycles; we forgo possibilities of combining and modifying any constructions. We introduce more incompatibilities, more problematic redundancies. In the end, we forgo the very social and cultural synergies that validate the notion of literacy in general—the convergence of multiple niches on common forms.

Inasmuch as our project has explored the issue, there seems no reason at this stage to bail out of the idea that a single form, more or less, can support the diverse uses necessary to constitute a literacy. For example, although Boxer does not do everything it might, we have uncovered no technical reason (as opposed to funding reasons, for example) why a system like Boxer could not be extended in any of the ways it seems limited now. The strain of satisfying too many demands at once might well break up the notion of a single, common medium, but before any widespread synergy emerges is too early to anticipate divergence.

An Essential Tension

So this is the state of the art. Most of this book explores the successes, both theoretical and in small-scale experiments, of the concept of computational media and new literacies. It appears that computational media *can* change the way people think and learn. Our project work has been successful far beyond my initial expectations, given what a big problem we took on and how few resources we had to put into the research. Our real-world successes especially surprised me because we never got to the stage where social forces and common intuitions in a significant community could begin to work with us, rather than against us. We saw that a technical basis for a new literacy is achievable. Even if Boxer is still not ideal, it surpasses critical thresholds of learnability and expressiveness. We saw children learning difficult things far earlier and in radically different ways than in current educational practice. We began to understand how different expressive possibilities could make this happen. At the same time, we peeked through cracks of newly opened doors to new *forms* of knowledge that can be enhanced with computational media—including intuition and the knowledge implicit in everyday activity—not just new methods of instruction or even new subjects to teach. We saw pockets of committed learning—of deep student engagement with intellectual enterprises—that we could understand as emerging from new, interactive representations and from individual and community ownership. We could in turn appreciate that ownership as conveyed, in part, by the two-way properties of the medium. We saw innovative use of the medium falling comfortably into tiny moments in a classroom and into the realization of impressive, long-term accomplishments by children and teachers.

We also understand, I hope, a little more about the power and importance of the social embedding of literacy. This understanding led us eventually to consider the processes of social change involved with the emergence of relevant social niches and to investigate the cultural resonance that is so important at early stages of emerging new paradigms. Seen through the lens of cultural resonance, the current state does not look encouraging. In contrast to the technical and cognitive pillars for new literacies, the social and cultural pillar looks spindly and uncertain.

I see two ways to summarize our analysis of macroculture and social change. The first is pessimistic. In view of the many interconnected and deeply embedded practices and ways of thinking that characterize cultures, how can we still expect a new regime with a new literacy basis to develop? On the other side, this chapter merely elaborates and exemplifies what we said from the beginning: literacies penetrate deeply into cultures and permeate not only everyday activity, but also priorities, values, assumptions about knowledge, assumptions about media, and expectations about what is intellectually possible for people. Were this not so, there would be little point thinking about old literacies or considering new ones. To boot, thinking about macrocultural issues should have made us just a little wiser about the scale of the change on which we may be embarking, about the timescale to success, and about what we can expect and should attend to along the way.

Complexity and seeming intractability notwithstanding, I do have some predictions about the future of computational media and new literacies. I do not believe the arguments of this book will carry the day. Analysis, data, and argument go only so far against the tide of self-evident judgments borne of culturally supported intuition. Instead, experience is the key. I believe we have really crossed a technical threshold. Cognitive challenges are manageable, so more and more people will experience the power of two-way computational media, even in bits and pieces. Their intuitions will change about what good software systems are like and about how learning in the context of computers should and can be. New literacies have a secret and most powerful ally: people *are* smart and creative, and they will soon enough be even smarter. Above all, children who are given a chance to show "newfound" intelligence will surprise and impress with their enthusiastic accomplishments.

Will Boxer be the first recognized new literacy basis? Despite the hurdles, I believe we need only one good break to cross into widespread visibility. That is likely, I hope, but not assured. In any case, Boxer has many good ideas to recommend to future designers of computational media.

I have a final word. This book has been, above all else, my attempt to lay out a road map of vastly underrated possibilities and understudied but fundamental scientific issues. I have regarded it as a challenging privilege to try to change some minds about how minds can change. In my most skeptical moments—regardless of what happens with Boxer or with the particular images of new literacies I have painted here—I can't believe it won't prove to have been worth the trouble.

Notes and Resources

In order to promote accessibility, I avoided scholarly trappings in the text, such as references, historical contextualizations, and footnotes. This addendum provides:

• References to technical work that contains details of concepts, theories, and empirical studies that are discussed in the text
• Some contextualization in terms of related (and contrasting) ideas and in terms of the history of the intellectual lines that show in the text
• An annotated bibliographic list related to some of the more important ideas in the book, for those who wish to pursue the issues

These notes and references are organized by chapter; they are also roughly in the same sequence as the corresponding discussion within chapters. Of course, the placement of notes related to general themes or to issues treated in several places is somewhat arbitrary.

In addition to the following notes and references, the Boxer Project will make available information about Boxer at our Web site as long as is possible—including software downloads, sample materials, and other information:

http://www.soe.berkeley.edu/boxer/

Chapter 1: Computational Media and New Literacies

What Value Is Literacy?

Jack Goody provides an interesting, if perhaps aging, attempt to describe what literacy has done for civilization. His orientation is more essentialist than mine. That is, he acts as if we can decide once and for all what literacy is about—in contrast to the diverse and probably ever-changing social niches that may alter the meanings and implications of literacies across time and for different groups of people.

Goody, Jack. 1977. *The Domestication of the Savage Mind*. Cambridge: Cambridge University Press.

A slightly more recent attempt is given in:

Ong, Walter J. 1982. *Orality and Literacy: The Technologizing of the Word.* London: Methuen.

The best, most recent account that I know of the consequences of literacy development, in the line of the works cited above, is:

Olson, D. R. 1994. *The World on Paper: The Conceptual and Cognitive Implications of Writing and Reading.* Cambridge: Cambridge University Press.

Scribner and Cole show that literacy is not the technical feat of learning to use a particular inscription system. Instead, what literacy does for people depends in a critical way on the community practices that use the technical competence. As such, their account is resonant with my social niches view and with the importance of activity (chapters 4 and 5) as a knowledge repository and knowledge generator.

Scribner, S., and M. Cole. 1981. *The Psychology of Literacy.* Cambridge, Mass.: Harvard University Press.

The History of Mathematical Thinking and Notation Systems

An excellent account of the development of mathematical notations, including algebra, is given in:

Smith, D. E. 1958. *History of Mathematics.* New York: Dover.

See also:

Cajori, F. 1928–29. *A History of Mathematical Notation.* Chicago: Open Court.

The mathematically interested reader may wish to look through Galileo for precursors to graphing and calculus. See, for example, Theorem 1 of Day 3 (p. 173 in the cited edition). There, Galileo seems to be "graphing" speed versus time, viewing distance as "area under the curve" of velocity, and viewing area as an accumulation of infinitely thin rectangular slivers (like the Riemann integral depicted in figure 8.7).

Galilei, Galileo. 1954. *Dialogues Concerning Two New Sciences.* Translated by Henry Crew and Alfonso de Salvio. New York: Dover.

Genres

My use of the idea of genres was inspired, in part, by the Russian literary theorist M. M. Bakhtin. He emphasized especially the diversity of forms and the complexity of their interaction (heterglossia). For his purposes, he included stylized forms of speech, as well as material forms, in the definition of genre:

short rejoinders of daily dialogue . . . , everyday narration, writing (in all its various forms), the fairly variegated repertoire of business documents . . . , and the diverse world of commentary. . . . And we must also include here the diverse forms of scientific statements and all the literary genres (from the proverb to the multivolume novel). (pp. 60–61)

Bakhtin, M. M. 1986. *Speech Genres and Other Essays.* Translated by V. W. McGee. Austin: University of Texas Press.

Chapter 2: How It Might Be

The Range of Expressiveness of Programming

What kinds of things are well said in programming is an open issue. One fundamental unknown is exactly what programming means! For example, there are different paradigms of programming, and each seems adapted to expressing different things. Early on, some people thought *logic programming* would be better adapted to helping people think than the kind of programming that emphasizes process, which is evident in Boxer. Logic programming involves programming by making assertions and adding inference rules without organizing them into a process (e.g., of reasoning or proof). The hopes for logic programming have not been realized, although issues of language learnability may well have prohibited effective exploration of expressive possibilities. The extinct (I believe) language Prolog was used to experiment.

Mitchel Resnick's article explores an interesting variant of procedural programming called parallel processing. His book contains extensive detail.

Resnick, M. 1995. "New Paradigms for Computing, New Paradigms for Thinking." In *Computers and Exploratory Learning,* edited by A. diSessa, C. Hoyles, and R. Noss, with L. Edwards, 31–43. Berlin: Springer.

Resnick, M. 1994. *Turtles, Termites, and Traffic Jams: Explorations in Massively Parallel Microworlds.* Cambridge, Mass.: MIT Press.

Programming As a Representation in Learning Physics

Our group has written a fair amount about how programming affects the learning of physics. For example, the following article describes many of the ways in which a learning activity that uses programming as a representation differs from using simply natural language, for example.

diSessa, A. A. 1995. "Designing Newton's Laws: Patterns of Social and Representational Feedback in a Learning Task." In *Dialogue and Interaction: Modeling Interaction in Intelligent Tutoring Systems,* edited by R.-J. Beun, M. Baker, and M. Reiner, 105–22. Berlin: Springer.

Bruce Sherin's thesis is an inquiry into how choice of representation affects concepts. He studied how students think about and learn physics using contrasting representational systems, algebra and programming. His conclusion is that representations are involved at the deepest levels in conceptualizing, and in his data he shows where the connection lies.

Sherin, B. L. 1996. "The Symbolic Basis of Physical Intuition: A Study of Two Symbol Systems in Physics Instruction." Ph.D. diss., Graduate Group in Science and Mathematics Education, University of California, Berkeley.

Probably the best single reference concerning the course we gave to sixth-grade children on physics is:

diSessa, A. A. 1995. "The Many Faces of a Computational Medium." In *Computers and Exploratory Learning,* edited by A. diSessa, C. Hoyles, and R. Noss, with L. Edwards, 337–59. Berlin: Springer.

Boxer Vectors

Boxer vectors and some of the other materials we used with students in teaching physics are available in the demonstration programs that come with Boxer. Check our Web site for download instructions:

http://www.soe.berkeley.edu/boxer/

Flexible Toolsets

The following reference describes the ideas behind flexible toolsets in more detail, particularly explaining some technical features of Boxer that facilitate building and using such tools:

diSessa, A. A. 1997. "Open Toolsets: New Ends and New Means in Learning Mathematics and Science with Computers." In *Proceedings of the 21st Conference of the International Group for the Psychology of Mathematics Education,* vol. 1, edited by E. Pehkonen, 47–62. Lahti, Finland.

This paper is available on-line in the papers section of the Boxer web site:

http://www.soe.berkeley.edu/boxer/papers.html

Chapter 3: Snapshots

Learning Motion with a Computational Medium

diSessa, "The Many Faces of a Computational Medium" (cited in the references for chapter 2) gives an overview of the course from which many of the vignettes in chapter 3 are taken.

Rare Ideas

Eleanor Duckworth writes eloquently about the importance of rare occurrences.

Duckworth, E. R. 1996. *"The Having of Wonderful Ideas" and Other Essays on Teaching and Learning.* 2d Ed. New York: Teachers College Press.

Teachers' cultivation of unusual occurrences and counting on student contributions are explored in:

diSessa, A. A., and J. Minstrell. 1998. "Cultivating Conceptual Change with Benchmark Lessons." In *Thinking Practices,* edited by J. G. Greeno and S. Goldman, 155–87. Mahwah, N.J.: Lawrence Erlbaum.

Collaborating in Boxer

Boxer has many features that facilitate collaboration, such as we saw in the student library Tina started. See:

diSessa, A. A. 1995. "Collaborating via Boxer." In *Technology—A Bridge between Teaching and Learning Mathematics,* edited by L. Burton and B. Jaworski, 69–94. Bromley, Kent: Chartwell-Bratt.

The same features of Boxer are implicitly referenced in the discussion about tools, tool sharing, and organic growth (chapter 7).

Henri's Infinity Class

Henri's infinity class's box, in which I have overlaid a few of my own observations, is distributed with the mathematics demonstration materials in the current release of Boxer:

http://www.soe.berkeley.edu/boxer/

Appropriation

Appropriation is discussed intermittently in this and other chapters. For a more expansive treatment, see:

Newman, D., P. Griffin, and M. Cole. 1989. *The Construction Zone: Working for Cognitive Change in School.* Cambridge: Cambridge University Press.

Chapter 4: Foundations of Knowledge and Learning

Words and Concepts

The relation of words to concepts is treated in:

diSessa, A. A., and B. Sherin. 1998. "What Changes in Conceptual Change?" *International Journal of Science Education* 20, no. 10: 1155–91.

In short, thinking of concepts as words is an unhelpful oversimplification.

"Activity Theory" and a Theory of the Structure of Activities

Those who know relevant literature may be puzzled that I claim no theory of the structure of activities and engagement exists. Many thinkers, from philosophers to social theorists, have studied activity and developed theories of it. None of these theories comes very close to what I feel is needed, however. Philosophical accounts of activity appear far too high level and incapable of handling the manifest and important diversity of people's engagement and activity structures. Self-described "activity theorists," such as Alexei Leont'iev and especially more recent Scandinavian thinkers, tend to emphasize large-scale and persistent social structures as opposed to either the diverse trajectories of individuals or generativity, how activity structures change. None of these thinkers is interested in what it feels like to a person to be engaged and committed or in how interest intertwines with competence.

At least some researchers are beginning to try to integrate theories of competence with theories of activity. Geoff Saxe is one; he situates cognitive change in the larger context of human action, even if activity is still typically described as relatively fixed in social structures.

Saxe, G. B. 1990. *Culture and Cognitive Development: Studies in Mathematical Understanding*. Mahwah, N.J.: Lawrence Erlbaum.

Theorists of engagement, such as Csikszentmihalyi, put personal experience front and center.

Csikszentmihalyi, M. 1996. *Creativity: Flow and the Psychology of Discovery and Invention*. New York: Harper Collins.

See also his book on talented teenagers.

Network of Enterprises

How Darwin managed a diverse but synergistic collection of research enterprises is explored in:

Gruber, H. E. 1981. *Darwin on Man: A Psychological Study of Scientific Creativity*. Chicago: University of Chicago Press.

Scaffolding Incompetence

The regime of competence sounds a lot like Vygotsky's zone of proximal development.

Vygotsky, L. S. 1978. *Mind in Society: The Development of Higher Psychological Processes*. Translated and edited by M. Cole, V. John-Steiner, S. Scribner, and E. Souberman. Cambridge, Mass.: Harvard University Press.

In fact, one might define Vygotsky's zone of proximal development as the gap between individual and collaborative regimes of competence. However, I find Vygotsky 's epistemological perspective limiting. Like Piaget, he emphasized limits, rather than strengths, of intuitive knowledge. He seemed to believe knowledge is passed down rather than re-created, and he backgrounded the "feel," texture, and generativity of activities and their relationship to learning.

Children as Little Scientists

At least as far back as Piaget, people have put forward the metaphor of "child as scientist." Piaget had an excellent point to make. Children are active learners. He believed that one could determine universal epistemological principles that governed both the development of children's intellect and scientists' knowledge. At least, he wanted to see scientific progress as a natural continuation of the children's intellectual development.

However, one can easily take this metaphor too far. Particularly with respect to activity structures and interests, children do not match scientists very well. Furthermore, it is dangerous to take aspects of a scientist's activity fabric, such as "doing an experiment," and project it unaltered into a child's life. I made the point in the text that although my electronics activities developed naturally into scientific learning, piece by piece, they did not look very scientific. We need to look more deeply at the continuities and differences between being a child and being a scientist. The following reference further explores images such as "child as scientist":

diSessa, A. A. 1992. "Images of Learning." In *Computer-based Learning Environments and Problem Solving,* edited by E. De Corte, M. C. Linn, H. Mandl, and L. Verschaffel, 19–40. Berlin: Springer.

Chapter 5: Intuition and Activity Elaborated

P-prims and Epistemology

The idea of intuitive knowledge as p-prims has a long history. An early reference that still gives an excellent and not very technical introduction is:

diSessa, A. A. 1983. "Phenomenology and the Evolution of Intuition." In *Mental Models,* edited by D. Gentner and A. Stevens, 15–33. Mahwah, N.J.: Lawrence Erlbaum.

A slightly later reference, which also makes the connection between p-prims and instruction using computers, is:

diSessa, A. A. 1988. "Knowledge in Pieces." In *Constructivism in the Computer Age,* edited by G. Forman and P. Pufall, 49–70. Mahwah, N.J.: Lawrence Erlbaum.

The full theory of p-prims as knowledge, with many examples and relevant data, is provided in:

diSessa, A. A. 1993. "Toward an Epistemology of Physics." *Cognition and Instruction* 10, nos. 2–3: 105–225; "Responses to Commentary," 261–80. (*Cognition and Instruction,* monograph no. 1.)

In the following paper, we try to uncover hidden assumptions about knowledge that make past research on conceptual change less valuable than might be.

Smith, J. P., A. A. diSessa, and J. Roschelle. 1993. "Misconceptions Reconceived: A Constructivist Analysis of Knowledge in Transition." *Journal of the Learning Sciences* 3, no. 2: 115–63.

P-prims and the Social World

The connection between how people think about the physical world and how they think about the social world is extremely interesting and much debated. In the following paper, I take the unpopular position that the relationship is not simple: social knowledge is not completely grounded on physical knowledge, nor is the reverse true, nor are they completely separate knowledge systems. Instead, there is an interesting partial overlap and mutual developmental history.

diSessa, A. A. (In press). "Does the Mind Know the Difference between the Physical and Social Worlds?" In *Culture, Development, and Knowledge,* edited by L. Nucci, G. Saxe, and E. Turiel. Mahwah, N.J.: Lawrence Erlbaum.

Is Intuitive Knowledge Misconceived?

A great many people have researched intuitive ideas and their contribution to or detraction from learning science. One good review is:

Confrey, J. 1990. "A Review of the Research on Student Conceptions in Mathematics, Science, and Programming." In *Review of Research in Education,* vol. 16, edited by C. Cazden, 3–56. Washington, D.C.: American Educational Research Association.

Researchers studying naive or novice conceptions have varied greatly in their sensitivity to the distinction between intuitive knowledge and conventional knowledge forms such as logic, facts, or concepts. In contrast, near unanimity has reigned concerning correctness. Very few researchers, especially early on, have seen any positive value in intuitive ideas. Mainly, naive ideas were seen to interfere with learning and hence had to be overcome. A landmark is the work of Michael McCloskey because of his unusually direct claims and because his work was probably the most widely read of this genre. He claimed intuitive physics is theoretical, he named the theory he believed it to represent, and he proposed only negative influence for such ideas.

McCloskey, M. 1983. "Naive Theories of Motion." In *Mental Models,* edited by D. Gentner and A. Stevens, 299–324. Mahwah, N.J.: Lawrence Erlbaum.

Two contributors have stood out in championing the productivity of naive ideas: Jim Minstrell and John Clement. Even Clement, however, describes the use of intuitive ideas productively in instruction as something that requires great care and finesse.

Minstrell, J. 1989. "Teaching Science for Understanding." In *Toward the Thinking Curriculum,* edited by L. B. Resnick and L. Klopfer, 133–49. Alexandria, Va.: Association of Supervision and Curriculum Development.

Clement, J. 1987. "Overcoming Students' Misconceptions in Physics: The Role of Anchoring Intuitions and Analogical Validity." In *Proceedings of the Second International Seminar on Misconceptions and Educational Strategies in Science and Mathematics,* edited by J. D. Novak, 223–34. Mahwah, N.J.: Lawrence Erlbaum.

"Misconceptions Reconceived" by Smith, diSessa, and Roschelle (cited earlier for this chapter) reviews the history of researcher evaluations concerning the form (are they theories or concepts?) and validity (can they be dismissed as wrong?) of intuitive ideas. DiSessa and Sherin, "What Changes in Conceptual Change?"

(chapter 4 references), provide a more elaborate model of the relation between intuitive knowledge and scientific concepts.

Rare Events and Wonderful Ideas

Again, see Duckworth, *"The Having of Wonderful Ideas"* (chapter 3 references).

Another Enrichment Frame

The existence and richness of intuitive knowledge actually provides a basis for a very easy enrichment frame. Engage it and talk about it! Many teachers build lessons on this basis, and some have a well-elaborated practice of drawing out intuitive knowledge in productive learning discussions. See diSessa and Minstrell, "Cultivating Conceptual Change with Benchmark Lessons" (chapter 3 references).

Chapter 6: Explaining Things, Explainable Things

Knowledge Telling versus Knowledge Transforming

That using a medium ("writing") is not just translating preexisting ideas into it is a fundamental fact about literacies. Writing is a reasoning medium, not just a memory or storage medium. Scardamalia and Bereiter have documented that students who believe writing is merely a matter of saying what you think perform less adequately than students who understand that in writing we transform our thinking.

Scardamalia, M., and C. Bereiter. 1987. "Knowledge Telling and Knowledge Transforming in Written Composition." In *Advances in Applied Psycholinguistics*. Vol. 2, *Reading, Writing, and Language Learning*, edited by S. Rosenberg, 142–75. Cambridge: Cambridge University Press.

Thinking with a Medium

diSessa, "Designing Newton's Laws" (chapter 2 references), provides an example of how a group design project is transformed when it is done using a computational medium.

From Logo to Boxer

Logo is a computer language for learning, very much in the spirit of a computational medium. In fact, the ideas that led to Boxer took root while I was a member of the Logo group at MIT. Logo was the first highly visible example of educational software that aimed both for a very broad expressiveness and for preserving the ability of every "user" to be a creator as well as a consumer. Given the landscape of educational computing, the philosophy behind Boxer is substantially aligned with that presented by Seymour Papert, Logo's chief exponent. An early and extremely popular presentation appears in:

Papert, S. 1980. *Mindstorms: Computers, Children, and Powerful Ideas.* New York: Basic.

More recent popular accounts of this line are:

Papert, S. 1993. *The Children's Machine: Rethinking School in the Age of the Computer.* New York: Basic.

Papert, S. 1996. *The Connected Family: Bridging the Digital Generation Gap.* Atlanta: Longstreet.

A good fairly recent representative of Papert's group's work is:

Harel, I., and S. Papert. 1991. *Constructionism.* Norwood, N.J.: Ablex.

Boxer's biggest breaks from the Logo tradition are probably two-fold. The Boxer group has steadfastly pursued the intellectual, political, and practical entailments of computational literacy. Probably for reasons of cultural nonresonance (chapter 9), the literacy metaphor has been muted in the Logo community. The second difference is that we believed essential changes in the basic medium—toward comprehensibility and broader usefulness—would make big differences in the feasibility of computational literacy. For example, the current descendent of Logo (called Microworlds) aims more toward encompassing currently popular func-tionalities (adding particular built-in subapplications, such as a paint program). Boxer, in contrast, has concentrated on structural change that would enable easier creation and use of any tools and subapplications. See:

diSessa, A. A. 1997. "Twenty Reasons Why You Should Use Boxer (Instead of Logo)." In *Learning and Exploring with Logo: Proceedings of the Sixth European Logo Conference,* edited by M. Turcsányi-Szabó, 7–27. Budapest, Hungary.

This paper is on line at:

http://www.soe.berkeley.edu/boxer/papers.html

Antitechnology Rhetoric

Generally, I avoid responding in this book to blanket antitechnology rhetoric. Weizenbaum and the Dreyfus brothers have provided good examples of such rhet-oric. The second reference, below, specifically targets education.

Weizenbaum, J. 1976. *Computer Power and Human Reason: From Judgment to Calculation.* San Francisco: W. H. Freeman.

Dreyfus, H. L., S. E. Dreyfus, and T. Athanasiou. 1988. *Mind over Machine: The Power of Human Intuition and Expertise in the Era of the Computer.* New York: Free Press.

For an update, consider:

Dreyfus, H. L. 1992. *What Computers Still Can't Do: A Critique of Artificial Reason.* Cambridge, Mass.: MIT Press.

Larry Cuban is an influential current exponent of the theme (at the risk of over-simplification) "computers are no different from film-loop projectors or televisions; they won't make a dent in education." This book—especially chapters 1, 2, 6, and 7—makes it clear we must distinguish technologies for how they may or may not have influence. In particular, computers introduce new representational forms (chapter 8) that are impossible to dismiss in areas such as scientific work. Computers may not transform education; however, if they do not, it won't be because all technology is indistinguishable.

Cuban, L. 1986. *Teachers and Machines: The Classroom Use of Technology Since 1920.* New York: Teachers College Press.

Tyack, D. B., and L. Cuban. 1995. *Tinkering toward Utopia: A Century of Public School Reform.* Cambridge, Mass.: Harvard University Press.

Chapter 7: Designing Computer Systems for People

Function, Structure, and All That

Probably the most complete article on technical aspects of Boxer's design is:

diSessa, A. A. 1991. "Local Sciences: Viewing the Design of Human-Computer Systems as Cognitive Science." In *Designing Interaction: Psychology at the Human-Computer Interface,* edited by J. M. Carroll, 162–202. Cambridge: Cambridge University Press.

The paper also explains some methodological aspects of designing while maintaining a scientific focus, two tasks that are at odds in the conventional wisdom about scientific versus design practices.

An easier and more accessible exposition specifically concerning function and structure in designed systems is:

diSessa, A. A. 1986. "Models of Computation." In *User Centered System Design: New Perspectives on Human-Computer Interaction,* edited by D. A. Norman and S. W. Draper, 201–18. Mahwah, N.J.: Lawrence Erlbaum.

An early and technical article on mental models that helped instigate some of my own thinking about comprehensible systems appears in the next reference. In this article, Richard Young also demonstrated that calculator design can be a good foil for broader design issues, which I followed up here.

Young, R. M. 1981. "The Machine Inside the Machine: User's Models of Pocket Calculators." *International Journal of Man-Machine Studies* 15: 51–85.

Halasz and Moran were among those who empirically validated (in the context of calculators) expectations such as functionally defined designs are less adapted to innovation.

Halasz, F., and T. Moran. 1983. "Mental Models and Problem Solving in Using a Calculator." In *Proceedings of the CHI '83 Conference on Human Factors in Computer Systems,* 212–16. New York: ACM.

An excellent thesis about the trajectory of structural and functional knowledge in learning programming is:

Mann, L. 1991. "The Implications of Functional and Structural Knowledge Representations for Novice Programmers." Ph.D. diss., Graduate Group in Mathematics and Science Education, University of California, Berkeley.

The Role of Programming

Mike Eisenberg has written eloquently against "feature mania" (a particular manifestation of too great a focus on function and of neglect of structure) and in favor of programming as a basic function of applications.

Eisenberg, M. 1995. "Creating Software Applications for Children: Some Thoughts about Design." In *Computers and Exploratory Learning,* edited by A. diSessa, C. Hoyles, and R. Noss, with L. Edwards, 175–96. Berlin: Springer.

Bonnie Nardi argues convincingly for the importance and plausibility of programming to enhance the effectiveness of computers for "ordinary people" (people who are not professional programmers). She emphasizes, as I have, the importance of the social setting of programming and the organic growth of software in contexts of use. One apparent difference is that Nardi advocates domain specific programming systems and believes general programming languages—of which Boxer is an example—are too esoteric and complex for ordinary folks. I haven't the space to explain how our points of view are more compatible on this issue than they may seem.

Nardi, Bonnie, A. 1993. *A Small Matter of Programming: Perspectives on End User Computing.* Cambridge, Mass.: MIT Press.

The Psychology of Everyday Things

Especially if you enjoyed discovering a bit about how calculators are designed, you might enjoy Donald Norman's investigations into the design of everyday things.

Norman, D. A. 1988. *The Psychology of Everyday Things.* New York: Basic.

Norman, D. A. 1993. *Things That Make Us Smart: Defending Human Attributes in the Age of the Machine.* Reading, Mass.: Addison-Wesley.

Chapter 8: More Snapshots

Inventing Graphing, Blow by Blow

The inventing graphing part of our course on motion for sixth-grade students is described in the following reference. The reference also adds more analysis of activity structures compared to the present text.

diSessa, A. A., D. Hammer, B. Sherin, and T. Kolpakowski. 1991. "Inventing Graphing: Meta-representational Expertise in Children." *Journal of Mathematical Behavior* 10, no. 2: 117–60.

Refer to diSessa, "The Many Faces of a Computational Medium" (chapter 2 references) for a description of the course in which this activity occurred.

Meta-Representational Competence

My project's recent work on meta-representational competence is just now being published. Contact us or consult our Web site for further references.

diSessa, A. A. In press. "Meta-Representation: Native Competence and Targets for Instruction." In *The Development of Notational Representations,* edited by S. Strauss. Oxford: Oxford University Press.

Computational Essays on Fractions

Idit Harel took a big step for the field in her thesis work at MIT in which elementary school students learned about fractions by producing learning materials for younger students.

Harel, I. 1991. *Children Designers.* Norwood, N.Y.: Ablex.

Knowledge Spaces and Concept Maps

The idea of knowledge spaces is explored in a bit more detail (p. 313 especially) in:

diSessa, A. A. 1990. "Social Niches for Future Software." In *Toward a Scientific Practice of Science Education,* edited by M. Gardner, J. Greeno, F. Reif, A. Schoenfeld, A. diSessa, and E. Stage, 301–22. Mahwah, N.J.: Lawrence Erlbaum.

Knowledge spaces are a generalization (involving a much broader representational range—including student innovation at representation) of the idea behind *concept maps.* Concept maps express the important meanings concerning some topic by identifying concepts as nodes and using labeled links to show their relation to other concepts.

Novak, J. D. 1998. *Learning, Creating, and Using Knowledge: Concept Maps as Facilitative Tools in Schools and Corporations.* Mahwah, N.J.: Lawrence Erlbaum.

Commercial software exists for making concept maps. In contrast to Boxer, such software can't be extended beyond node and link representations, nor can it include any other representational forms at all beyond words, nodes, and links.

Activity Components of Inventing Graphing

"Cultivating Conceptual Change with Benchmark Lessons" (chapter 3 references) highlights activity aspects of the final day of inventing graphing, when Tina broke from the designing representations plan to follow students on a wonderful debate about the concept of "stop." "The dance of ownership" is explored in some detail.

Designing Newton's Laws

"Designing Newton's Laws" (chapter 2 references) provides an account of using design as an enrichment frame for learning physics. It also gives an analysis of why a computational medium surpasses both text and algebra in thinking about physics. A more extensive empirical presentation is given in:

Sherin, B., A. A. diSessa, and D. M. Hammer. 1993. "Dynaturtle Revisited: Learning Physics through Collaborative Design of a Computer Model." *Interactive Learning Environments* 3, no. 2: 91–118.

Expertise at Reasoning about Motion

Carol and Ming's work is reported in more detail in the next reference. As with many of the accounts in this book, video is available for interested analysts.

diSessa, A. A. 1989. "A Child's Science of Motion: Overview and First Results." In *Proceedings of the Fourth International Conference for Logo and Mathematics Education,* edited by U. Leron and N. Krumholtz, 211–31. Haifa: Israeli Logo Center, Technion—Israel Institute of Technology.

A newer version of the microworld that Ming and Carol used is distributed as a physics example with the current version of Boxer. It is called "Elmira."

http://www.soe.berkeley.edu/boxer/

Using Intuitive Knowledge Wisely

I elaborated in the text how intuitive knowledge may enter into learning science and how easily it may seem a problem rather than a resource. Ming and Carol didn't guess correctly all the time; on certain problems, almost all students guess wrong, but refining intuitive ideas and changing the contexts in which children will think of using them are critical moves. Most educators don't believe this. In fact, they believe the opposite. Consult Smith, diSessa, and Roschelle, "Misconceptions Reconceived" (chapter 5 references).

Collaborating via Boxer

Once again, the ways Boxer supports effective collaborations are relevant. See diSessa, "Collaborating via Boxer" (chapter 3 references) for more detail than the text of chapter 8 on how people manage to collaborate using a computational medium.

Chapter 9: Stepping Back, Looking Forward

Transparency

The assumption that the best software should be transparent has a long history. *Direct manipulation* is one component of this history. The idea behind direct manipulation is that even for programming, one should act directly on problem-specific graphical objects, not on abstract things such as variables and procedures.

Shneiderman, B. 1983. "Direct Manipulation: A Step beyond Programming Languages." *IEEE Computer* 16, no. 8: 57–69.

One of my early critiques of this point of view is contained in:

diSessa, A. A. 1986. "Notes on the Future of Programming: Breaking the Utility Barrier." In *User Centered System Design: New Perspectives on Human-Computer Interaction,* edited by D. A. Norman and S. W. Draper, 125–52. Mahwah, N.J.: Lawrence Erlbaum.

A different treatment is provided by:

Hutchins, E. L., J. D. Hollan, and D. A. Norman. 1986. "Direct Manipulation Interfaces." In *User Centered System Design: New Perspectives on Human-Computer Interaction,* edited by D. A. Norman and S. W. Draper, 87–124. Mahwah, N.J.: Lawrence Erlbaum.

Although he does not deal with programming per se, Hancock provides an excellent discussion of transparency (the "transparency dialectic") and what it means to learn to use mathematical tools.

Hancock, C. 1995. "The Medium and the Curriculum: Reflections on Transparent Tools and Tacit Mathematics." In *Computers and Exploratory Learning,* edited by A. diSessa, C. Hoyles, and R. Noss, with L. Edwards, 221–40. Berlin: Springer.

Component Computing

In chapter 7, I didn't discuss Boxer's properties that make it an excellent medium for component computing, although that would have been appropriate. In brief, these properties are exactly what make Boxer a superb "container" system in which to implement and use families of tools that are easy to combine and modify, supporting organic growth of software as depicted in figure 7.1. See diSessa, "Open Toolsets" (chapter 2 references).

Technologists Resonate with Computational Media

There have been several important exceptions to technologists' disinterest in computational media. Doug Engelbart, inventor of the mouse, saw computers' most splendid promise in augmenting human intellect. Although I did not know of Engelbart's work before starting Boxer, Alan Kay's work at Xerox PARC was directly inspirational.

Engelbart, D. C. 1963. "A Conceptual Framework for the Augmentation of Man's Intellect." In *Vistas in Information Handling,* edited by P. Howerton, 35–65. Washington, D.C.: Spartan.

Kay, A., and A. Goldberg. 1977. "Personal Dynamic Media." *IEEE Computer* 10, no. 3: 31–42.

Large Experiments in New Literacies

There are many sites in the world where technology has deeply penetrated teaching and learning communities. Few of these employ a model of technology use that is much like the literacy model of this book. In general, the United States seems less resonant to the possibilities of new literacies than other parts of the world, such as Europe and Australia. Unfortunately, I am not aware of any site that is both committed to literacylike use of technology and has the resources and inclination to constitute a scientific testbed.

Improving the Technical Bases for Computational Literacy

Probably the most important historical line relevant to computational literacy emerged with Seymour Papert's Logo Group at MIT. Given the revolutionary grounding of the group, it is ironic that technological innovation in that community has not touched the core structures, hence learnability and expressiveness, of their adopted medium. See the discussion and references under "From Logo to Boxer" in the notes for chapter 6.

Antiprogramming Backlash

One of the original and central papers aimed at debunking the claims for programming's general, positive value was:

Pea, R., and M. Kurland. 1984. "On the Cognitive Effects of Learning Computer Programming." *New Ideas in Psychology* 2: 1137–68.

A detailed critique of that research is given in:

Noss, R., and C. Hoyles. 1996. *Windows on Mathematical Meaning*. Amsterdam: Kluwer.

A broader analysis of the scientific and nonscientific basis for rhetorically central events in the antiprogramming backlash is given in:

Hoyles, C. 1995. "Exploratory Software, Exploratory Cultures?" In *Computers and Exploratory Learning,* edited by A. diSessa, C. Hoyles, and R. Noss, with L. Edwards, 199–219. Berlin: Springer.

A reprise and update of the central debate is given in the three main articles in the "Books and Ideas" section of:

Journal of the Learning Sciences 6, no. 4 (1997).

The best single reference I know for irresponsible antitechnology statements concerning education, including most of those used in this text, is:

Teachers College Record 85, no. 4 (summer 1984).

The Big Problem Problem

There has been a faint rustling of realization that the core issues behind educational change require scientific (rather than "practical") experiments beyond currently assumed scales. One of the reflections of this realization has been increased discussion of "design experiments." The article "Local Sciences" (chapter 7 references) contains some of my own thoughts about the issue. See also:

Collins, A. 1992. "Toward a Design Science of Education." In *New Directions in Educational Technology,* edited by E. Scanlon and T. O'Shea, 15–22. New York: Springer.

Brown, A. L. 1992. "Design Experiments: Theoretical and Methodological Challenges in Creating Complex Interventions in Classroom Settings." *Journal of the Learning Sciences* 2, no. 2: 141–78.

Index

Activities
  continuity of, 105
  and graphing adventure, 204–206
  and information, 221
  and knowledge, 66
  mediated, 105
  and metarepresentation, 186–190
  and social niches, 103
  structure of, 78–87, 99–107, 253
Adaptable materials, 55–63
Algebra
  and Galileo's theorems of motion,
    14, 16
  infrastructural aspect of, 14, 19
  vs. programming, 31–33
Antilearning bias, 224–225
Applications, 145–148
Athanasiou, T., 258
Automobile steering, 125–128

Bakhtin, M., 250
Ball drop
  representing, 167
Bereiter, C., 257
Big problem problem, 242–243, 264
Bouncing babies video game, 51
Boxer, 30
  and adaptability, 203–206
  after-school library, 53
  alternatives for, 110, 112, 244
  and collaboration, 202–204, 252,
    262
  and commercial development, 244

and component computing, 227,
    263
description of, 148–160
and educators, 227–231
and Logo, 118, 257–258, 264
and menial utility, 119
multifunctionality in, 156, 160
network browsing, 154, 158
physics course, 47, 166
principles for, 149–151
project and funding history, 235–
    237
and representational intelligence, 175
and reusable software, 240
and teachers, 54–55
and technologists, 224–227
and thresholds of learnability and
    expressiveness, 246
and tools, 41, 44, 119, 252
tutorial, 55–56
Web site, 249
Boxes
  data, 30, 155
  doit, 30, 155
  file, 154
  graphics, 158
  port, 54, 159
  sprite, 158
Brown, A., 265

Cajori, F., 250
Calculators, 131–139, 259
  structural model for, 134, 135, 259

Calculus, 7, 9–11, 166, 183, 194, 250
  derivative and integral 172
  Fundamental Theorem of, 34, 172
  infrastructural aspect of, 10–11, 58
  vs. programming, 31, 34
Canceling p-prim, 193
Carol and Ming, 193–198, 206, 262
Chalk representation, 169–170
Chaos theory, 73
Clement, J., 256
Cognitive basis for literacy, 8
Cole, M., 250, 253
Collins, A., 265
Committed learning, 66, 78, 83–86, 104–105, 107, 186–189, 207, 247
  artifacts designed for, 139
Communities
  educational, 227–231
  funders and developers, 234–242
  scientific, 26
  and social niches, 26, 27
  teacher, 43, 44, 54
  technological, 223–227
  tools and, 40
  and the World Wide Web, 217
Complexity
  assessing, 131, 135, 139, 140, 142, 145, 146, 151, 156, 161–162
Component computing, 227, 262
Composing motions, 191
Computational essay, 185, 207, 261
Computational medium, 1, 24, 32, 45, 48, 52–53, 56, 58, 131, 175, 209, 216, 252
  and appropriation, 57
  commercial development, 243–244
  complexity, 161–162
  and the culture gap, 209, 222–244
  and dynamic representations, 190, 197–198
  and economics, 244–245
  and educators, 227–231
  and funders, 234–242
  history of, 231–234
  and intuitive knowledge, 98

learning, 59, 143–145, 212–213
  and metarepresentation 175–178, 207
  and multifunctionality, 124, 146–148
  and patterns of development, 151–152
  principles for, 111–119
  summary discussion, 246–248
  and technologists, 223–227
  and tool building, 41
  and the World Wide Web, 221–222
Computational structure
  principle of, 150, 152, 204
Computer literacy, 4, 109, 222, 234, 245
Computers
  expense, 211–212
  numbers of, in schools, 3
Confrey, J., 256
Continuous incremental advantage, 144–145
Csikszentmihalyi, M., 254
Cuban, L., 259
Cultural resonance, antiresonance, 211, 213–218, 222–241, 247
Culture gap, 209, 222–244
Cyberspace, 148

Dance of ownership, 187
Darwin, 83, 254
Database structure in Boxer, 156
Davy, J., 233
Descartes, 14, 166, 183
Design as an enrichment frame, 190
Dinosaur activity, 99–104
diSessa, A., 251–253, 255–256, 258–263
Dots representations, 169
Dreyfus, H., 233, 258
Dreyfus, S., 258
Duckworth, E., 252
Dynamic media, 218, 222
Dynamic representations, 190

Ecology, 24
Economics, 27, 244–245

Educational research
level of funding, 241–242
standard program, 238–239
Efficiency in learning, 85, 87
Einstein, 17, 131, 209
Eisenberg, M., 260
Electronics hobby, 66–78
Engelbart, D., 263
Enrichment frame, 106, 189–190, 257
Expressiveness, 31, 111–113, 203, 207, 218, 226, 232, 251, 257, 264

Feynman, R., 183
Flower program, 155
Force as mover, 93
Force as spinner, 93
Fractals, 59, 60

Galileo, 9, 12–19, 29, 166, 183
Dialogues Concerning Two New Sciences, 12, 15, 250
model of a toss, 36–37
six theorems of motion, 12–19, 30, 34, 197
Gearing, 120–123
Geiger counter, 68–69
Generativity, 80, 95, 103, 253–254
Genres, 22–28, 207, 250
Goldberg, A., 263
Goody, J., 249
Graphing adventure game, 199
Griffin, P., 253
Gruber, H., 83, 254

Halasz, F., 259
Hammer, D., 260, 262
Hancock, C., 263
Harel, I., 258, 261
Henri, 58–63, 180, 202, 237, 253
Hierarchical organization, 152, 154–158, 160
Hollan, J., 263
Hoyles, C., 264
Hubble telescope, 178
Hutchins, E., 262

Hypertext, 7, 109, 114, 147, 159, 175, 185
Hysteresis, 72

Implementing
new ideas, 117
representational intelligence, 175
Infinite structure in Boxer, 159–160
Infinity class and box, 41, 58–63, 253
Information, 217
illusion, 219–222
Inscription systems, 7, 18, 27, 32, 35
Intelligence, 8, 78, 166, 175
implementing, 175
Interactive media, 218, 222
Interest, 78–82
Internet, 43, 214–222
Intuitive knowledge, 66, 71–78, 89–99, 185, 174, 190, 195–197, 221, 247, 256, 262
Inventing graphing, 166, 177, 186–190, 260

Jan, 170–174, 188
Java, 217–218
Jerk (motion), 50

Kay, A., 263
Know-how, 220
Knowledge space, 185, 207
Kolpakowski, T., 260
Kurland, M., 264

Law of the little, 47, 51, 177, 180
Learning/use cycle, 118, 119, 161, 213
Leibniz, 9–10, 19, 58, 183
Linearity, nonlinearity, 72–75
Literacy, 1–3
central hypothesis, 25, 245–246
computational, 2, 4, 29, 113, 142, 165, 209–210, 222–223
and cumulativity, 230
definition of, 19, 24
grand canyon view of, 26

Literacy (cont.)
  history and theory of, 249–250
  infrastructural aspect of, 2, 5
  invisibility of, 46, 64
  material forms for, 20, 24, 27, 106–163
  skills basis for, 20–21, 25
  three pillars of, 6
  and transparency, 225
  two-way, 113, 207, 218, 221
  and values, 21, 27
Literature of representational forms, 178
Logic and intuitive knowledge, 93–97
Logo, 118, 257–258, 264

Macintosh design personality, 137
Mann, L., 260
Material basis for literacy, 6–7
Material intelligence, 5, 18, 29, 115, 166
  cognitive view of, 12
  social view of, 19
Maxwell's equations, 17
McCloskey, M., 256
Menial utility, 117–119, 213, 246
Metamedium, 166, 177
Metarepresentation 166, 175, 178, 183, 190, 206–207, 261
Mickey's tutorial, 56
Microworld, 47
  motion, 193
Minstrell, J., 252, 256, 257
Misconceptions, 97, 107
Modes and mistakes, 140–141
Mohammed, 180
Molecular toolkit, 181–184
Moran, T., 259
Multifunctionality, 26, 32, 122, 123–124, 138, 139, 146–148, 156, 160
Multimedia, 110, 114, 147, 178

Nardi, B., 260
Newman, D., 253
Newton, 9–10, 19, 37, 58, 166, 183
Newton's laws, 186, 190, 251, 262

Nightmare bike, 120–123, 134
Norman, D., 260, 263
Noss, R., 264
Novak, J., 261

Ohm's p-prim, 90–91
Olson, D. R., 250
Ong, W., 250
Oompht, 50–51
Orbit example, 95
Ownership, 47, 49, 54–55, 187

P-prims, 89–98, 107, 121, 126, 138, 191, 255
  and computational media, 98
Papert, S., 118, 258, 264
Patterns of change, 75–76
Pea, R., 264
Piaget, J. 254
Pocket organizers, 139–142
Pokability, 156, 201
Potential energy, 76–77
Programming, 29
  analytic property of, 34
  expressiveness of, 31, 251
  history of in schools, 231–234, 264
  learnability of, 212–213
  and metarepresentation, 207
  and motion, 30–37, 207
  as the "new Latin," 233
  synthetic property of, 34–35

QWERTY keyboard, 28

Rare events, 104, 257
Rare ideas, 50–51, 252
Regime of competence, 84–85, 98, 105, 195, 204, 254
Representational tools, 39, 40
Representations and scientific thinking, 117, 251
Resnick, M., 251
Resonance, antiresonance, 211, 213–218, 222–241, 247
Roller coaster metaphor, 80–81, 83, 106, 188, 204

Romance novels, 22–23
Roschelle, J., 255, 256

Sam's images, 178–180
Saxe, G., 254
Scardamalia, M., 257
Schneiderman, B. 263
Schroedinger's equation, 17
Science for All Americans, 75
Scribner, S., 250
Sean and Bob, 198, 201, 204–206
Sheena, 49–52
Sherin, B., 251, 253, 260, 262
Side effects, 133
Simon, H., 3
Skateboard vignette, 46
Skidding car, 126–128
Slants representation, 170–173
Sloan, D., 233
Smith, D. E., 250
Smith, J. P., 255, 256
Snow, C. P., 227
Social basis for literacy, 8–11, 19
Social niches, 22–28, 39, 44, 117,
    146, 148–151, 249–250, 261
  subway romance novel–reading,
    22–23, 26
  and the World Wide Web, 214–
    217, 235
Software development
  organic forms, 55–58, 62–64
  and social niches, 48
Sonar representation, 170
Spatial metaphor
  principle of, 149–150, 205
Star Trek, 112–113
Structure and function, 111, 120–
    121, 123–125, 127, 129, 131–
    148, 163, 259–260
  and learning trajectory, 143–145

T representation, 171–172
Teachers
  personalization, 52
  professionalization, 41–42, 44
Technological ancestor worship, 132

Technologists, 223–227
Ted, 180–184, 206
Telecommunities, 44
Textuality
  principle of, 149
Tick model, 29–37, 197–198
Tina, 52, 53, 58, 175, 187–189, 260,
    261
Tool-rich cultures, 39–44
Transparency, 225, 262
Two cultures, 227
Tyack, D., 259

Vacuum cleaner example, 90
Vectors, 35–37, 41, 176, 229, 252
Virtual reality, 112, 114, 226
Visibility, 156
Visual reasoning, 195
Visualization, 178
Vygotsky, L. S., 254

Weizenbaum, J,. 124, 258
Word games, 101–102
World Wide Web, 43, 53, 214–222

Yo-yo example, 92
Young, R., 259

Zajonc, A., 233